M000249198

FROM
COMPTON
TO
CONGRESS

Walter R. Tucker, III
with Martha Tucker

RayMar Publishing
1129 E. Dominguez St.
Suite A
Carson, CA 90746

Library of Congress Cataloging-in-Publication Data: An application to register this book for cataloging has been submitted to the Library of Congress for International Standard Book Number.

ISBN: 978-0-692-88732-5

RayMar Publishing
1129 E. Dominguez St., Suite A
Carson, Carson 90746
waltertuckeriii@gmail.com
www.fromcomptontocongress.net

Cover Design by Yolanda Scott-Allen & Angie Alaya

"It's been several years in the making, but without a doubt the most interesting, inspiring, and provocative autobiography in recent time IS FINALLY HERE!!!"

— RayMar Publishing

"I thoroughly enjoyed reading FROM COMPTON TO CONGRESS. Every conceivable emotion was captured– love, romance, joy, anger, betrayal, regret, sorrow, grief, humiliation, determination, courage, fear, pride, and so much more."

— Wanda Williams

"A human story of a leader pursuing his dream that dies and then resurrects into an unexpected destiny. It is our story as a nation set on the backdrop of the 90's Rodney King Riots, Clinton Administration, OJ Simpson trial and the beginning shift of the U.S. mindset."

— Kenneth Nye

"Great commentary on the life of a young black man from the inner city thrust into the world of politics. I couldn't put it down and after I was finished, I was at a loss for words!"

— Nedra Cooper

Special Honor to My Father
Dr. Walter R. Tucker

Dear Dad,

No matter how many years have passed, or events come and gone, you are still my mentor, and my best friend. Thank you, Dad, for being a great role model of faith, hope, love and service to your family, your community and your country. You remain forever in my heart and in the hearts of countless people whom you loved and served. This book is my way of keeping your life and daily habits alive in the minds and hearts of those who knew you and introducing you to the minds and hearts of those who didn't have the pleasure of meeting you in this life.

You were the inspiration for this book because you served Compton residents for over 20 years through the Compton Unified School Board, and the Compton City Council. You also served countless patients as a practicing dentist for years. "Without you, dad, I probably would have never served as an elected official, and I certainly would not have become the spiritual man I am today. You will always be known for your integrity and, as the Los Angeles Times labeled you, "Mayor with the 'nice guy' ways."

As you used to always say, "Nothing good comes easy, and anything that comes easy isn't good." This autobiography that you inspired was a monumental undertaking, but it's because of the years of struggle that I feel its tribute to you and your legacy is GOOD!

Your son, Walter

Foreword

The year was 1993 and Congressman Walter R. Tucker, III invited me to speak at the Congressional Black Caucus' Annual Legislative Conference in the fall. The Congressional Black Caucus is comprised of African-American members of the United States House of Representatives. Their annual Black Caucus meeting is a renowned gathering of national political, business, and social leaders. I was, at that time, a little known Executive Director of the faith based non-profit corporation named FAME Renaissance—the economic arm of First AME Church of Los Angeles, California.

I was awed by the invitation to speak in front of that body of highly regarded national Black leaders. More importantly, as an African American in his 30's, I felt especially excited that I had been invited by the young visionary, Congressman Walter R. Tucker, III. He was innovative, and liked bringing economics to the community in an impactful way. I remembered that it was just a few years since I had been homeless, but now with his help I was "center stage" before the rich and powerful.

Congressman Walter Tucker III was a black man on the rise in Los Angeles. His election to Congress represented a legacy of Black leadership in Southern California—Walter Tucker, II, Mayor of Compton, Tom Bradley, Mayor of Los Angeles, and Congressman Mervyn Dymally, U.S. Representative of Compton. These were just a few of the shoulders Walter R. Tucker, III stood on.

I, and many others will never forget the 1992 images of violent and destructive civil unrest following the acquittal of Rodney King's white police attackers and Walter Tucker, III standing in the streets of Compton—amid flying bullets and burning buildings—demanding the National Guard's help. He inspired me. He was the voice for those muted by racism, discriminatory practices in multinational corporations, and neighborhoods without friendly neighbors. He carried the hopes and dreams of Black people living in low-to-moderate income communities. Yet, we knew something would happen to this intelligent, bold, brash, and brave Black brother.

Something did go very wrong for this courageous and progressive community activist/politician. The FBI targeted him. It seemed par for the course for a successful Black politician to be wrongly brought down. According to the Joint Center for Political and Economic Studies, a Washington-based research organization, Congressman Charles Diggs of Michigan, and Congressman Mel Reynolds of Illinois were wrongly convicted. The legendary Congressman Adam Clayton Powell was wrongly accused of mismanaging his committee's budget. Beginning in 2008, Congressman Charles Rangel was wrongly convicted of 11 counts of violating House ethics rules. America has a history of wrongly convicting Black men.

Congressman Tucker, in many ways, became a national scapegoat for the O.J. Simpson acquittal. America's reaction to O.J.'s acquittal was visceral. I remember watching the Oprah Winfrey show's live broadcast of the Simpson verdict. It was like watching two different worlds. The Simpson case revealed the truth about race relations in America. The national media attention created a great racial divide between blacks and whites and targeted successful Black men.

Walter Tucker's case was tried simultaneously with the O.J. Simpson murder trial. The Simpson 'not guilty' verdict was reached on October 3, 1995. Ironically, two months later, Walter R. Tucker, III's guilty verdict was reached on December 8, 1995. Interestingly, Johnny Cochran who represented O.J. during his criminal trial initially represented Walter and was supposed to represent him during his criminal trial. I, like many, truly believe Walter was careless, but not guilty, and O.J. Simpson was very guilty.

Twenty five years later, Congressman Walter R. Tucker, III is now a pastor, preaching the Gospel of Jesus Christ. This comes as no surprise, as he always stood up for social justice for the underserved, marginalized, and the least. The history of Black preachers called by God to change low-to-moderate income communities is well documented. I had not seen Tucker for years, but when asked to write the foreword for this book, I was honored.

I believe God is leading Pastor Tucker in the same path as Rev. Martin Luther King. I still believe Walter will do a great work for the good of those who need a voice of sound reasoning, humility, and productivity. The Bible says, "For a righteous man falls seven times, and rises again: but the wicked stumble in time of calamity." (Proverbs 24:16)

Walter R. Tucker, III's book, FROM COMPTON TO CONGESS, speaks to the heart of our nation's need for restoration and unity. It is my pleasure to share my thoughts about this exceptional man I've known almost 30 years.

Rev. Mark Whitlock, Jr.,
MSSE., Senior Minister COR Church
Executive Director, USC Cecil Murray Center for Community Engagement Center for Religion & Civic Culture

Table of Contents

Foreword... vii

Acknowledgments... xiii

Introspection xix

Chapter One: The Hill 1

Chapter Two: Out of The Black and Blue 11

Chapter Three: Dad...21

Chapter Four: When It Rains, It Pours 27

Chapter Five: Sudden Death....................................33

Chapter Six: Face The Music...................................41

Chapter Seven: A Star Is Born.................................45

Chapter Eight: Hooked...51

Chapter Nine: Off and Running 59

Chapter Ten: Closing The Deal 69

Chapter Eleven: The Godfather 79

Chapter Twelve: Face-To-Face................................85

Chapter Thirteen: Briburn 93

Chapter Fourteen: The Trap...................................101

Chapter Fifteen: Targeted.....................................109

Chapter Sixteen: Home Again 115

Chapter Seventeen: A Date with Destiny....................121

Chapter Eighteen: Dating Robin 125

Chapter Nineteen: The Bar....................................129

Chapter Twenty: New Lawyer, New Life...................137

Chapter Twenty-one: Reflections of A Mayor 145

Chapter Twenty-two: A Twist of Fate 151

Chapter Twenty-three: Rising Star 163

Chapter Twenty-four: Indicted 173

Chapter Twenty-five: Fallout 183

Chapter Twenty-six: Changing Horses 193

Chapter Twenty-seven: The Die Is Cast 199

Chapter Twenty-eight: Elementary 209

Chapter Twenty-nine: Junior High 217

Chapter Thirty: Tichenor Street 225

Chapter Thirty-one: High School 231

Chapter Thirty-two: Round One 239

Chapter Thirty-three: Round Two 247

Chapter Thirty-four: First Blood 257

Chapter Thirty-five: Fighting Back 267

Chapter Thirty-six: Charging Ahead 275

Chapter Thirty-seven: The Best Defense 281

Chapter Thirty-eight: Life-Changing Lunch 289

Chapter Thirty-nine: The Whole Truth 293

Chapter Forty: Rolling with The Punches 301

Chapter Forty-one: Offspring 309

Chapter Forty-two: Final Round 319

Chapter Forty-three: Pins and Needles 329

Chapter Forty-four: Verdict 331

Chapter Forty-five: Beyond The Horizon 341

Footnotes 347

Acknowledgments

First, I want to thank and praise God for His mercy which kept me until I received His saving grace through His Son, my Lord Jesus Christ. I realize that every good thing I have and any good thing I can do comes from God the Father through Christ. Therefore, I give God all the praise and glory for giving me the gift of writing because I could not have written this book without His grace.

To Robin Tucker, my great wife, and life partner. I thank God for sending you into my life because you are perfect for me. I still light up when I gaze at your beauty. I still praise God when I consider your wise counsel to our family and friends. You are the best helpmeet imaginable. Thank you for all the countless things you have done and continue to do to keep our home, our family, and our ministry running smoothly. Thank you for also being a great mother to our two children and now a wonderful grandmother to Spencer, Jr., our first and only grandson.

Thank you, Robin, for sharing all the happiest moments of my life. But also, and perhaps most importantly, I thank you for your strength and loyalty; for standing with me during the toughest times of my life.

Lastly, thank you for all those times, over the last seventeen years, you left me alone in my office to make the extra sacrifices I needed to make to perfect and finish this book.

To Martha Tucker, my mom, thank you for being my first teacher; the one who taught me the love of learning. Thank you for always being my # 1 cheerleader, even from my childhood. Thank you for causing me to think big and believe that big dreams are possible in this world.

Thank you for inspiring me to one day become a writer like you, and agreeing to be my co-writer and editor of my autobiography. Thank you for the countless hours you sacrificed for development and editing, which were and are priceless. Even when we disagreed, we knew the truth was always "somewhere in the middle." Your keen sense of literature, unique writing style, and ability to make words come alive on the page can't be compared. Without it, I could not have accomplished this wonderful work that cements a significant portion of my life in the annals of time.

To Keta Tucker-Brown, my sister who always had my back in "the sandbox of life." We have always been more like twins, sharing the closest childhood experiences from the past, and having a similar passion for the future. Thank you for your tremendous energy and creativity, which planted a seed in me at a young age. Your potential for ministry and entertainment is limitless!

To Richard Brown, my brother-in-law, thank you for your zeal for and knowledge of politics, for being a good match for my sister, and for being a fierce "weekend warrior" throughout my political campaigns.

To Kenneth Tucker, my younger brother, thank you for being the "scud missile captain" during my campaigns, and for sticking with me through the storm. Praise God for the great man of God you have become. I truly appreciate your ministry. Thank you for your support of my endeavors—political or spiritual— even until this day. Thanks for your feedback on the book that caused me to improve on some characters' descriptions. Blessings to your family!

To Camille, my younger sister, who also stood with me through the storm. Praise God for what He has done and is doing in your life. From bratty baby sister to brilliant screenwriter, Christian University professor, and evangelist! I'm honored to have, in some small way, contributed to your love for the arts when I cast you in your first acting role and took you to see Star Wars as a teenager. I'm glad to finally be writing with you creatively. The best is yet to come!

To Walter, IV, my namesake—my only biological son. I'm proud of your exceptional educational, business, and personal accomplishments, but most of all I enjoy our friendship and am excited about the great plan that God has yet to reveal for your life. You were a big part of what inspired me to write this book. I wanted you to know your legacy, and be ready to carry the baton.

To Autumn Tucker-Rodney, "baby bear," thank you for carrying on our family standard of excellence in your educational, business, and personal pursuits. Like your mom, you are wise and caring, and a tremendous wife, and mother. I especially thank you for giving us our first grandchild – "SJ" (Spencer Junior). He is the smartest, most handsome little man. He has stolen our hearts forever!

To Spencer Rodney, my son-in-law who has become my son. Thanks for becoming a vital part of our family, and taking great care of Autumn and SJ the way you do. I pray this book inspires you to place no limits on what God can do in your life.

Thanks to all the dedicated people who worked on my campaigns and helped catapult me into an elected position to help countless citizens through my public service. Thank you, residents of Compton for the love and support you gave my dad and family over the years and the love you still show me every day, reminding me that I was "your mayor."

Special thanks to my congressional staff! You all were the best ever! I'd take the field with you all any day!

Thank you, Attorney Mark Stephen Smith, my brother-in-law. You were there for me when I needed you most, and you know I will always be there for you! Seems like the Smiths and the Tuckers were destined to be one big family. Thank you, Robert and Pauline Smith for your undying support, treating me like your son. Thank you, Steve and Nedra Cooper for your lifelong support, taking care of our children as your own, and all the joyous times we've spent together over the years.

Thank you, Pastor Major Johnson, for being a true and loyal brother in Christ and friend. Thank you for teaching me about God's kingdom and covenants, and for being a great example of a true shepherd.

Thank you, Apostle Ronald Hill for your sound spiritual wisdom and precious fellowship. Praise God for the tremendous work your ministry has been and is doing in the City of Compton and throughout the world.

Thank you Tucker-Watson-Hinton family for giving me a great spiritual and educational legacy to live up to; Nye James Tucker, Sr. and Carrie Tucker who fasted and prayed weekly and had all eight of their children to achieve postgraduate degrees; the "Tucker brothers" who set the bar very high as doctors, and gave me a stellar example of great African-American, male leadership that touched lives and made a huge difference in our community; Uncle Wallace for inspiring me to fall in love with words; Aunt Mary Jane for teaching me to tie my shoes, butter my toasted bread, and stay out of the "dog house."

I am grateful for the influence of all the educational institutions that played a role in shaping my life: Charles Bursch Elementary School, St. Albert's the Great Elementary School, Longfellow Elementary School, Escuela de Montessori, Walton Junior High School, Compton High School, Princeton University, University of Southern California, and Georgetown Law Center.

Thanks to Yolanda Scott-Allen and Angie Alaya for a beautiful Cover Design.

Thanks to my proofreaders, Karen McLaren, Lynel Washington, and Angie Anomalous, for their keen eyes.

Thanks to John F. Kennedy, and Dr. Martin Luther King, Jr. who inspired me to dream big at a young age.

Introspection

Writing a worthy autobiography roams into fields of secrets and truths, and I really struggled with that. What good is an autobiography if you do not allow yourself to be vulnerable in the illumination of human foibles?

It wasn't about whether I could deliver facts, but would I have a handle on what was worth sharing? What were lessons worth learning? Who would be helped? How would they be changed?

People who knew my story suggested that I write it long before I did, as I still struggled with the thought of writing an autobiography. That undertaking would be much more demanding than the countless songs, plays, poems, and sermons I had written over the years. Yet, my unique political, legal and spiritual story was compelling to me and worth telling. I believed it would help to shape a better world, even if someone embraced only one chapter, paragraph, quote, or line.

First and foremost, I had two children, and I believed one day I would have grandchildren and great grandchildren who would want to know more about me. I wanted them to know who I was, the depths of my soul, my commitment to life from my own words, my own perspective.

I remembered the many family gatherings in my childhood when my parents would try to tell me about my ancestors. Walter R. Tucker, my dad's grandfather (on his father's side), was the first hero. He and his siblings refused to be slaves and ran away into the woods of Mississippi. They were eventually discovered by white Methodist missionaries from Ohio who taught them to read and write. His son, and my grandfather, Nye James Tucker, Sr., became secretary to now-famous Booker T. Washington, and later became the principal of Booker T. Washington – an elementary and secondary school where all his eight children attended.

All eight Tucker children received their Master's degrees, and three of the five sons—Booker, Walter, and Sebron—graduated from Meharry Medical College, became doctors, and moved to Los Angeles. They constructed the first multi-level medical building in the Watts area of Los Angeles after the Watts Riots in the summer of 1965. Despite racism and political attacks, they became very successful in their medical practices and community service

As the stories of my forefathers were passed down to me, I received them proudly. There remained, however, a deep desire in my heart to have held an actual book in my hands that told all these great and terrible events that were a part of shaping me, Walter R. Tucker, III.

Over the last seventeen years, I came to believe that God wanted me to leave a legacy to my family and the world. I have come to realize how connected we all are as humans and how one person's life affects many. This is especially true when one becomes a public figure, is known by many for his public service. I also wanted them to know my private life, my triumphs, and my failures.

Because so many people knew my father and were witness to my meteoric rise in politics, and my unceremonious fall from grace, it was important for me to share how God gave my life miraculous restoration. Surely, mine was the story of redemption that needed to be told to the next generations, since a disproportionate number of black men were in prison.

So seventeen years ago, I slowed down to write my unique story, knowing that while it involved me, it wasn't about me. It was about a certain time, a certain place, a certain circumstance that made my story much bigger than me. It was really about exposing the facts and conditions leading to my rise by grace, my fall from grace, and my redemption by grace. I wanted the reader to know about the grace of God available to anyone who will seek His help.

When I first started writing this autobiography, I aspired to tell my life's story from my fall from political prowess to the fruitfulness of my current day ministry. However, after I began writing the story, I sought help from my co-writer/editor/mother, Martha Tucker. She convinced me that there were three books there. Needless to say, the first of the three is the one you are about to read. It is not my entire life's story, but it is the story that covers the political and legal years of my rise and fall from grace, which occurred some twenty years ago.

My prayer is that From Compton To Congress will not only enlighten, entertain, and move you, but also inspire you to find comfort and confidence in Christ in spite of the storms of life.

Even as I write this introspection, I realize that perhaps my greatest weakness has always been impatience. Now in the process of writing my book, I have grown in patience and allowed "patience to have her perfect work." I am now perfect and whole, wanting nothing (James 1:4).

Oh, just in case the thought crossed your mind, that doesn't mean it will be another seventeen years before the second book comes out, but I guarantee you I'll wait until it's true from the depths of my soul before I release it. Thank you for your time, interest, and engagement.

Walter R. Tucker, III Family
(Spencer Jr., Spencer Sr., Autumn, Walter III, Robin, Walter IV)

The Extended Tucker Family

Congressman Walter R. Tucker, III walking down the U.S. Capitol steps.

CHAPTER ONE

The Hill

Each day brings a world of new possibilities, but one day brings
a moment that changes your life forever.

January 3, 1993: The 103rd United States Congress, with a Democratic majority in the House and the Senate, was about to be sworn in on Capitol Hill. The Democratic Party was walking tall as if we had accomplished a strategic plan for war. It was Camelot revisited. The young, virile, good-looking, newly elected president, William Jefferson Clinton, was about to lead the country in a new direction, despite all the attacks hurled against him during his presidential campaign.

America was excited again. Young voters were involved again, talking politics in every bar, restaurant, office party, and family gathering. Minority voters took notice that there were more blacks in the Congressional Black Caucus than before, and more blacks were appointed to the president's cabinet than at any other time in American history. This was the America that so many had been waiting so long to see, especially since the devastation of President Kennedy's assassination in the 60s. It was as if when JFK died, the country went into a coma, and now a sudden awakening had occurred. The dream of Camelot was resurrected.

As the youngest African American to ever be elected to Congress from California, I, Walter R. Tucker, III, was also about to be sworn into office. I was a part of an electrifying political history in the making. I was a rising star in the Democratic Party—a man who many said could be the first black president of the United States. Why not? Walter R. Tucker, my great-grandfather, and namesake refused to be a slave and was educated by white Methodist missionaries. His son, Nye James Tucker, Sr., became secretary to now-famous Booker T. Washington. The name "Walter" means "Powerful Warrior" and that name was passed on to my father, Walter R. Tucker, II. My father, and his two brothers, Booker T. and Sebron Edward Tucker, were doctors. They graduated from Meharry Medical College, a prominent medical school in Nashville, Tennessee. Those brothers built the first multi-level, elevator-equipped medical building in the Watts area of Los Angeles after the 1965 Watts Riot. Furthermore, my dad was the first black man to be re-elected mayor of Compton, California. I felt that diligence running through my veins.

Despite how exhilarated I felt about the democratic movement and being the newly elected representative of the 37th Congressional District, which included Compton, Carson, Long Beach, Wilmington and Watts, the bitter-cold winter morning in Washington D.C. was sobering. My family and I exited our car, put on our wool scarves and overcoats, and walked briskly to the East Capitol entrance. The huge, white U.S. Capitol dome stood prominently against the bleak, gray sky, and barren oak trees. As I moved closer to the East Capitol steps, not even the cold January wind could stop my shivering six-foot-one, 180-pound body from feeling the warmth of our nation's breath—the warmth of promise, progress, and power.

Capitol Hill was always busy with bills, lobbyists, and votes, but not this day. This was a day of congratulations; a day to celebrate successful elections. With police barricades in the streets, and a host of media gathered on the lawn in front of the East Capitol steps, several legislators marched up those steps, while others stopped below, taking gleeful photos with their families and supporters. I carefully watched the style and standards of the elder statesmen—experienced congressmen like Julian Dixon, Ron Dellums, Charlie Rangel, John Conyers, and Louis Stokes. They breathed knowledge and connections that reached all around the world. *Because of our common interests as members of the Black Caucus, we are instant allies. We'll be working together. I'm so honored.*

My family and I were having our own personal day of euphoria in the midst of this national political renaissance. After a photographer snapped photos of my striking and strong wife, Robin, our well-groomed kids, Walter IV, six, and Autumn, four, and me in front of the Capitol steps, I shared a quick kiss with Robin, grabbed the kids' hands and led them into the Capitol. We walked down a long hall and, then, as congressmen had done for decades, entered into that awesome, airy, spacious room called "The House Chamber." *I've seen this on TV many times, but this is really it, and I am actually here.* The chamber of the House of Representatives was the place that millions of Americans saw when they tuned into C-Span to see how our nation's laws were made. It was the crucible of national politics and the pinnacle of public sentiment.

Like several of my freshman colleagues, I took advantage of a longstanding tradition of the House which allowed only the congressman's children to stand by his/her side on the House Floor for this once-in-a-lifetime moment. Spouses were not allowed then, but afterward, they could come down and take photos. While I fully intended to be reelected and do this again in two years, I realized that this first oath of office as a freshman congressman was a moment in time that could not, and would not ever truly be repeated. I wished Robin could have been on the floor with me. Nevertheless, she was right there in my heart.

In time, my children probably wouldn't remember being there, but the record would show that I thought enough of them to make sure they were there. As we entered the House Chamber, we took a quick left turn into a small private area called "the Democratic Cloakroom." This was the place where the Democrats could momentarily retire from the spotlight of the House work and talk with one another about everything from the next bill to how their children were doing in school.

The Democratic Cloakroom also featured a Snack Bar that served sandwiches, coffee, cold drinks, and even ice cream. As soon as we entered the Cloakroom, my children zeroed in on the Snack Bar.

"Ooh, ice cream! Dad, can we have some ice cream?" Walter asked.

"Yeah, Daddy, pleeease!" Autumn joined in.

"Well, there's a bit of a line right now. Let's go get some seats, get through the ceremony, and we'll see about the ice cream later. Okay?"

"Oookay," Walter and Autumn reluctantly conceded.

We dashed out of the Cloakroom and entered the large House Chamber with its incredibly high ceiling. My children immediately looked all around the huge room with amazement. I also glanced up and over the fully-seated gallery to see if I could spot Robin and the rest of my family and supporters, but all I saw was a sea of people.

Family and friends from all over the country were seated somewhere in the packed gallery. Most important to me was that

Robin, my mother, Martha, and all my siblings were present: my sister, Keta, who felt like my twin; her husband, Richard, who had become like a brother to me; my brother, Ken, the kid who looked up to me; my baby sister, Camille, the brat, who was becoming a young lady right under my nose; my sister-in-law Nedra Cooper and her husband, Steven; my brother-in-law, Mark Smith, and his wife Olivia were present. Even Grandmother Bell and Aunt Barbara were there from Michigan. Of course, I made sure that my campaign workers and supporters who had come all the way from Southern California were well taken care of. I was especially glad that my pastor, Major Johnson, and his wife, Sylvia, were able to attend.

"Never forget the bridge that carries you across safely," my dad always said.

While we were waiting for the Oath of Office to take place, I gave my children a brief orientation.

"Okay, kids, see this little box in front of you? This is where Daddy sticks in his voting card when he makes his votes on certain things."

"Well, where's the card?" Walter asked.

I pulled it out of my front pocket and said, "Right here."

"Ooh, can I do it, Daddy?"

"Me too!" Autumn added.

"Yes, yes."

Fortunately, the House had anticipated such requests from our kids and had set up a system for mock voting.

"See kids, look up at that wall. See, my name lights up when you vote. If you vote yes, a green light comes on to the right of my name, and if you vote no, a red light comes on instead."

"Cooooool!"

Suddenly the august, white-haired Speaker of the House, Thomas Foley, took to the Speaker's podium. He pounded the gavel, and in the two-hundred-year-old tradition of the House called the session to order.

"It is with great pleasure that I welcome you to the installation of the one hundred and third United States Congress."

Any legislator not already standing stood instinctively. Speaker Foley took a moment and looked over us pensively before leading us in the oath of office.

There we were standing in front of seats where the likes of Daniel Webster and Thomas Jefferson once labored. Without the great sacrifices of the Civil Rights Movement, I knew I would not have made it into this traditionally white, male, exclusive club.

"Gentlemen and ladies on the floor, please raise your right hand," Speaker Foley said.

The large crowd of legislators and I proudly raised our right hands.

"Now, please repeat after me... I do solemnly swear that I will support and defend the Constitution of the United States..."

"I do solemnly swear that I will support and defend the Constitution of the United States..."

My God, is this really happening? Dad always said, "Take care of business, and good things will come to you."

"That I will bear true faith and allegiance to the same..."

"That I will bear true faith and allegiance to the same..."

Who would have ever thought it would be me—a United States Congressman? Now I know why my dad checked me when I returned from Princeton and had refused to stand for the National Anthem at a Rams game in the L.A. Coliseum: *"Son, this country is far from perfect, but it's the best the world's got. Be careful what you do today because you never know where life will take you tomorrow."*

"That I take this obligation freely, without any mental reservation or purpose of evasion…" [1]

"That I take this obligation freely, without any mental reservation or purpose of evasion…"

"Congratulations to you, one and all."

I made it! I've climbed up a high, hard hill and now I'm standing on the top.

The House Chamber erupted with jubilation. With just a few words, we 110 freshmen became part of that great institution that shapes and influences the entire country. We had officially become a part of the 435 members of perhaps the most impactful body in the country— the House of Representatives. And yes, membership did have its privileges.

Member of 103rd Congress.

Speaking to my kids loudly over all the noise, I asked them, "Well, what do guys think? Wasn't that awesome?"

"Can we have that ice cream now, Dad?"

"Yeah, ice cream, ice cream!"

"Ooookay, let's go get some ice cream."

Oh, how my life has changed. It wasn't that long ago that I was a kid thinking about nothing more than going to the movies and getting some popcorn or ice cream. Now I have a chance to help change the world.

After the Swearing-In Ceremony, Robin joined me down on the House Floor and we took photos with Speaker Foley at the Speaker's Podium. He allowed us to take turns holding the gavel to the House as we posed for the camera.

A few days earlier a lottery had been held for freshman office placement. That lottery set the tone for what a newcomer's life was going to be like on the Hill. The favor of God was with me, and out of the 110 freshmen, I drew the ninth pick. Although the choice Rayburn Building was already filled with senior members of Congress, that pick saved me from having to reside in the dreaded Longworth basement. I was able to choose one of the nicer offices in the Cannon House Office Building and I chose a fourth-floor office with a view of Southeast Washington—419 Cannon.

The Cannon Building was the oldest congressional office building. Completed in 1908, it was a majestic display of our nation's history and architecture. Its Beaux Arts design, Corinthian columns supporting a huge coffered dome, brass railings, statues, and vast marble foyers made me feel the pulse of the Hill's history. The footsteps of a solo pedestrian on its marble floors reverberated down the hallway like the rhythmic moves of a tap dancer's shoes. Like most buildings on the Hill, its activity was not only experienced above ground, but also below ground as one walked through its tunnels.

These tunnels represent the deep work and planning that must take place under the surface to build connections. If done right, my plans, like these tunnels, will stand the test of time and cause generations to be delivered to their desired destinations. From poverty to prosperity, from violence to victory, from illiteracy to education. I'm gonna build some tunnels for Compton and the 37th Congressional District!

My office sat at the end of the fourth-floor hallway. The maroon draperies, Victorian furniture, and chandeliers painted a classic picture of America long ago. This was a place where the Declaration of Independence might have been drafted by steady hands, brilliant minds, and ink-dipped pens.

To the right of my office's reception area was my private office. Behind the stately mahogany desk, my nameplate gave off a dull shine: *Walter R. Tucker III, U.S. Representative, D-37th District.* I leaned back in my black executive chair and glanced to the right. I appreciated the tall, sky-blue walls, and thought about all the pictures I would soon hang on them.

Walter seated in Cannon Office on Capitol Hill.

Glancing down to my left, I focused on the congressional pin that rested on my left lapel. That pin would act like a key to unlock highly secured doors, the password into private parties and high-level meetings. It was a metaphor for shaping American history and dreams—the secret handshake of respect. Despite an office void of personal effects and photos, that small pin spoke volumes about the great things to come.

My family and supporters from the District eventually found their way to my Cannon Office and filled it with their hope and cheer. As I gave them the "nickel tour" of my office, their pride rose like the sun. They were proud of their native son who made it all the way from the mean streets of Compton to the historic halls of Congress.

CHAPTER TWO

Out of The Black and Blue

N ow a couple of months after my inauguration, I had settled into my position as the U.S. Representative of the
37ᵗʰ Congressional District. The Democratic Leadership had appointed me to two congressional committees that were
important to my district: The Transportation Committee as my primary committee, since a billion-dollar rail project called the
Alameda Corridor was going to be built in the middle of my district, and The Small Business Committee as my secondary one,
since small business was the greatest creator of jobs—a top priority
for a district like mine with high unemployment. The Transportation Committee Chairman, Norman Mineta, was not only well-
respected, but was also from California.

Mineta and I had hit it off immediately. Like the chairman,
I could see myself making my way up the Democratic leadership
ladder in time. Committee Chair, then Majority Whip, Majority
Leader, Speaker of the House, and then, one day a presidential candidate. But first things first.

I wasted no time hanging photos, plaques, and certificates
for outstanding service to my country and community on my once-
bare, sky-blue walls. There were photographs of my family: my
parents, Walter and Martha; my wife, Robin; my children, Walter,
IV, and Autumn; my siblings, Keta, Kenneth, and Camille.

Thoughts of my family darted in and out of my mind while I sat at my desk studying the 356 pages of The Violent Crime and Control Act of 1994—simply known as "The Crime Bill."

Mayor & Mrs. Walter R. Tucker, II

With so many of our friends having grown up in single-parent homes, my sisters, brother, and I recognize how fortunate we were to have been raised by a good father and mother. We're not a perfect family by any stretch of the imagination, but we know we have something special. We're always there for one another. But now here I am on the other side of the country. God, I miss them.

There were also photographs of leaders—the powerful and the famous—now filling my office walls: Dr. Martin Luther King, Nelson Mandela, President John F. Kennedy, President William Jefferson Clinton, and again, my dad.

Like my role models, within a few months, I was rising even faster and higher. I had assembled a staff of 18 people—9 on the Hill and 9 in the District—and we were churning out the work. We were taking care of the nation's business and responding to the needs of our constituents back home. Life couldn't have been better.

Thursday morning, March 24, 1994: As I did each morning on Capitol Hill, I fell easily into the rigorous rhythm of my congressional office. I talked on the phone and, at the same time, shuffled papers on my desk. My private line rang and I answered. It was the chairman of the Congressional Black Caucus.

"Congressman Kweisi Mfume!" Saying his full name was my playful greeting to him.

"Congressman Walter Tucker. Man, you really did a great job co-hosting the Congressional Black Caucus' first Regional Meeting in Los Angeles. Everybody's saying, 'Who is that young, articulate, handsome congressman from L.A.?' "

"You mean after they say, 'What about that new dynamic and debonair CBC chair!' "

"Hey, we're just two young black elected officials trying to do good."

"I know that's right."

"Speaking of which, did you get the CBC's Executive Summary about the mandatory minimums?"

"Yeah, I agree. We've really gotta dig our heels in and stop those mandatory minimums from being attached to the Crime Bill. Don't worry, I'll be ready to take the floor tomorrow morning."

"See you then."

I hung up the phone with Congressman Mfume and immediately picked up another call. "The majority leader wants another party meeting with the president, next Wednesday at eleven."

"Alright, I'll be there. My regards to Congressman Gephardt."

I recorded the appointment and methodically placed piles of papers in my outbox. There was an enormous volume of information, issues, constituent requests, research, and assignments. Thankfully, I had an excellent staff to help me manage it all.

"Okay, I'm heading for the floor..." I called over the intercom line to Wanda, my scheduler. "...and don't forget to book my reservation for L.A. tomorrow morning, nine o'clock."

"Gotcha, boss."

Wanda responded with the snappy characteristic of a workaholic who worked for a workaholic.

"Oh, and Wanda, round up the legislative staff and send them in here right now before I go to the floor."

"Got it."

Patience had never been my strong suit. I kept thumbing through messages: Ron Brown returned call...draft of crime bill speech in your inbox...transportation committee meeting after lunch. Suddenly, the legislative staff rushed into my office, each of them mumbling under their breaths about the pending crime bill. They were led by Marcus Mason, a stout former safety from Arizona State University. Marcus, a 22-year-old African American, and a product of my congressional district, answered submissively out of admiration, not fear. While I was the second youngest black congressman in the nation, Marcus was the second youngest chief of staff on Capitol Hill. As far as I was concerned, he was the best—a rock.

I was proud to do more than preach about the problems facing young, black males. Anyone who was honest about the matter knew that black men have suffered arguably more than any other Americans. When we weren't being beaten, enslaved, shot or lynched, we were being emasculated and imprisoned. Nevertheless, countless, courageous and irrepressible black men had forged a path for me to succeed, and I was determined to repay them by "paying it forward."

I mentored and gave Marcus the job, opposing everyone who said he was too young and too inexperienced. When it came to his political judgment, he could fence with the best of them. Our relationship was one of mutual hope for improving conditions for our community and for future generations. We were both committed to doing that which would empower them, making them free of excuses to achieve success.

"Hey, boss, I'm sure you want to know if the crime bill is going to hit the floor by tomorrow?" Marcus said.

"You got that right. What's the word?"

Marcus cut a quick look at Larry Risley, my legislative director, who with his conservative glasses and mustache looked like a law professor, and lived for the pulse of the Hill.

"Ugh, we're not one hundred percent, boss, but we think so." Larry hunched his shoulders in a state of uncertainty.

"Find out for sure, Larry. If it hits the floor, I need to cancel my flight to the District. I can't wage a floor fight from the friendly skies, now can I?"

"Okay, Dave, I know there's six point one billion dollars for prevention programs, but I need more specifics on those prevention dollars like yesterday."

"It's coming, boss."

"And Bob, do you have my speech against the federal guidelines that create mandatory minimum sentences for low-level offenses?"

"Right here, boss," he said, handing me a copy.

"Great, thanks!"

The 1994 Crime Bill, originally written by Senator Joe Biden,and sponsored by Representative Jack Brooks, was the largest crime bill in U.S. history. President Clinton was lobbying hard for it. The bill promised to put 100,000 more cops on the streets, ban assault weapons, and funnel billions of dollars to cities to help prevent crime. But the members of the Black Caucus and I had our concerns about it creating more prisons, and putting more black men in them for longer sentences based on low-level offenses.

In light of the rise of crime in inner cities like Compton, I know we need all the help we can get. Still, I'm not going to give my vote to something that in the long run may do black people more harm than good—not even for the Democratic president I'm trying my best to support!

As the meeting broke up and my legislative staff left my office, I cornered Marcus and handed him some paperwork.

"Marcus, here are some high priority constituent matters. That was code for responding to the concerns of some of our "big contributors." Please let Attorney Albright, Mr. Kerdoon, and Emile know we're looking into their concerns. I need an update by next week."

"No problem, Congressman."

Just like his last name, "Mason," Marcus was a "builder." I trusted him to take several units and bind them together with the mortar of political savvy and bring forth the construction that would stand the test of time.

Marcus was out the door in a flash. I pressed the intercom for Wanda again. No answer. Usually, this meant she was on the phone haggling with the airlines. I darted out of my office again.

"Wanda, change my flight to Saturday!"

"Change again?" Her frustration rose over the high counter. She scratched her head, lifted her brow, and sighed.

"Gotta do it. We don't really know when the crime bill's comin' down and I'm not out of here 'til the fat lady sings!"

I was back in my sanctuary with the door closed before some lobbyists could corner me with their particular causes: anything from saving spotted owls to revising our nation's policy on gays in the military. There would be time for those issues, but right now, I had "crime" on my mind. The prevention dollars, under the authority of the crime bill, were in jeopardy. It represented millions that could help high-poverty, crime-ridden communities like my District.

I was known to be the one who "fights for what's right." I was no longer impressed by the powers that be, and I no longer trusted the big boys to help the people in need. They betrayed me on the National Economic Stimulus Package, the Long Beach Naval Shipyard, and the Alameda Corridor. I knew I would have to lobby strongly to see a crime bill I could support. I got back on the phone and called the majority leader's office.

Latonia Smith, my young secretary, quickly knocked and charged through my door, nervously waving a slip of paper in her hand. While I was on hold with the leader's office, Latonia said, "Congressman, *The Wall Street Journal* wants to speak to you—right away!"

The Wall Street Journal? They've never called me before. What could they want? Probably a follow-up on the Rebuild LA story previously run by the LA Times.

"They'll have to wait on those Rebuild L.A. stats," I said.

"But, but…" Latonia said.

Before she could continue, I waved her away and resumed my call with the leader's office. "Yes, this is Congressman Tucker. Is the leader available? Yes, I'll wait."

Latonia reluctantly shoved the message slip in front of me.

"Take a message," I said, holding my hand over the phone.

"But, sir..."

I raised a "stop sign" hand. "Not now! I'll call 'em back."

Mounting stress moved up and down the back of my neck. I swept my hand over it and sighed.

"But, Congressman," her eyes and voice pleaded for consideration. "I think you *need* to take this call...it's something about charges being filed against you."

I leaned forward, took the message slip from her hand, then leaned back, eyeing it. I quickly dropped my call with the leader's office.

The Wall Street Journal? My opponents must be on the attack early this election year. "Okay, Latonia, put him through."

"Line four, sir."

I picked up.

"Hello. This is Congressman Tucker."

"Hi, Andy Pazstor with *The Wall Street Journal.*"

"How can I help you?"

"Congressman, thanks for taking my call."

The voice seemed eager and cunning, but somehow, credible.

"I've been informed by a reliable source that pursuant to a three-year investigation by the FBI the Justice Department will be filing extortion and tax evasion charges against you tomorrow. Do you have any comment?"

This is a bad joke on a busy day.

"Who are you?"

"My name is Andy Pazstor, P-A-Z-S-T-O-R, a reporter with *The Wall Street Journal.*"

"Look, I have no idea what you're talking about."

Gotta be an old college buddy playing a sick prank. Or a friend of my father's, trying to see what kind of stuff I'm made of. Maybe?

"The charges apparently relate back to the time when you were mayor of Compton, California in 1991. Can you think of any reason the Justice Department would want to indict you?" the reporter asked.

I let out a breath and spoke carefully. "Well, it's an election year, and I can think of a lot of people who have political agendas."

"So are you denying any wrongdoing?"

"Absolutely!" I felt defensive and agitated.

The whole thing was very mysterious, and yet something seemed real. Being an attorney, I knew that whatever evil was lurking out there would require an attorney.

"But, Congressman, you did serve as mayor of Compton, California in 1991, didn't you?"

"Where's all this coming from?"

"All I can tell you is what I know, not who I know it from."

"Surely you can tell me who in the Justice Department is making the allegations?"

"You might want to talk with the U.S. Attorney's Office in L.A. Other than that, I can't help you, Congressman. I'm sorry."

Abruptly, I hung up and stared blankly at the photos of those powerful leaders on my wall. Suddenly their internal voices rang through my twirling mind: *"Don't fret, Walter. All great men suffer trials."*

Everything became surreal as Dr. King spoke to me. "The ultimate measure of a man is not where he stands in moments of comfort and convenience, but where he stands at times of challenge and controversy."

Then Nelson Mandela spoke to me, "...courage is not the absence of fear, but the triumph over it."

My dad took his turn. "Remember, son, you might feel lonely, but you're never really alone."

Finally, my mom spoke, the way she always did in times of trouble, "This too shall pass."

Even the white dove amidst my favorite poster's ominous blue sky took flight and recited the poster's caption: *Faith is not knowing what tomorrow brings, but Who brings tomorrow.*

I yanked my tie loose, perspiring. I pulled a number out of my Rolodex. "Johnnie!"

There were not many defense attorneys, white or black, whose first name brought instant recognition. Attorney Johnnie Cochran, Jr. was one of them. My fingers hurriedly dialed the phone number to his L.A. office. As Johnnie's number rang, I stared at Andy Pazstor's name and kept thinking...three years ago...when I was Mayor. *What in the world is this all about?*

CHAPTER THREE

Dad

"Attorney Cochran, please!"

"Who's calling?"

"This is Congressman Tucker and—"

An aloof, "Hold please," on the other end.

"Wait! This is an emergency—!"

Too late. The line went silent.

The reception area of my congressional office swelled with visitors' voices from back home. Their concerns were rising and tumbling like the howling March winds outside my office windows. Most days, my constituents' voices were like string music and violins. But now, my head was spinning with the mysteriously droning voice of a reporter from *The Wall Street Journal*:

"Hi, Andy Pazstor with *The Wall Street Journal*...I've been informed by a reliable source that pursuant to a three-year investigation by the FBI, you're about to be indicted..."

The FBI! An acronym that makes even the strongest soul cringe like a child about to be spanked. I'd always thought of them as trained hounds that sniff out really subversive activity: targeting organized crime or catching terrorists. I imagined them locking away people whose crimes traversed interstate lines.

I nervously tapped my finger on the top of my desk, seething through my teeth. "Come on, Johnnie. Where are you?" *Probably still hassling with Michael Jackson's case. He might be the "King of Pop," but my life is the king of need right now…I need you!*

I pressed the phone hard to my ear like it would make Johnnie come on the line, like it was going to stop my stomach from looping, my heart from racing. Suddenly, a click. Jan, my homegirl from Compton, came on the line. "Congressman, he's in trial. I'll have him call you as soon as he comes up for air."

"Jan, you gotta page him now. This is an emergency!"

"Okay, I'll have him get back to you as soon as I can."

As soon as I hung up the phone, I knew I needed a minute to catch my breath. I buzzed the intercom.

"Latonia, please hold all my calls for a little while."

"Yes, sir."

I leaned back in my executive chair and pondered.

Extortion?! Tax evasion?! Three years ago? I heard myself groan in the loneliness of my inner office, with its walls full of silent mementos and its oblong windows covered in Victorian drapes that shut out the blustery wind swaying in the trees outside.

Walter R. Tucker III. Three years ago. 1991. Serving as mayor of Compton, California. They had to be looking for someone else. Something that happened three years ago? As I sat back in my office, I realized that three years can make a world of difference.

* * * * * *

1989 was a little over three years ago and I wasn't even in politics. My dad was the mayor of Compton, California, a unique, independent, black-run city boasting 100,000 largely middle-class residents. Nestled between the ports of Los Angeles and Long Beach and downtown L.A., and surrounded by every major freeway in L.A. County, this 10-square mile city was known as the "Hub City." [2] My dad, a 6'3, 220-pound dynamo for justice for African Americans was Compton's captain. Most women throughout the community noted that his light skin and straight black hair reminded them of *Super Fly's* strikingly handsome star, Ron O'Neal. But it wasn't his good looks alone that got him elected or the fact that he was a successful community dentist who did excellent work, charged a reasonable price and gave his patients the option of a payment plan. It was his warmth, his affection for anyone in need. The people of Compton loved him for it.

Big Willie Duhon from the west side of Compton was known to say, "Man, nobody betta mess with Tucker! He's down for the brothas in the streets and we down for him!"

No, my dad's accomplishments never affected his attitude toward the great and mighty or the poor and downtrodden. They were all the same to him and I admired him for that.

In 1985, my dad had been re-elected Mayor for a second term. Of the three black mayors elected before him, he was the first ever to be re-elected. During his second run in 1985, I was just getting my law practice established. I played a significant role in that re-election campaign. In 1989, my father was poised to make one last re-election run—a third term. By then my practice was well-established and knowing this election was going to be special for him, I got more involved.

"So, Dad, I heard that Janet's not going to run your campaign this time. What happened?"

"Nothing. She's just bogged down with that 52nd Assembly race and doesn't feel she'll have the time," he said.

"Don't worry, you got my help if you want it."

"You ready to run the campaign?"

"Sure, if you need me."

"Well, yeah, that would be good," he said matter-of-factly. My mom chimed in. "I hear Congressman Dymally is pulling out all the stops to unseat your father. They're putting a lot of money behind a newcomer—Chuck Esters, Jr. He's young and educated, and the son of Reverend Esters."

"Umm," I pondered.

"But since he has no political track record, he can't be held accountable for any political mistakes like your dad can," my mom added.

"Yeah, but that also means he can't take any credit for political accomplishments like Dad can!" I said. "Dad says this is his last run and we have to have a victory!"

Since my father had led me to Christ in 1983, our relationship had grown so strong that it was fair to say he was my best friend. I guess that's the way it goes with parent-child relationships. It starts off with the parent being the authoritative figure, but as years go by, there's a wonderful opportunity to peek into the prospect of true friendship.

Over the years, I gave my dad many gifts for his birthday or for Christmas. But I believe giving my time and service to his political life was the best present I ever gave him.

As the weeks and months passed by, I learned more and more about the inner workings of a mayoral campaign while caucusing daily with my father in our library. It was all about our political platform, attending candidates' forums, walking precincts, putting out posters, door knockers, mailers, and press kits. There was a checklist of entities we needed to contact: the Baptist Ministers' Alliance, the NAACP, Block Clubs, the Chamber of Commerce, the seniors at the Dollarhide Center, and the Women's Coalition. Those daily hour-long sessions just after dinner were so consistent and intense that campaign issues and strategy oozed out of our pores.

"Walter, are you still prepping your dad for the candidates' forum at seven tonight?" my mother asked.

"Yes, he'll be ready. Like any incumbent, Dad has voted for some things people liked and some things they didn't. We need to clarify his position on every issue, and remind everyone about all the good he's done."

"I agree," Dad said.

Kris Bailey, our savvy media consultant, walked in and interjected, "Walter, we need a shot of the mayor with S.E.I.U. Local 660 for our mailer."

"No problem, they're having a rally this Saturday. I'll call the photographer."

"Since our opponent is yelling "change," we need to drive home to everyone the mayor's proven leadership," Mom said.

"Exactly!" I said.

"Cities are the front line of American politics, and it's the mayors who actually touch and change people's lives," Dad said.

"Yes and you have definitely done that," I said.

This political boot camp lasted all the way to election night. On that night, I was mentally and physically exhausted. Some had said that it was going to be a close race in light of the amount of money the opposition had poured into Chuck's campaign. But in the end, we trounced our opponent. It wasn't even close.

"Son, you did a great job!" my dad exclaimed above all the raucous celebration in our campaign office.

"No, I had a great candidate and we had a great team!"

All was well in the black Camelot called Compton. The king was back on the throne. The progress he had made was safe to continue and the future looked bright for the many projects he had started along with Councilman Bob Adams and Councilman Floyd James: the Auto Plaza, the Lazben Hotel, the modern Sunny Cove Housing Development, and the Compton Town Center. Although many white developers said there would never be a new shopping center in Compton because black dollars wouldn't support it, these three political trailblazers gave a chance to a young, black, firebrand developer named Danny Bakewell, and the Compton Town Center became a reality. That project broke the perennial economic log jam in the city. Now with the voting block still in place and Mayor Tucker remaining at the helm, things looked good for all Compton citizens. But no one had the slightest idea of the tragedy the city would face in just a few years.

CHAPTER FOUR

When It Rains, It Pours

A s I sat at my desk reflecting, the video in my head was suddenly interrupted by the buzz of the intercom.

I reluctantly picked up the phone. "I thought I told you to hold my calls."

"I'm sorry, Congressman, but Jan from Attorney Cochran's office said you were expecting her call."

"Sorry, that's right. Please patch her through."

Thank you, Jan, for keeping your promise to have Johnnie get back with me right away.

"Hello, Johnnie?"

"Hey, Congressman, what's hapnin'?"

"Listen, Johnnie, some reporter called from *The Wall Street Journal*...said something about an indictment being brought against me tomorrow by the U.S. Attorney's Office. Something about a three-year investigation by the FBI."

I could imagine Johnnie scratching notes feverishly on his legal pad, as was his custom.

"You didn't say anything, did you?" he asked.

"No. I just asked a few questions."

"Good. Do you have a name to give me?"

"No, except that it's coming out of the U.S. Attorney's Office in L.A."

"No problem, baby. There's a Rick Drooyan I know over there. I worked with him in the District Attorney's Office. Just give me a couple of hours, 'cause I'm still in trial. I'll get back with you this evening."

"Thanks, Johnnie."

I sighed with relief. Johnnie was on the case, but my greatest enemy was still there—the unknown. Yes, "this thing" had become real. Everything my dad had taught me about keeping your nose clean and staying out of trouble was throbbing in my brain. Prison—the worse possible situation for a human being. *I'm never going to prison!*

I attempted to write a speech for the upcoming floor debate on the crime bill. But suddenly I changed direction. I called Marcus into my office and handed him the phone message.

"Marcus, call *The Wall Street Journal* to verify that this man, Andy Pazstor, is on staff there and that he just placed a call to me."

I could hear Marcus dialing in the outer office, but his voice wasn't clear enough for me to hear what he was saying. Moments later he walked back into my office and said, "Yep, he's legit."

This thing was for real. Something happened three years ago, and it was in my face today like a boxing opponent staring you down before the match begins.

It was nearly 3 p.m. when Latonia crept back into my office like a scared mouse.

"Sir, pick up line four, it's—"

"I don't want to speak to any more reporters."

"Congressman, I'm so sorry, but little Walter got hit in the mouth with a baseball bat."

"What! Oh, my God!" I was halfway out the door when Latonia cut me off.

"Wait, your wife is on line four."

I returned to my desk and grabbed the phone in a panic. "Honey, how's Walter?"

"Walt, this is Tony. He's fine. There's been some bleeding, but he's gonna be fine."

Tony Williams was my special assistant and had been working with Robin on a Congressional Black Caucus Spouses' Event.

I inhaled deeply.

"We've got him here at Mount Vernon Hospital. They gave him a shot in his upper lip, and he's gonna need some stitches."

My heart sunk. "I'll be right there."

"No, there's nothing you can do. Robin and I've got it covered, and you've got votes you can't miss."

I hung up and stood there in a daze. On one hand, what Tony said made sense. The press just loved to report when a congressman missed votes. But all I could do was think about my son. I headed for the door again. This time it was more like a drunk man trying to walk the sobriety line. Before I could get there, Marcus knocked and came in without waiting for an answer.

"Hey, boss. I'm really sorry, but I gotta remind you about your three o'clock with Jim Quillen and the machinists."

"Reschedule."

"This *is* a reschedule. He came three thousand miles for this meeting, and they've been waiting a half hour."

My knees were weaker than a newborn calf's. I sat down. I looked up at the ceiling and sighed. The intercom buzzed.

"Congressman, I'm really sorry to bother you, but Mr. Quillen says they're on a tight schedule," Wanda said.

I dug deep down and rubbed my hands over my face. I knew my staff members were just doing their jobs, the jobs I trained them to do. I sighed again.

"Send them in," I said reluctantly.

The machinists lit in on me. "Congressman, we've really got to have those jobs in San Diego. We need your help!"

They had no idea what kind of mental burden I was under at that moment; that I was worried about my son in the Emergency Room and about a pending indictment against me. So they kept bending my ear, waiting for me to make promises and jump through the proverbial, political hoops when suddenly the House bell rang. I was literally "saved by the bell."

"This is the Democratic Cloakroom. Five bells, pause, three bells. Members have fifteen minutes to record your vote on the previous question."

Like time, House votes waited for no one, regardless of personal or political crises. Missing too many votes was tantamount to political suicide.

"I'm sorry gentlemen, I have to go vote."

I darted out of my office and walked briskly to the House floor to record my vote. Truly my mind was out there in the ethers as I walked. Speedily Marcus caught up to me in the hallway.

"Hey, boss."

"What's up now?"

"Remember what you always told me?"

"What's that?"

"Family first. Look, I found out there's only one vote left tonight. We got you covered with the machinists and everything else."

"You're right. I can't do this. I'm outta here."

My thoughts were set in cement: *I can't focus on any legislation tonight. I've got to see about my son, then find out what happened three years ago.*

CHAPTER FIVE

Sudden Death

The drive down the winding George Washington Parkway to Alexandria, Virginia seemed like the longest, loneliest ride of my life. Although Tony had assured me that my son was fine, my memories of visiting my loved ones in hospitals were anything but reassuring. Of course, the most recent and regrettable hospital memory involved my father some three years ago.

* * * * * *

After the dust settled from our re-election victory, my father got back to business as usual.

6:00 a.m. jogging track

7:00 a.m. shave and shower

7:30 a.m. read the *LA Times* from cover to cover while eating cereal and fruit

8:00 a.m. off to work!

While continuing to run his full-time dental practice from Monday through Friday, my dad, the mayor, attended 5-10 events a week. He kept a fast pace that perhaps few much younger men could measure up to. He never turned down one resident's call, nor did he ever refuse to answer his door bell. At the age of 65, he still seemed invincible to me, always walking briskly in his Tony

Lama Ostrich cowboy boots, and as straight as an arrow. Only my mom could call his bluff.

One noonday in his third term, I stopped by my father's house and found him and my mother in the library. They were going over their taxes that were due next month. Suddenly, he belched out a foul odor. My mother looked up at him, and said, "What did you eat? That belch smelled like rotten eggs!" She grimaced. He laughed.

"You have to start taking better care of yourself—start living like someone who wants to retire one day," she said.

"After this term, I am gonna retire."

"And then what, Dad?" I asked.

"Well, son, that's when you and I are gonna start our church."

"In the meantime, you're going to check with your doctor," Mom warned. "I'll call and make the appointment."

In a week, my dad went to his doctor for an exam. That was the last I had heard about the matter from my mom until the next Wednesday when I'd dropped by my old home to see my parents.

"Hey, Walt, come on and join us for lunch at the beach. I have to stop by the doctor's office on the way. That shouldn't take long. Just to get some test results," he said.

"When have you known me to pass up a free lunch?"

Riding in the car with my father and mother, I realized that the three of us hadn't been together like that since I had passed the bar. It was a nice day in March, with a good breeze, and we all anticipated the lunch at the Bluewater Grill—my mother's favorite seafood restaurant in Redondo Beach. Once we were at the doctor's office, my mother and I sat in the reception area while my father went inside. In less than an hour, he came out and we stood up and walked with him toward the car. As we were walking he said, "Well, I have stomach cancer."

My mother and I stopped in our tracks and said in unison, "What are you talking about?" We were struggling to find some reality in that moment. Was it a joke, or some aberration? Mom just looked at him. She repeated those words, "stomach cancer," in strong denial. I began to internalize my feelings, trying to convince myself that he would be fine.

Later at the restaurant, my mother ordered her usual fresh, grilled salmon, but she never ate a bite. She stared at the bountiful, calm blue Pacific waters just outside the plate glass window. As I stared at my dad, I could barely touch my food either. Meanwhile, my dad and I talked quietly.

"Dad, in the name of Jesus, you're gonna beat this. By the stripes of Jesus Christ, you are healed!"

"I know God's with me," he replied.

Over the next six months, our family members prayed for him, as my mom continued her weekly trek to the doctor's office at Kaiser in Harbor City. But week after week, I watched my Superman lose weight and become thinner and weaker.

One night as he was lying in bed at home and I sat by his bedside, he said in a low, raspy voice, "It takes a lifetime to learn how to live…by the time you do, it's time to die."

"Dad, don't say that!"

I couldn't stand to hear him speak those profound words, but deep down, I knew he was preparing me for the worst. Those words proved to me that he had never been more coherent or courageous. He was sharing his homespun philosophy with me until the very end. I held back the tears with all my strength.

"Hey Son, don't worry 'bout a thing." He grabbed my hand and continued, "I love you."

"I love you too, Dad."

"It's all about love. Love sweet love."

Finally, my role model lay in a Kaiser Harbor City Hospital bed, gaunt and motionless. His eyes were peacefully closed. I bent over him, holding his hand. The smell of sickness, laced with Lysol, filled the air, and the sounds from all the medical equipment connected to his body carved out its own rhythm.

In the presence of my father, the living legend, I was often referred to as "Junior" by Compton residents. My aunts and uncles often referred to me as "little Walter." That day I didn't know who I was. All I knew was that I was trying to gather my thoughts, as my father lay there dying of cancer and a distant hospital bell kept ringing every few minutes, droning in my ears.

"Paging Dr. Lawson. Dr. Lawson to station five, please."

Although Dad seemed peaceful, his intermittent grimacing signaled to me he was writhing in silent pain.

"Paging Dr. Lawson. Dr. Lawson to station five, please."

The community's most handsome and virile dentist, mayor, and minister lay powerless, and it was up to his family to do something. My mother, wife, siblings, and I hung close by. We insisted on every known medical treatment that could possibly comfort him through the pains of this terrible disease.

Surely, a man who has given so much to so many deserves better than this.

Everyone concerned was "grasping at straws," groping for a solution. Our family had heard of some experimental drugs being used at St. Jude Children's Research Hospital in Mexico. Once

Robin and I talked to our friends at City Hall about this, the Compton Fire Department was standing by, ready to transport their mayor south of the border. But, in my dad's weakened state, it was not to be.

Dr. Lawson finally arrived at my dad's hospital room at Kaiser, apologetic about his heavy caseload. Being the oldest son, I took charge and addressed him as he approached my father's bedside. My family looked on as they huddled together a few feet away from my dad's bed.

"Doctor, you gotta do something, anything!" I urged.

The doctor reviewed the chart before him and checked his watch.

"Okay, it's been a few hours. We can give him another shot of Demerol."

"Thanks, Doc."

"I wish I could do more. Like so many others, I have heard about your dad—what a great man he is. I'm just sorry that I had to meet him under these circumstances."

After Dr. Lawson left, I noticed that a dim morning light had crept through the tiny hospital window. It shone on Dad's face, but his eyes were still closed. I leaned back and sighed deeply.

I couldn't think of my father, "Big Walt," lying there in bed, helpless with his eyes closed. When I had been a boy, my father always had his eyes open, making his "old school" hook shot like Kareem Abdul-Jabbar, teaching me to compete. His eyes were wide open when he saw me turn the lights off at one of our infamous teen house parties and he insisted that I turn them right back on. They were wide open again when he and my mom insisted on homework, household chores, and no television during the week to keep us grounded.

During the summer, he took me down to his medical build-ing in Watts to serve as one of the janitors. The pay was minimum wage, but it kept me out of trouble and with a little change in my pocket. There would be no hanging out in the streets where gangs were getting tougher and tougher. Those dental office floors I mopped, stripped and waxed seemed bigger than the world. But nothing was as big as my dad, "Big Walt."

Now, as nurses shuttled in and out of his room, Dad's eyes intermittently closed. Perhaps some of those visions floating through his head were complete: graduating from dental school; a successful dental practice; all four of his children having college degrees; becoming the mayor on his third attempt; and becoming an ordained Baptist minister at 61 years of age, on the same day his first grandchild was born. But there were some visions that were not quite complete: the construction of Compton's new civic cen-ter, the new hotel, the Auto Mall, and the North Side Shopping Center. I think the most important accomplishment he never got to complete was a personal one—the establishment of a church.

When I compared my life to his, it was, in many ways, an empty canvas. I had finished my education, as was the family re-quirement. I became a deputy DA and later, started my own law practice. But as for a longstanding track record of public service, I had yet to come close to his accomplishments.

I was content to praise myself for things I had done for my dad, things my dad could or would never do for himself. When I ran his mayoral campaign in 1989, I decked him out in a new tux-edo for the grandest tribute he had ever experienced. I fought off all his foes when we were in battle. And when our camp was at peace, I rented him movies to try to get him to relax and escape from the maddening pace.

Most importantly, I became his "boy Friday," making runs for him and with him every time he needed a hand. I was his "go-to guy." Block clubs, banquets, churches, you name it. I got so good at it that he trusted me completely to represent him.

The more I thought about it, the more tears tried to flow out of my eyes. But somehow the tears were sacked away. I felt like there was something more I could have done. He had done so much for me. I just wanted to give back. My dad's prolonged silence and stillness raised my concern.

"Dad?"

Finally, Dad opened his eyes, touched my wrist, and whispered slowly, "Matthew six, thirty-three. Keep, God, first...and take, care, of family..."

"I will, Dad. I promise."

From that moment forward, I knew in order to keep my promise to Dad to take care of the family, Robin and I would have to immediately move out of the apartment we currently rented in the neighboring city of Bellflower and move into his house in Compton. The family was going to have to be closer than ever if we were going to survive.

I could sense my mom and sisters wanting to draw near to kiss him, so I moved over a bit and gave them room.

"I love you," he said to each family member.

They kissed him gently, but he still held onto my hand. Suddenly, he let go of my hand. His arm dropped and he became silent again. A little cough, then he was still. The life monitor went flat and a lone monotone drifted in the air.

I looked straight up to heaven, where my father always told me to look in times of trouble. All I saw was a dull white ceiling.

When my mother, wife, and sisters realized that Dad was really gone, they broke out in violent tears. We all huddled in anguish, but I still didn't shed a tear. Not because I felt men weren't supposed to cry, but because by vowing to be the strength of the family, I had abdicated that privilege, at least for the time being.

I just stood there, outwardly the soul of strength, but inside, dying. I was feeling pain beyond anything I'd ever known. The death of my mentor and best friend had shattered my faith. I wasn't sure what hurt most: the loss of my father, or my inability to cry. But there would be a time to cry. Another day, another time.

CHAPTER SIX

Face The Music

Having calmed my fears about what I would find at Mount Vernon Hospital, I parked my car and headed for the Emergency Room. After checking in at the front desk, I walked into room eight where I found Robin and Tony trying to comfort my son, lying still on a gurney. Robin looked up and we quickly folded into a desperate hug.

"Blood was everywhere," she said.

"What happened?"

"Eric and Walter were playing baseball in the field and Walter was too close to the bat when Eric swung. One tooth is chipped, but thank God his front teeth aren't knocked out."

"Thank God," I said.

"Walt, you shoulda seen your wife move into action. I thought I was watching Carl Lewis at the Olympics the way she cleared those fences in her white dress, and quickly made her way to your son's side," Tony interjected.

I glanced at Walter on the hospital gurney where red-stained white sheets revealed the bloody debacle. His eyes were droopy and sad. Robin looked at me—tears welling in her eyes. I just dropped at Walter's side and wept. I wept for my young, injured son. I wept for all the times I wasn't able to weep for my father. And lastly, I wept because I'd have to tell Robin about the strange phone call from The Wall Street Journal. I had to tell her that night because tomorrow the country could easily be lit up with headlines mentioning me. I wept because I had very little information to give her. Johnnie hadn't called me back yet.

Johnnie, call me!

After Robin and I made it home and put the kids to bed, I was at the kitchen table trying to review some work, but I couldn't focus. I was desperate to hear from Johnnie. The phone finally rang around 10 o'clock. I snatched it off the hook. It had to be Johnnie.

"Hello."

"Hey, Congressman."

"Johnnie, I've been waiting for your call."

"Sorry it took so long, baby. This trial I'm in is lasting way longer than expected. Anyway, I made contact with the U.S. Attorney's Office here in L.A., and I'm sorry to say there is something afoot. Couldn't get a lot of details, but it has to do with some FBI sting in nineteen ninety-one/ninety-two. Some businessman was acting undercover. I'm working on a meeting between them and us at their office. Probably Monday or Tuesday of next week. When can you be in town?"

In a flash my entire calendar changed its course: floor votes, committee hearings, golf, and dinners were suddenly put on the back burner.

"I'll fly in tomorrow and be there throughout the weekend. I'll be ready to stay over a couple of extra days next week. Let's update soon as I get to L.A."

"Sounds good, baby."

"Johnnie, what's the name of the businessman?"

"Macardican…John Macardican."

My heart skipped a beat and sweat popped out on my forehead. John Macardican. I hadn't heard or thought about that name for three years.

I prided myself on having thorough communications with my wife—full disclosure. However, every spouse has their secrets and John Macardican was one of mine. In light of the shock of our son's injury, there was no right way to tell Robin about everything else that happened that day; about everything that happened three years ago. I walked into our bedroom and closed our door. Robin was lying still on the bed. I came up behind her, held her and stroked her hair. I knew I couldn't hold back much longer, but at the same time, the moment had to be right. We laid together in silence, hoping for some solace from the day's traumatic events. Finally, she turned around and we were face to face. I knew that was the moment—a tiny window before the exhaustion of our trying day would quickly overtake us. I looked deeply into her eyes.

"Robin…I need to talk to you about something."

This was Robin, my wife, the only person in the world, besides my mother, who knew when something was wrong with me just by the timbre in my voice. I expected to see fear and rebellion in her eyes, but somehow a deep strength appeared, inviting me to proceed. I moved in closer to her and turned up some music on the clock radio. At that point, I couldn't be sure that our house wasn't bugged. Everything was now suspect. I whispered into her ear everything I knew.

"Robin, I got a strange call at the office today…."

When I finished briefing her, I expected a thousand questions. But perhaps due to her exhaustion from the day, she asked none. The only questions I got were the ones I saw in her eyes. What about the things she had planned? Our children's future? Our vacation with them to Disneyworld? The important volunteer work she was doing in the community with the Congressional Black Caucus Spouses? Our weekly candlelight dinners in my office just so we could spend time together? What would happen to them?

For me, it was too much for one person to handle in one day. For Robin, there was an inner toughness that came from somewhere I didn't know. It was something maternal which defies anything that attacks the nest. She held me close to her bosom and our embrace receded into the night.

I leaned over to check on her and she had finally drifted off to sleep. I laid there, eyes wide open, trying to decompress from the day's tension. All I knew was that somewhere in New York City, in a tall high-rise that housed The Wall Street Journal, a lone reporter was working away at his computer, determined to scoop the rest of the media. Nothing was going to hold him back. My mind was racing a million miles a minute, trying to figure what they had on me. All I knew was a name—John Macardican, and that I needed to get some rest, and get back to L.A. right away. I was physically exhausted, but I couldn't sleep; I tossed and turned all night long. My mind kept racing back to the past where all the answers lay.

CHAPTER SEVEN

A Star Is Born

My father's death had been very emotional for our entire family and community. We chose to hold his funeral at Double Rock Missionary Baptist Church, the only church in Compton with the capacity to hold the 3,000 people who would attend. That day, the Compton Police Department blocked off the streets and our family limousine trailed an official police motorcade to the church. The service started at noon and now, after several prayers, songs, poems, and acknowledgments, family and close friends spoke.

It was nearly three in the afternoon when I finally took the podium to deliver the Eulogy. I really don't recall how I got from my seat to the podium. All I recall is the band playing a song I had never heard before—"God Has Smiled On Me." I knew then that song would forever be associated with my dad.

I paused and looked at the sea of faces staring at me, some familiar, and some not. Silence and great anticipation covered the sanctuary. Befitting my dad, I quoted a Scripture:

Verily, verily, I say unto you, Except a corn of wheat fall into the ground and die, it abideth alone: but if it die, it bringeth forth much fruit. (KJV John 12:24)

"Yes, my dad has died, but I believe the death of this good man will bring forth much good fruit."

Suddenly, I felt that I was speaking from the wings of my father's spirit. A melodic saxophone, not saddened, but rhythmically blowing the tune of his triumphant life. Up and down the scale, the notes rang out. "If Mayor Tucker could speak to us today, he would say, don't cry—unify! Reach high, reach wide—don't cry, unify! Unify all races in this community, so that we all may share in its progress and prosperity!"

Heads nodded in agreement and a couple of people mumbled, "Amen."

My voice elevated to a resounding pitch. Emotional, yet controlled. Insightful, yet practical. Piercing, yet pleasing. A voice touched by the Spirit of God; one much wiser than my years. Then I added, "Today we are all here, physically together, but through love and faith we can make Compton better! When we unify, we dignify. When we unify, we edify. When we unify, we can reach high, reach wide—unify!"

"Amen! Reach high! Unify!" a few people up front added.

In that moment, I sensed a shift of hope sweeping through the audience. A woman in the second row pointed with excitement toward me. I read her lips when she leaned close to a man next to her, seeming to say, "That's our next mayor." The man nodded.

Her spirit swept across pews as other people in the audience began to whisper to each another earnestly. The city councilpersons, seated in the first row, also glanced at each other, but kept more of a "poker face." They seemed to be holding some internal rage in tow. Maybe it had to do with the rumors that each of them had already laid claimed the mayor's seat.

The man sitting next to the woman in the second row was a middle-aged white man with white hair. He smiled politely while seeming to study the audience's reaction to the woman's statement. As I continued to speak, he followed my every word. When the funeral ended and the family and I proceeded toward the exit, I glanced to my right, but the white-haired man seated in the second row was gone.

Right after my father's funeral, his longtime ally, Compton City Treasurer Wesley Sanders, eased into the repast at our family home. This dark complexioned, six-foot-one-inch, 280-pound cowboy was affectionately known in Compton as "Big Wes." Rolling his big brown eyes like a searchlight in the dark, he offered a passing "hello" to hundreds of sympathizers until he found me. With a big gap-toothed smile, he pulled me aside, speaking real low. "Junior, you got to take your father's seat." He made that statement as if such a move was a given.

Is he out of his mind?

Wes turned his back to two people standing too close to us. "Let's go talk—privately."

He walked into the family library, I followed behind him, then closed the door.

As soon as I turned around, he was right in my face. "Look, Junior, the folks in this city depended on your daddy and me. I can show you the programs—everything. See, your dad looked out for the people, not the fat cats. Now, if you don't take that seat, all your daddy did to keep the sharks from eatin' up the city's revenue will be in vain. See what I mean."

Big Wes must have known anything that favored my dad's legacy would catch my ear. I could feel the weight of this big man without him laying a hand on me. He leaned in closer and said,

"Listen to me, now." He shook his right index finger in my face. "I'm gonna make 'em appoint you to that seat."

Wes was often regarded as the city's "boss man" because he influenced a lot of voters, yet he listened to my father. People respected him because he was one of them. Raised in Watts and founder of a local butcher shop, he became a local hero. But to me, he was like an uncle. When my father was alive, Wes would stay up nights, working on Dad's campaigns, making crude posters, and mailers that highlighted the dirt on my dad's opponents. He would ride out late at night in his blue Ford pickup to hang posters, scaring off the opposition with the Colt .45 he kept strapped to his belt. Everyone knew he wasn't packing just for show. He brought along his friend, a man named Walter Lewis. That rough-riding pair kept my father in tune with the pulse of the streets.

I eyed Wes right back. "Look, I'm a young lawyer, married with two kids and here's Compton, an inner city sandwiched between L.A. and Long Beach with close to 100,000 people with all their problems: lack of jobs, poverty, drugs and gang violence, and racial tension between blacks and a growing Latino population. Being an elected official is all about a lot of local people who boss you around without much appreciation for what you do. I don't know, Big Wes. I've seen my dad take that ride, and it wasn't always pretty."

His eyes shifted past me to the west wall. He pointed to a large photo of my dad and him, smiling big, arms around each other's shoulders. Such smiles. So much youth, so many dreams. Beneath the photo was written, *November 1965*. Both of us stared at it as if it were the first time we'd seen it.

That was a time when blacks struggled for Civil Rights, and began to live in neighborhoods they could have never lived in before; a time when they made coalitions they'd never enjoyed before. The Tucker family had just moved into a ranch-style home in the Richland Farms area of Compton along with other middle-class blacks: doctors, lawyers, a handful of engineers, a banker, a few businessmen, and teachers. Big Wes lived in a ranch-style home in a similar neighborhood on the east side of town. It wasn't long before my dad decided to run for a seat on the Compton Unified School Board. Big Wes was one of the first men to have his back and Dad was elected.

I believe my dad ran for the Compton Unified School Board largely because of his experience as a boy in Haskell, Oklahoma. His father, Nye James Tucker, held the prestigious position of principal of Booker T. Washington—the local segregated elementary/high school. The State of Oklahoma funded that school through the Haskell Superintendent's office. Every four years, the white Superintendent would put the principal's position out to bid. As the position gave the Tucker family of 10 a home, food, clothing, and prestige, Nye planned to beat out any bidders. So, once a year he assigned his young son, Walter, the job of walking five miles a day throughout the community to pass out flyers full of school information aimed at convincing the community that Nye James Tucker was worthy of their continued support for that position.

My dad wore holes in his shoes to keep his father's name and position alive. The holes in his shoes were nothing to be compared to the joy he received when his father praised him for dropping off the flyers in the most remote parts of the town. Dad once told me that the fulfillment he felt passing out those flyers was a sensation he found no other place. Maybe it was because of the importance of helping his father. Maybe it was because of the opportunity to interact with countless members of the community. Whatever the reason, his life was never the same.

CHAPTER EIGHT

Hooked

After Dad's first taste of Compton politics on the School Board, he was hooked. By 1969, Compton's population was about 70% African American and the residents were excited about the possibilities of electing their first African American mayor. My mother started talking about Compton becoming a model independent urban city. Certainly, that would give our city's name the grandness she liked and Compton residents something to boast about—a phenomenon of black achievement. In May of that year, my dad entered a historic mayoral race against a crowded field of candidates to earn that distinction.

I was 12 years old when I got my introduction to politics. Climbing onto the back of an old pick-up truck with a group of campaign workers holding "Tucker for Mayor" signs was such a thrill. While the song *Tighten Up* played over the truck's portable PA system, the driver rolled us slowly through the neighborhoods of Compton. Then, intermittently, the man in the passenger's seat holding the microphone blasted out election information.

"Don't forget to vote this Tuesday. Vote Tucker for Mayor. Remember, Tuesday is Election Day. Vote for Walter Tucker. Vote Tucker for Mayor!"

Dad gained enough votes to get into a run-off with Douglas Dollarhide, a former postal worker, and automobile salesman by trade, who had become Compton's first African-American councilman in 1963. Though it was a hard-fought runoff, when all the dust settled, Dollarhide became Compton's first African American mayor in June 1969, and the first African American elected mayor of the biggest city west of the Mississippi.[3]

My mother's dream of "Compton's Urban City Model" came to a halt and she started contemplating the family's move to Beverly Hills, but in 1973, Dad ran for the City Council seat in the 3rd District and won. He was determined to stay and Mom decided that she could help him make Compton a model independent city. Nothing was more important than that dream, so she chose to defer her own dreams for his. One day I asked her about "the dream," and she shrugged, "Oh, I guess we'll be here until it's done."

With Doris Davis becoming the first black female mayor of Compton in 1973 and other prominent blacks serving on the City Council, like Dr. Ross Miller, Compton was experiencing its own renaissance of professional black leaders with progressive ideas. Suddenly our sprawling ranch-style home on Tichenor Street was transformed into the unofficial community center. My dad and mom were always hosting something for the likes of Martin Luther King, Jr., Andrew Young, Jessie Jackson, Paul Robeson, World Affairs Council dignitaries, Sister City representatives, and a host of luminaries from the Dorothy Chandler Music Center. Barbecues and swim parties were always just a thought away, but bigger than the pool and the backyard was my dad's heart.

He was a gentleman who would literally give the shirt off his back. He took the phrase, "Mi casa es su casa" (My house is your house) literally. There were always people at our house whom I called uncle and aunt, but mostly, they were just people who loved being around my family. No matter who came to visit, there was always enough room and food.

In 1977, my dad ran for Mayor again. This time against Lionel Cade, an unassuming African American accountant who had served on the City Council from 1964-1973. Dad and mom were exhilarated about the prospects of that election, but much to their dismay, Dad lost again. The unassuming accountant had paid his political dues for over a decade and now he was the mayor.

To that disappointment, Dad offered another one of his southern quotes, "Every dog has his day."

Meanwhile, with Dad's dental practice booming, he purchased Mom the car she always wanted—a brand new black Rolls Royce! I believe the gift was to appease her for not moving to Beverly Hills when many middle-class black families were leaving Compton for the west side. Riding in that Rolls seemed to bring Beverly Hills to Compton. It wasn't long before some notable socialites tapped Mom to join the crème de la crème of the Dorothy Chandler Center Theatre Group. Life was good for the successful dentist and his socialite wife who especially enjoyed elite parties and travel. Dad, though, being out of political life for the next four years, seemed to me like a wounded bear.

* * * * * *

Over the years, I often thought: *Why isn't Mom content to live in Compton anymore?* It wasn't until years later that I understood her hopes and dreams.

My mother, Martha, was born in Wynne, Arkansas to Dennis and Lola Hinton, local farmers who owned land and had sharecroppers. Unfortunately, her father died when she was only six months old. When Martha was three, her older sister, Bernice, the local teacher, took her to school and exposed her to the joy of reading books, plays and acting. When she was four years old, she started writing one-page stories. By the time she was 10 years old, her 11-year-old brother and best friend, Isaiah, was killed in a hunting accident, swept out of her life forever. About the same time, her stepfather, William Bell, was signing papers to buy a large adjoining farm that a white farmer wanted. The white man and his posse came in the middle of the night to kill him. William fled to Gary, Indiana to work in the steel mills.

A month later, Lola took Martha and her baby sister, Barbara, to rejoin their stepfather in Gary. There, Martha read stories to entertain her baby sister and take herself on imaginary trips around the world. During those voyages, Martha learned to rely on the comfort, stability, and wonder of reading books. As she continued to read about great people and places of the world, she began to long for more than the black smoke of Gary steel mills. Those hopes lead to good grades, good manners, and heeding the advice of a high school teacher to attend one of the most prestigious black universities — Fisk University in Nashville, Tennessee. At Fisk, she met an aspiring dental student at Meharry Medical College. The couple married and Martha left family and all she was familiar with for love, Los Angeles, and the promise of becoming a part of the world she had read so much about.

* * * * * *

In the fall of 1980, Dad decided to run for Mayor against Cade one more time and Mom gave him her full support. Although Cade was credited with balancing the city's budget in his first year as mayor, in 1978 California voters overwhelmingly approved Proposition 13. That measure severely reduced property tax revenues. Since much of the fat was already eliminated from Compton's budget, Compton was one of the hardest hit by the measure.[4]

With Compton reeling from rising gang violence and limited revenues, in June 1981, Dad soundly defeated Cade. He had finally become the mayor of Compton! My mother immediately turned her sights again toward encouraging a model independent urban city.

Photos on the library wall that I walked by every day, without so much as a glance, suddenly gripped me. In one shot, I stood proudly beside my father, wearing an Afro. June 12, 1974: I was the valedictorian of my senior class and had just urged 2,500 fellow students who filled up the Compton High football stadium to join me in making a difference. Another photo of Dad and me was snapped at Princeton University, standing proudly in front of the ivy walls of my dorms. My dad came to visit me during my freshman year, and I couldn't have felt more special.

Choices. The course of a man's life begins with one tiny decision made at the fork in the road. Big Wes stared at me and was waiting for an answer.

What answer should I give him?

Being a Princeton alumnus, a USC honor graduate, a Georgetown lawyer, and an ex-deputy district attorney who was now in private practice at only thirty-three years old, I prided myself on being my own man. But since Dad's death, I had moved Robin and our two young children from our Bellflower apartment into my father's huge house. Nevertheless, I wasn't sure if I was ready to try to fill his large shoes. Most people said my dad gave too much to Compton, fighting for its citizens to get into colleges, go into businesses, and get good jobs. But the attendance of those thousands of people at Dad's funeral made it apparent that he hadn't given too much, after all.

Right there in the library, another one of Dad's favorite quotes came to my mind, "A man doesn't seek the office. The office seeks the man."

"I'll let you know, Wes."

"I'm sure you want to carry on the things your daddy started...."

Sweat beaded on my face as I remembered him walking tall in his Tony Lama cowboy boots, and one of his neatly pressed Armani suits, graced by some government-related pin in the lapel. The smell of Kouros Cologne would linger in the room after he left. I could still hear his wise answers and the genuine concern in his voice when he talked patiently to irate constituents on the phone throughout the night. I always saw admiration on senior citizens' faces when they saw him. Like he was their very own son who'd come home from a long journey. Who was I fooling? I had inherited my dad's legacy of service and vision. Still, I couldn't rush into this life-changing decision.

"I'll have to sleep on it, Wes," I said. That was code for *I have to talk to my wife about this one.*

That night in our bedroom, Robin and I started our nightly talk. "Honey, Wes really has faith in me and he's waiting for an answer," I said.

"Yeah, but you have to know if this is something you really want to do. I never wanted to be some politician's wife."

"But, baby, I can't just let my dad's life's work die."

When Robin became quiet, I knew she was showing her objection to the idea. We'd been married only six years, but I knew when to back off and allow her to think. We went to sleep.

When we woke up, something strange seemed to be in the atmosphere. Robin was staring at me without saying a word. The quiet was annoying. Then suddenly, her words came pouring out.

"Walter, your father came to me last night. Here in this room—I'm serious! He was powerful and shining so bright! His power held me still on the bed. He said, 'Don't be afraid.' We were communicating spirit to spirit. I couldn't say a word! He said, 'Walter's going to be the next mayor of Compton and he's going to need your cooperation, your complete support. Listen to me! Listen to me! You'll have tough trials to endure, so you're going to have to be very strong—stronger than you've ever been.' Honey, you're going to be the next mayor of Compton."

I nodded.

What she didn't know was that same night I had a dream. I saw myself walking down the halls of the Compton Courthouse where I practiced criminal law. An angel was walking beside me. He pointed to the courtrooms and said, "See these courtrooms…take a good look because you won't see them again as a practicing criminal lawyer."

Robin and I stared at each other quietly. We were now in agreement because she knew it was the will of God. We realized we were part of a destiny greater than either of us had imagined. God had given us a vision of the victory line, but now we were back to reality and we'd have to walk it out to reach it. The first order of business was to give Big Wes my answer.

Off and Running

I t was a typical overcast day in February 1991 when Big Wes and I strolled inside the 70s glass and brick City Hall. All the usual, self-interested parties packed the City Council Chambers' lobby.

"They'll appoint you tonight 'cause they owe me a few favors. Truth be told, they owe me a lotta favors and I'm calling 'em in," Big Wes whispered in my ear.

Once Wes and I stepped inside the City Council Chambers, some citizens' heads turned and they whispered to each other. We sat in the back of the chamber and focused on the four councilpersons in front of us. They were seated at the council table, heads down, pouring over the preliminary agenda. Representing District 1, there was the opinionated and outspoken Councilman Maxcy Filer, acting as Mayor pro tem since my dad's passing. He was known around town as "Mr. Compton," largely due to his commendable community and civil rights work done through the NAACP when he and his family first moved to the then predominately white city. Anyone who knew Maxcy knew that his personality could be summed up in one word—unrelenting! In fact, everyone knew how this City Councilman aspired to become a lawyer and took the California State Bar 48 times until he finally passed it!

From District 2, Councilwoman Patricia Moore sat properly on stage. "Pat," as she was affectionately called, was truly one of a kind—a real diva. Rumor had it that she had been planning her climb to the top all her life. Her flashy outfits, fancy cars, and well-kept hair and nails declared that she had arrived. But her polished exterior belied the fiery lava that lay just below the surface and could erupt in a moment's notice. Like a powerful racing car, she could speed forward from 0 to 60 in just a few seconds.

Pat made it her business to establish relationships with the right people at the right time. Everyone from the most prominent ministers in Compton's churches to the most feared gang members in Compton's streets to the families most grieved by tragedy. Those families allowed her to speak for them because they knew she would manipulate the media to garner public attention for their cause. Insiders whispered that her opportunistic character always sent her searching for any injustice she could rally around to further her political career.

Representing District 3, was Councilwoman Bernice "Momma" Woods, who wore her church hats as her own brand. The "Momma" brand, coupled with her involvement with the black churches, elected officials, and organized sports her children played, endeared her into the hearts of many Compton residents. When Momma Woods wasn't walking around carefully on her cane quoting Scripture, she was incessantly on her phone with residents, keeping abreast of all the issues. She kept the biggest prayer and hotline going in the city.

Finally, from District 4, sat the elder stateswoman of the city—Councilwoman Jane Robbins. She was the only white person still on the Compton City Council. The soft-spoken, seventy-year-old woman who wore black, cat-eye-shaped glasses right out of the 50s, boasted that her father had been the first mayor of Compton back in 1924. I used to think Jane spent more time telling the city about its past than planning for its future. However, in time, I came to appreciate Compton's rich history, and, after she died, I wished I had an opportunity to talk with her about some of the finer details of the city's beginning.

After the preliminary agenda was finished, the council persons looked up at the audience. It seemed they stared straight at me, then quickly looked away. The City Clerk called item number 6574 and the councilpersons stared down at their agendas.

"Those in favor of appointing someone to serve out Mayor Walter R. Tucker's unexpired term."

Big Wes and I watched intensely as the Council answered in a matter-of-fact manner.

"Councilman Filer?"

"No."

"Councilwoman Moore?"

"No."

"Councilwoman Woods?"

"No."

"Councilwoman Robbins?"

"No."

Wes' face bucked in disbelief. He had been double-crossed. The citizens in the audience looked unhappy too.

The City Clerk added another matter-of-fact item. "That leads us to Item number 6575 – approval of a Special Election on April sixteenth, nineteen ninety-one to elect someone to fulfill Mayor Tucker's unexpired term. Councilman Filer?"

"Yes."

"Councilwoman Moore?"

"Yes."

"Councilwoman Woods?"

"Yes."

"And Councilwoman Robbins?"

"Yes."

"Alright, the item passed and the Special Election to complete Mayor Tucker's unexpired term will be held next year, April sixteenth, nineteen ninety-one."

Just in front of us, the gray-haired Momma Harris, once a block club powerbroker, stood on her cane and headed for the exit. As she passed by her friend, Willie Duhon, she blurted out, "They shoulda just made Junior the mayor and saved us all a lot of time and money."

"You know what that was all about. They all want to be Mayor," Willie responded.

"You right about that!" Momma said, and limped out on her cane.

I shot a look of disappointment at Big Wes and could see anger and embarrassment all over his face. He and I quietly left the council chambers.

At home, I hurriedly told Robin what happened.

She chimed in, "I could have told you that. I've worked at City Hall for twelve years and I know this is not going to be easy. Your father's name carries weight, but they play hardball. They've been waiting for a moment like this and now they want the power. If you run for Mayor, just be ready for things you never thought could happen. They will fight dirty."

"I know, baby, I'll be ready. I won't just turn away from a fight because somebody's gonna get some licks in. I've gotta carry on Dad's legacy."

A few days after the vote, Maxcy Filer, Bernice Woods, and Pat Moore petitioned to run for Mayor. That was the entire council, except Jane Robbins, who had served on the council for twenty years and now, was just going along for the ride.

Congressman Mervyn Dymally, D-31st District, had held a grip on the City Council for the last ten years and now was supporting all three candidates. That way, whichever one won, he would have ousted the entrenched Tucker name and been in good with the new mayor. Stop a "Tucker Dynasty" at all costs. If I'm going to be the next mayor of Compton, I'm truly going to have to earn it, notwithstanding all of my father's good works.

Big Wes and my mom, affectionately known as "Marti," ran my campaign, with Robin contributing in every meeting and learning with me along the way. My beautiful mom was a behind-the-scenes power. Her sophisticated manner made it seem that all she did was give dinner parties for visiting dignitaries, write books, buy designer clothes, and attend club meetings with her bourgeois friends. But it was her high ideals for all of her children to finish college and to get exposed to different cultures that caused Tina Griego, an LA Times writer, to label our family, "The Kennedys of Compton": "They're attractive, educated, wealthy, well-traveled, and fiercely loyal." [5]

All those years hanging with my dad at countless community events had prepared Marti to be a good campaigner. She knew the ropes and where all the bones were buried. For starters, she was loved at the Dollarhide Senior Citizens' Center. She took me there, and taught me how to "work a room." In one way or another, I've been working a room ever since.

"You don't know them, but they know you because you're "a Tucker." So just go and speak to everyone at the table. Be friendly. Smile and shake hands."

At first, when I attended an event, I just sat in my seat and tried to talk to the nine other people around the table. But that day, I learned my lesson. There'd be time for eating later. This was the time to go table by table and make friends, one by one.

The seasoned politicians called it "pressing the flesh." The seniors were the solid voters of Compton, and they solidly supported my dad. We needed them to touch my hand and know that Mayor Tucker's son was touchable and worthy of their support—just like his dad.

"You the first son, right? Well, you got that chin, just like your daddy. He was my dentist, you know and he was the best," Momma Harris said. She took her index finger and pulled the right side of her mouth open. "See, right here. He put this bridge in twenty years ago, and it's still good. I paid him for it over ten years. But I paid him like I said I would."

I smiled. That's my dad.

She changed the subject. "And you gonna be our first black President one day? I know your momma sure would be proud."

I just smiled politely and wondered.

* * * * * *

Reflecting on the challenges ahead, I talked to my pastor, Major Johnson, after one Wednesday night Bible Study.

"Major, I believe it's time for me to become a licensed minister, anything to bring me closer to God."

"Well Walter, you've been faithful in your study and service for years; I've seen good growth in you. I agree that it's time."

Little did I know that what I needed at that moment to gird me up for the political battle ahead, God would use later for His purpose throughout my entire life.

* * * * * *

As the campaign progressed, Big Wes was determined to bring Omar Bradley along. He was a young black man close to my age, named after a World War II U.S. Army General. He was known to be a street fighter. Big Wes had a plan. He would draft Omar to run for Maxcy's council seat. Wes was determined to have a cadre of young lions elected to be loyal to his plans. The city treasurer needed a team to be effective and make Compton turn out like he had planned with my dad.

"Look, Omar, you need to join us. I'm mobilizing Junior's whole campaign and he's going to be the next mayor."

"I dunno. The whole City Council's running against him," Omar argued.

"Don't matter. I know the streets. See, I'm the one that put Mayor Tucker in office back in '81. This time, I see Junior as Mayor, and you and Pat take the council seats—that's a winning slate! Can't you see it?" He gestured. "Omar Bradley, City Councilman. You in?"

"Yeah. Count me in."

"Good! I'll set up a meeting between you, Junior, and Pat."

* * * * * *

When I walked into the Ramada Hotel's restaurant with Wes, Omar rose from his seat and shook my hand like we were veteran politicians. He smiled and we sat and talked. He seemed to share my own hopes and dreams for Compton.

"Your dad started a good thing. Now let's make Compton better than when the white people were here."

"We can do it. Bring in new businesses, lower taxes, and reduce crime."

"First, we gotta get a truce between the gangs. I can help with that."

Some people said that Omar was a "wannabe gangsta." But as I sat across the table from him that night, all I saw was a young black man who was well-read, well-spoken, and bent on fixing the city he grew up in and loved.

Because Omar was a young, political unknown who had once run for Mayor in a huge field of hopefuls against my dad, people paid little attention to him. But together, with Wes' slate in place, we could be a force to be reckoned with. We were going to save this 100-year-old, decaying city. We were going to bring back the pride!

Young lions roar!

My mom's background as a teacher and writer proved useful in helping me shape my issues and write my speeches— Newspaper publicity was her forte. But her tenacity was greater. She vehemently defended the issue of my youth with the NAACP, the Rotary Club, Chamber of Commerce, City Commissioners, and anyone else who questioned my maturity. Her wise anecdotes, which she said came from hanging out with my dad and hearing his plans for the city, were effective.

It was also great that Mom understood and had favor with the block clubs. Next to the power of the churches to put someone in office in the black community, the block clubs were key; they were the soul of "grassroots politics." They were essentially the coming together of neighbors on the same street, block, or neighborhood to unify around the issues that directly impacted their street or neighborhood. Things like crime, poor lighting, tree trimming, or speed bumps. She knew that block clubs in Compton were generally well-organized, highly vocal, and adamant about their issues. Mom knew how to win their respect. Under no circumstances did she ever allow my dad to miss one of their candidates' forums. Spending all day Saturday with them, sampling their home-cooked treats—barbecue, potato salad, peach cobbler, and homemade ice cream—and meeting their families went a long way. She wrote them up in the local papers and reminded Dad to honor them at the City Council meetings.

Before the block clubs were polled to endorse a candidate, she made sure I followed in Dad's footsteps.

"Make sure you attend all their forums, listen carefully to all their issues, and hang out the whole day with them. The residents need to know that you're accessible and that there's no other interest more important than them."

"Got it."

It made for a lot of long Saturdays, but I followed her advice to the tee. She was right. When the block club endorsements came out weeks later, I won most of them.

The woman who had for years wanted to leave Compton had learned it was bigger than her selfish desires; she learned to truly love and appreciate it. So she laughed with community cornerstones like Willie Duhon and Clarence Reed, and they willingly filled their trucks with sandwiches, yard signs, posters, and flyers to fuel the campaign. She was the lady who women admired up close, but often hated from a distance. She kept smiling at all of them because her singular goal was making Compton great.

CHAPTER TEN

Closing The Deal

The special election was war. Winning would take political acumen, unity, and a lot of courage and persistence. As soon as we opened our headquarters, someone threw eggs all over our windows. Then, I was notified that our campaign literature had been thrown in the L.A. River that angled through Compton, not far from our office. We knew it was our opponent's dirty work, but since we were fighting three major camps, we'd probably never know which one did it. Soon we discovered spies were planted in our office, but we kept them "out of the loop." The good news was that we were a family and all hands were on deck.

My family and supporters were present at every candidates' forum. And that was a good thing because new drama dominated every one of them. From one event to the next, some gadfly was always on the attack.

"So what makes you think you're qualified to be our mayor when you've never even held office?"

"That's true, but I've been prepared for this job all my life. I'm a product of Compton schools and I'm a licensed lawyer with my own practice right here in the city. I watched and assisted my dad over the years as he gave his life to serve this city. I'm qualified, alright."

"I heard you don't even live in the city. That you live in Bellflower!"

"That's not true. When my dad died, I moved back into the house I grew up in—five o one West Tichenor."

"But you don't own that house—"

"I don't have to. I pay the rent there just like I did at my residence in Bellflower. That's my residence. It's where my mail is delivered and that's where I'll be living should I take office."

"Oh, you not taking nothing here—this is our city!"

One of our campaign workers yelled, "This is out of order!"

"You're right. Who's next?" the moderator asked.

Yes, our campaign had to be ready for anything, but as I stated at the candidates' forum, I was prepared.

Our opponents had forgotten how tough of a campaigner I had become under my father's tutelage. I had been the consummate campaign manager and now I was the candidate. From dawn to midnight, I was in the streets, shaking hands, kissing babies, galvanizing youth, and hugging seniors. It was love at first sight. I was making my own friends, forging my own trails, getting the word out.

While I was working the streets, Robin was working on my behalf at City Hall, where she was employed. There, the powers that be did their best to keep her in the dark but because of her intuitive personality, she could detect what they were up to.

We'd stay up half the night sharing information and planning, and wake up early the next morning doing the same.

"Honey, Little Zion's having their Pastoral Appreciation Service this Sunday. Maxcy, Pat, and Bernice are sure to be there with a city resolution, and a plug for their campaigns. Make sure you're there early so you can get a good seat. In fact, even though Reverend Fisher is staying neutral in this race, I'm sure he'll recognize you because of his longstanding friendship with your father."

"Not only that, but it's protocol to allow all ministers to sit in the pulpit."

"Right. The councilpersons might be able to speak on behalf of the city, but all you have to do is stay visible at every community event and talk to people one on one."

I took the wisdom Robin gave me and put it to good use, following leads, trails, and dark rabbit holes. When she wasn't working City Hall, she, too, was working the community. I never really realized what a social butterfly my wife was. She knew everybody and everybody knew her.

Robin's father and mother, Robert and Pauline Smith, had lived in Compton almost all their adult lives and influenced a lot of votes.

"Mrs. Smith, now who do I vote for? For Mayor?"

"Child, please. Right there, my son-in-law, Walter Tucker. He's the best!"

"Ah, yeah. Sure 'nough."

My campaign didn't have a lot of money, but we had enthusiastic campaigners—youth, seniors, singles, and strangers. And, because we spoke Spanish, nearly every Latino we talked to promised to vote for me. With my family and friends visibly involved, people who might have thought of opposing us began to walk ever so carefully, just in case we won.

At that time, a lot of Robin's family worked in law enforcement. Robin's brother, Mark Smith, then a bailiff with the Sheriff's Department, was always packing. So, every wannabe gangster in town knew not to put his hands on me.

Of course, my mom ran the campaign headquarters with my sister, Keta, serving as campaign treasurer, making sure our books were straight. Even my baby sister, Camille, who was up to her eyeballs in textbooks at college, stole away for a few Saturdays to help make phone calls or pound the pavement.

My younger brother, Ken, tall and lean, who came home from D.C. when my father became ill, was the commander in charge of the "Scud missiles," our yard signs that were delivered to almost every house in every city block. When a call came in for a sign, Ken and his team packed the signs in a 1974 blue Ford LTD and delivered them promptly to the residents' home and anchored them in the yard. In a matter of weeks, neighborhood streets began to look like "Tucker Territory."

But placing signs on the main city streets was a greater challenge. When we put signs up on the telephone poles that lined the main boulevards by night, they would mysteriously disappear by morning. We knew our opponents were doing the damage, but we didn't know exactly who. I heard that one night Big Wes and some of his men were hanging out late at a local bar, hoping to catch the culprits.

As Big Wes threw back another bourbon, he said, "I'm tellin' y'all, the way they been doin' us, it's jus' a matter of time. They musta lost they mind. They forgot I'm from Watts!"

Suddenly, a lookout from the streets ran into the bar.

"Big Wes! Big Wes! I seen't 'em! They out there right now, man, pullin' down our damn signs!

"Where they at?"

"On Rosecrans, between Willowbrook and Wilmington!"

"Hell, let's roll!"

Wes and his men grabbed their coats and ran for the parking lot. Once inside his truck, Wes opened his glove compartment, pulled out his .45, and laid it between his legs. He pressed on the gas like a fireman speeding to a fire, and the rest of the campaign workers followed in their trucks behind him.

As Big Wes and his men rolled down Rosecrans, they could see some shadowy figures standing on the back of a flatbed systematically pulling down Tucker signs from the street poles. Wes pulled right up alongside the truck.

"Hey, them's Tucker signs!"

He fired off a few rounds over their heads, hitting the poles.

The driver of the flatbed yelled, "Oh, hell no!" He burned rubber, and the men in the back held onto the flatbed for dear life as they swerved from street to street. Wes and his men chased them for a couple of blocks, running red lights, honking their horns, shooting in the air, and yelling obscenities at them.

"We gonna get *yo'* ass!"

After Big Wes and his men let them get away down a narrow alley, they returned to their bar and toasted their success to the wee hours of the morning, throwing back more bourbon and slapping high-fives!

Needless to say, from that night on, the Tucker for Mayor campaign signs lit up the main boulevards.

April 16, 1991. Election Day finally arrived. Since Compton elections were notorious for their reported improprieties, we assigned "poll watchers" at the various polling places to make sure that no one would think of cheating. Once the polls closed at 8:00 p.m., it was time for the real high drama in the jam-packed City Council Chambers. Workers from each campaign huddled together in their respective areas.

"Junior, we watched till every ballot was sealed, boxed up, and put into the vans. Then we followed them here." Big Wes said.

"And our people are overseeing the delivery of those boxes into the City Clerk's office?" I asked.

"Right, even though police cars are stationed out front for the drop-off."

"Great. Keep me posted."

I was checking every detail because as my dad used to say, "There's many a slip between the cup and the lip!"

Throughout the night everyone was eyeing everyone else like gunfighters at the O.K.

Corral, preparing to draw and fire. The entire audience was starkly divided along campaign lines, but all eyes were on the City Clerk, Charles Davis, in all his fluster. His deputy clerks recorded the precinct tallies and periodically handed them to him.

As the City Clerk announced the latest tallies over the mic, it became apparent the race was tight. Tension gripped the packed room. God forbid there was a glitch or even the slightest appearance of impropriety. Finally, around midnight, the City Clerk was handed the final tally and he nervously grabbed the mic.

"Well, folks, with thirty-four of the thirty-four precincts in, I can now give you the final results: Bernice Woods, 394 votes, 5.9 %, Patricia Moore, 1,863 votes, 27.8%, Maxcy D. Filer, 1,593 votes, 23.8%, and Walter R. Tucker III, 2,389 votes, 35%." [6] Walter R. Tucker III is our new mayor.

My campaign workers and supporters erupted into loud cheers, and the sound filled the entire Council Chambers. Yes, I had shocked the entire city, winning over projected front-runners Maxcy Filer and Pat Moore. Overnight, at age thirty-three, I had become the youngest Mayor in the city's 100-year history. The celebration was intoxicating. I tried to hug everyone who had helped my campaign in any way. In addition to the hugs, there were tears of joy and a plethora of high-fives. In a blink, the euphoria in the chambers dissolved into the victory party at our family home in Richland Farms.

Richland Farms was arguably the most respected neighborhood in Compton. When Griffith Dickenson Compton donated his land settlement to incorporate and create the city of Compton in 1889, he stipulated that a certain acreage be zoned solely for agriculture. That acreage was and is named Richland Farms.[7] It was comprised of large residential lots which gave residents enough space to build a home and a farm. In the '50s, Richland Farms attracted black families who had begun migrating from the rural South. The lots were filled with barns, crops, and livestock.

Now, in the '90s, Richland Farms was where successful, middle-class, black families paid for single-family homes that were set on half-acre and acre lots. It was not uncommon to still see residents riding horses, growing gardens, or raising livestock amidst their beautiful ranch-style homes. This neighborhood, though not a gated community, was very close-knit. The families, which resided on only five streets, all knew one another and were invested in each other's well-being. Their children were raised to matriculate through the city's public schools, attend the nation's finest universities, return home and give back what they had learned to help elevate the city they loved.

Now it was party time in Richland Farms because one such favorite son had returned and was now in a prime position to give back. The city councilpersons and some city leaders put on their best-pasted smiles and dropped by. They tried to look pleasant and sound congratulatory, but I could see they were still in shock. They needed to go lay down, so none of them stayed long. After they cleared out, the party cranked into high gear.

My victory party in our big backyard was young and raucous. We were bouncing our bodies to the soulful sounds of a local band until three o'clock in the morning. Our sprawling home had hosted political parties for Jesse Jackson for President, Jerry Brown for Governor, Maynard Jackson, and Andrew Young, Jr. for Mayor (of Atlanta), and special receptions for baseball great, Don Newcombe, the late, great Paul Robeson, young Martin Luther King, Jr., and several stars of stage and screen. But that night, the party was for me! The music pumped louder and more people crowded into the moonlit, late-night celebration. We got loud, but no one called Compton PD—no, not that night.

Everywhere I turned, robust hand slaps, high-fives, and back slaps caught me faster than I could react. That moment was like the glory of a fantastic touchdown. Run, dodge, runnnnnnnnn over that goal line!

"We won, man! You da man!"

The guys' hugs of congratulations were so rough they nearly squeezed the breath out of me. Suddenly, tiny raindrops drizzled, threatening to explode into a full downpour. But no one was the least bit concerned. Rather, the moisture created a magical atmosphere that seemed to work the crowd into a fever pitch.

My homeboys yelled, "We did it, man! Compton for life!"

All the excited campaign workers kept the party pumping. Our sing-along and bragging echoed throughout the neighborhood.

"Good times...these are the good times! Boom, boom, boom, boom, boom, boom, boom! Good times!"

Suddenly, Robin and I took to the dance floor, throwing up our hands in jubilation. Everyone around us raised their hands in the air and cheered. Our motley crew had just squashed two seasoned Councilpersons and left an acting mayor in the dust. When I saw my mom walking toward me, her baby face blended into the youthful crowd of party animals. I just knew she was coming to tell us to pipe down. Her voice cut through the booming noise of the music.

"Your father woulda been so proud of you…the youngest mayor in the city's history! And I'm so proud of you too!"

"Me too!" Robin yelled. "Group hug." And just like that the three of us enjoyed a magical moment that seemed frozen in time.

I knew it was my father's good name and humble service to the community and my mother's unselfish dedication to her family that placed me in that seat. It was my father's death that made the people appreciate his allegiance to them. It was the people's desire to keep him alive that opened the door for me to enter this peculiar new world of politics. Now the rest was up to me.

Walter R. Tucker, III sworn in as youngest mayor of Compton, April, 1991.

CHAPTER ELEVEN

The Godfather

After a sleepless night at my home in Alexandria, Virginia, Robin drove me to Dulles International Airport to catch my flight to L.A. She pulled our car up to the curb in front of the United Airlines terminal.

"Call me as soon as you get more details from Johnnie. I'm planning on being out there in a couple of days."

"Okay, I'll see you soon." I kissed Robin, grabbed my luggage, and sped off to my gate.

I strapped into my seat on American Airlines flight 526, took a couple of slow deep breaths, and braced myself for the five-hour flight. I couldn't arrive in Los Angeles fast enough. I needed answers and I knew Johnnie would have them. A stately blonde flight attendant stood over me with a bottle in her hand.

"Champagne, sir?"

First class service could break all the rules of coach—things like not serving anything before takeoff.

"No, thanks."

The last thing I needed was champagne. My mind was already in a haze. What I needed most was clarity.

After takeoff, fatigue got the best of me. I drifted in and out of sleep, my mind reverting back to the past. Maybe my past held some secrets to this mystery. What could they be?

* * * * * *

Back in '91, the Beverly Wilshire Hotel's lobby was packed with a lot of California's power brokers—State Assemblywoman Teresa Hughes, State Assemblyman Willard Murray, Mayor Mike Mitoma of Carson, business magnates in aerospace, rubbish, and import and export. They always came out for Congressman Mervyn Dymally's birthday bash, an annual feast for elected officials, commissioners, and appointees who carried out his wishes in the district. The well-dressed, important-looking guests stood in little circles, mostly according to their affiliations in the district. Some were backslapping, joking and filled with raucous laughter. But most of them spoke in lowered tones. It seemed to me, the young mayor, the new kid on the block, that they were discussing high-ranking, and strategic secrets. With my wife on my arm, I cut through the crowd, my antenna picking up the stares and a few low-tone comments:

"He was always with his father. His father was a good man, a good mayor. Untimely death!"

"Is he twenty-one or what?"

"No, he's a lawyer...worked for the District Attorney's office...he's at least twenty-five."

A woman added, "All I know is he's fine!" They chuckled.

"Yeah, check out that suit and tie. Looks like he stepped straight out of *GQ*."

"It's not the clothes that got him elected, it's the education. They sent him to Princeton, U.S.C., *and* Georgetown."

I shook hands amongst the power brokers like I belonged, like I had seen my father do. *Just be cool. Lay back and watch the crowd.*

As Robin and I eased across the hotel lobby into a foyer outside the banquet room, Ken Orduna, Congressman Dymally's Chief of Staff, reached out with the friendliest hand I had seen all night. It was like nothing adversarial had ever happened between our political camps.

"Ah, the new mayor. Come on, let me introduce you around."

I was always a little leery of Ken because he was so glib, but I needed an entrance to this new world and he was it. In the blink of an eye, I was caught up in a whirlwind of introductions. A photographer appeared.

"Hold that handshake, Mr. Mayor, and we'll take a couple of shots."

The camera's flashes were blinding. By the time I refocused, I was standing face to face with Dymally.

"Congressman, I'd like you to meet our new mayor," Ken said.

We shook hands. While Congressman Dymally and I were in each other's space, everyone around turned toward us and began whispering.

In a Trinidadian accent, Dymally spoke without ever looking directly at me, "One helluva victory, young man."

And just that quickly, he departed. Then Ken leaned over to me and said, "Oh, Mr. Mayor, there's someone else you really need to talk to...John Macardican."

The name rang a bell. I raced through my brain, trying to place it. I recalled seeing his name on my dad's list of political contributors. I also recalled Councilwoman Moore saying that I should meet him. I turned and we were standing face to face. Ken made the introduction.

"John Macardican, this is Walter Tucker III, the new mayor of Compton."

At that moment, I realized he was the white-haired man on the second row I had seen at my dad's funeral. He offered a handshake and a polite grin. I shook his hand. "People keep saying we need to talk." That seemed like the power statement to make.

"Most definitely. I've been wanting to talk with you," he said. "I'll call you for an appointment."

I smiled, handed him a card to my law office, and continued to maneuver through the crowd of movers and shakers. Suddenly the lights flashed, signaling dinner was about to be served. The crowd started flowing into the banquet room, and I followed. Once inside, Ken began to point people to their respective tables. I checked the back of my ticket—Table 55—and led Robin toward our seats.

We arrived at our table where I greeted some familiar faces. Looking around, I noticed John Macardican seated at a table next to me. He nodded in my direction and smiled.

It wasn't long before Congressman Dymally took the stage and addressed the audience. His thick accent and the sound of waiters removing dinner plates made it difficult for me to hear every word he was saying. His small stature and calm demeanor were definitely misleading. When my father was Mayor, he used to tell me about the battles they'd had; about Dymally's explosive temper. Some people attributed it to him being from Trinidad. Others said that his temper was his own personality trait. One thing I did know, Dymally was a real force to be reckoned with in our community.

I watched the congressman carefully measure his words. No doubt about it, he was a giant to whom people showed great admiration. He had been a State Assemblyman, State Senator, and had made history as the first black Lieutenant Governor of California. As a member of the House Foreign Affairs Committee and Chairman of the Subcommittee on Africa, he had clout throughout the country and in a good portion of the world.

If there was ever a political godfather in our community, the six-term, seasoned congressman was it. Potential candidates and people with proposals and projects bowed and kissed his ring. They sought him out for political endorsements, financial support, or life-changing introductions to someone who could do them good. But my father, a successful dentist and well-respected himself, never bowed to Dymally. He did, however, support him when he ran for State Senate, and years later, expected his support when my father ran for mayor. Dymally's failure to return the favor was the beginning of their declining relationship.

In the years that went by, I heard my father's ire, "He's not from Compton, he doesn't live in Compton, and yet he wants to control everything in Compton!"

Later, when my father was Mayor, he set up a meeting in D.C. with officials from the Small Business Administration to receive tax credits for Compton businesses. He requested Congressman Dymally's presence and support at that meeting, but Dymally sent word that he would be out of the country. My dad went to the meeting in D.C., anyhow. When he went to dinner that evening at a restaurant downtown, there sat Dymally.

"That man's got his own agenda!" Dad complained. "He cares more about economic interests in Africa than he does about the interests of our Compton residents!"

The war was on. The bitter never left the gall.

With that background, I understood Dymally was not my friend or supporter. But I was the new mayor and it was my duty to try to work with him, and anyone else who could help me improve Compton.

That was three years ago...

CHAPTER TWELVE

Face-To-Face

"Excuse me, sir, please bring your seat forward, we're about to land."

I slowly opened my eyes and followed the flight attendant's direction.

After the long flight, I couldn't wait to get off the plane. I quickly grabbed my luggage, then stood at the curb searching for a black Lincoln Town Car with congressional license plates that read "CA 37." Thankfully, it wasn't long before I spotted Tyrone, one of my District Field Deputies, pulling up. Tyrone, like Marcus, was a product of the 37th Congressional District. Although he was a 21-year-old African-American male, what he lacked in experience he made up for with enthusiasm and an eagerness to learn. Neatly dressed in an olive-colored suit and tie, and sporting a close-cropped haircut, Tyrone pulled the car to the curb in front of me. He scooted out, grabbed my bags, and I ducked into the backseat.

Tyrone knew that with all I had on my plate, some days were better than others. He had learned how to gauge my disposition after my long flight. He'd take the initiative to strike up a conversation with a general greeting, then wait to see if my response was talkative or brief.

"Welcome home, Congressman?"

"Thanks, Tyrone."

"Where to?"

"The district office."

"Another busy weekend?"

"Yeah, a lot going on." I placed my hand on my forehead. "Please turn down the radio."

Tyrone knew then that I was not in the mood for much conversation. Unfortunately, I couldn't tell him my head was spinning from all the speculation concerning an impending indictment. Of course, I didn't know enough yet to share anything with him. The only thing I knew was that I wasn't leaving L.A. until I found out what was coming down from the U.S. Attorney's Office. Was it all a bluff to unglue me in the public eye? Or was it an eerie prelude to a thunderous storm? I took my phone from my briefcase and called Johnnie.

"Hey, Johnnie, so what's the update?

"Congressman, they called me back and said they want to meet us on Monday at two o'clock in the afternoon in the lobby of the U.S. Attorney's office—Three Twelve North Spring Street. Unfortunately, my schedule's jammed over the next couple of days, so instead of you coming to my office first, I need you to meet me at their office. We'll have a few minutes to talk before we go in, then we'll debrief afterward at my office."

"Okay. That'll give my wife time to get in town and also I'd like to have my brother-in-law, Attorney Mark Smith, at that meeting."

"No problem, baby."

I thought Mark, who was also a criminal defense attorney, could assist Johnnie. However, it was understood that Johnnie was running the show. The stage was set. My lawyers, my wife, my mother, and I on one side, and the U.S. attorneys on the other side. We would meet face to face for the first time. All the speculation and innuendoes would be confronted. Before the prosecution could play their game, they'd have to show us a few of their cards.

Later that day, at my district office on Compton Boulevard, I received a surprise visit from one of the city's most colorful characters. My District Office Manager, Audrey Gibson, walked into my office.

"Basil Kimbrew to see you, Congressman. He says it's important."

My first reaction was to avoid him since he was known to be Councilwoman Pat Moore's right-hand man, but I knew I had no conspiracy or collusion with Pat and that made me feel a bit more at ease with him. There was always the possibility, though, that Basil might be wired. Still, a small voice inside said, "Talk to him. Don't say much...just listen."

Basil, who was always willing to impress me with knowledge of recent developments in the community, sat down and rattled off the latest.

"Pat has already been down to visit the U.S. Attorney. I know 'cause I was down there with her. Past the reception area was a hallway and on both sides of the hallway, there were doors. Those doors each had one thing in common— a big sign posted on them: COMPTON PUBLIC CORRUPTION INVESTIGATION. At the end of the hallway was a room that Pat was escorted into for her conference with the U.S. Attorney."

Basil stood up and started nervously pacing back and forth, "I wasn't present for that meeting, but from my position in the hallway, I was able to see into a couple of rooms. What I remember the most were mounds of boxes, files, charts, and graphs with Compton officials' names on them. One huge chart was like a big target board, and it showed all of the faces and names of the members of the Compton City Council." He stood still and looked me squarely in the face, "Imagine that!"

Wow.

I listened. Following the advice of my inner voice, I kept tight-lipped and thanked Basil for sharing. My interest was piqued. I knew I was dealing with something massive, but I just didn't know what. Basil gave no further information as to any pending indictments against Councilwoman Moore or what they said to her. Apparently, even the close-knit relationship between Basil and the councilwoman had its limit. Either that or that's all he wanted to reveal.

The weekend in the District passed with me attending numerous community events, all the while trying to keep my mind from being preoccupied with thoughts of my meeting with the U.S. Attorney. By Sunday afternoon, I was ecstatic that Robin had managed to leave our children in the care of people we trusted and had arrived in L.A. Not know what was about to befall me, I needed her close to me for moral support. Nevertheless, by Monday afternoon my mind was racing a thousand miles a minute. My legal instincts said, no matter what the prosecution says or reveals in the meeting remain totally silent.

Though my wife and mom were right by my side, the drive downtown to the U.S. Attorney's Office for the afternoon meeting was not by any means a pleasant one—tension hovered in the air like a fog. We arrived first and waited in the austere lobby for Johnnie and Mark. The dingy concrete seemed to whisper gloom as we waited.

Here I am in their lair and there's no turning back.

After about five minutes, Mark arrived and sat with us. After ten more minutes, Johnnie arrived with one of his associates. As expected, Johnnie was dressed to the tee, sporting a custom-made, blue pinstriped suit, colorful silk tie, and power glasses. His associate, Carl Douglas, was also well dressed and appeared quite perceptive as his eyes scanned over me from head to toe.

"Hey, baby, sorry I'm late, just couldn't be avoided," Johnnie said.

"I understand, Johnnie."

"Let me just ask them if we can take a few minutes here in the lobby before we go back there to meet with them."

"That's fine."

When Johnnie returned, he indicated that the U.S. Attorney had no objection to his request. So there we were, my legal team, my wife, my mother, and I huddled in the lobby, just outside the security door.

"Congressman, these things are generally pretty standard," Johnnie said.

"Really? So, you've done a lot of these?"

"Well, to be honest, my criminal practice is principally in State Court and I haven't had many occasions to deal with these guys. But that's why Carl's here. You know Carl Douglas, my associate, right?"

"Yes, right." I glanced over at Carl and nodded, although it was my first time meeting him personally.

"He's an ex-U.S. Attorney and can give us guidance on any legal nuances."

Johnnie may not have had extensive experience with federal cases, however, given his excellent reputation with criminal cases in State court, I wasn't worried.

"Okay. Carl, tell me what we're looking at here?"

"Well, this is their 'informal conference' where they lay out for us, in summary, the case they have against you, Congressman. They may try to get you to comment under a form of immunity for today only."

"Oh, no. No comment whatsoever. I learned about that one a few years ago as a deputy DA. When they say anything you say, can, and will be used against you in a court of law, they do mean *anything*."

"No problem, Congressman. Just keep perfectly quiet and leave the talking to me," Johnnie said.

"Now, if I have a question, Johnnie, I'll whisper to you, and allow you to take it from there."

"Right. We're straight on that. Let's go."

Since the news broke that Johnnie was representing me, people speculated that I had put up a bundle to get LA's top criminal defense attorney. Not being wealthy, I had put up only a $50,000 retainer. Perhaps Johnnie agreed to it because he admired me as a young black congressman. On the other hand, he seemed to like me because he was a former assistant district attorney and I was a former deputy district attorney. Whatever the reason, I knew it was just God's favor.

My party and I stood waiting outside the bulletproof glass door. As it opened, Michael Emig, a white attorney appeared and said, "I'm sorry, Mr. Tucker, but only you and your attorneys will be allowed inside."

I glanced at Robin and Mom and sighed. They shot me a look back that said, *It's alright, we understand,* while Attorney Emig led my legal team and me through the security door. Once inside the secured area, I saw the infamous hallway, just as Basil had described it. *Oh, my God!*

As my attorneys and I walked down that hallway, we passed by a quirky-looking white man wearing a conservative suit. I wondered who he was. I would later learn that he was Assistant U.S. Attorney John Potter. His appearance and demeanor were as staid and cold as the concrete walls—a "gray guy." I instinctively knew there was more to him than met the eye. I had worked around enough prosecutors to know that they, like sharks, come alive when they smell blood. The sharks were circling. They were standing close to the mysterious room at the end of the hall. On the way to that room, my attention focused on the doors off the hallway, which, as Basil had said, had signs on them marked: COMPTON PUBLIC CORRUPTION INVESTIGATION.

I counted six doors. It suddenly dawned on me that an entire wing was dedicated to Compton as a target. *Deep!* As I glanced into an office space where one of the doors had been left open, I could see FBI charts and graphs on Compton. Files upon files, and mounds of paperwork in boxes. Perhaps most interesting was the sign, THE BRIBURN INVESTIGATION!

As quickly as the mind records subliminally, it was all locked and stored in my head. "Bri," short for "Bribery." "Burn," indicating a "setup," or a "sting operation." The bribery was the means by which the burn would take place. It was all so strategic. It had all been carefully considered and conceived—it reminded me of a plan to extinguish a group of people.

CHAPTER THIRTEEN

Briburn

"Right this way, gentlemen."

We walked through the doorway and entered the room at the end of the hall. All the important prosecutorial players stood facing us from behind a long, oak conference table—Michael Emig, Rick Drooyan, heading up the Criminal Division, Steve Madison, top gun Assistant U.S. Attorney, and the "gray guy," Assistant U.S. Attorney John Potter—the sleeper. I stood at a distance as the usual exchange of greetings took place between the attorneys. Then, we all took our seats at the table. It was clear by the setup of the room —U.S. Attorneys on one side of the conference table, and my attorneys and me on the other side—that this was no social gathering.

Rick Drooyan took control and introduced the government's team. Johnnie introduced our smaller contingent. We sat perched to hear the government's presentation. Steve Madison, a sandy brown-haired, well-groomed, intense young white man, took charge. Copies of a report were quickly handed to us. My team leafed through them, and Madison's confrontational spirit broke loose without provocation.

"The U.S. Attorney, in conjunction with the FBI, has conducted an investigation of Mr. Tucker for the past three years since he became mayor of Compton. As a result of that investigation, we have amassed evidence that Mr. Tucker has violated the Hobbs Act, a federal statute that regulates interstate commerce involving extortion by elected officials.

"Specifically, we have evidence that during the years nineteen ninety-one to ninety-two, our undercover agent gave a total of thirty thousand dollars to Mr. Tucker in order to influence him to put certain business items on the City Council's agenda. The Hobbs Act, gentlemen, does not require extortion by force or fear, but recognizes it where an elected official accepts money under 'color of official right.' In other words, where they accept money in exchange for the clout that they wield by nature of their public office—money to which they knew they were not entitled. We can show, through several video and audio tapes secretly recorded, that Mr. Tucker accepted the undercover agent's money; that he wasn't entitled to it; and that he subsequently voted favorably on a matter connected to the undercover agent who gave him the money. That's a violation of the Hobbs Act, gentlemen."

As Madison spoke, Johnnie scribbled copious notes. The faces of my attorneys were phlegmatic and careful. All eyes were on me for a reaction. I gave none.

"Furthermore, we can prove that Mr. Tucker demanded another two hundred fifty thousand dollars from another one of our undercover agents. This is another Hobbs Act violation, although no monies were received by Mr. Tucker from this demand. We can prove that the thirty thousand dollars in bribes received by Mr. Tucker were deposited into his bank accounts and thereby became his personal income. Our charts show the income Mr. Tucker received in nineteen ninety-one to ninety-two, and that he did not report the bribery money to the IRS. This, of course, represents tax fraud; one count per each year. We believe that when we are all said and done with the Grand Jury, we'll be able to indict Mr. Tucker on a total of ten counts, including the two tax counts I mentioned. The eight Hobbs Act counts carry a maximum of twenty years each. Bottom line, Mr. Tucker could be going away for a very long time."

It felt as if I had just plunged down the steepest roller coaster in the entire world, or taken a sudden leap out of an airplane from 3,000 feet, wondering if the parachute would open. What was supposed to be a routine conference, with the expectation that the U.S. Attorney was going fishing, turned out to be a declaration of death.

We gotcha! You're dead!

They weren't probing to see what I may have done. They were telling me that it was a done deal, and they wanted the pleasure of seeing me squirm as they pronounced judgment. I wouldn't give them any such satisfaction.

I'd been in some tough spots, I'd heard some tough talk, but at that precise moment, I knew I was facing the worst hell I'd ever been up against. My head was between the proverbial lion's jaws. It took everything in me to remain cool. My faith, in the face of this imminent danger, was truly something to witness—even for me. My attorneys peeked over at me to see if there were any cracks in my armor. Not a crack.

"Mr. Tucker, we can understand if this is all hitting you rather fast. We can appreciate the fact that you may be saying to yourself, this is the biggest bluff I've ever heard in my life. Tapes, videos, undercover agents. Let me assure you, the U.S. Attorney's office does not bluff," Attorney Emig said. Then, he turned to Attorney Madison, "Steve, the transcripts please."

This is much worse than I could have ever imagined. I'm in a dark alley and there is no light. I'm surrounded and there seems to be no way out.

"Mr. Tucker, I'm now reading from selected excerpts of the transcripts of the tapes."

TUCKER: Well, I guess I'm not unlike any other politician. I just came off of the campaign and I have a debt to retire. What I'm comfortable with is— and again it depends on how you'd like to do it—it's probably to yours, mine and the project's benefit to not have checks.

SOURCE: Absolutely.

TUCKER: Right, yeah, that's right, that's just a deal breaker; you wouldn't want to do that. But I would be comfortable with a check or checks in some other name. That would be very comfortable with me.

SOURCE: Okay.

TUCKER: As I say, you know, I have a relatively considerable debt. It's not that bad, but whatever you can muster, something in the area of, maybe ten grand could help.

SOURCE: Okay.

"And then in another reference, we heard the following."

SOURCE: That plus the eight thousand we agreed on should secure your vote.

TUCKER: We'll be friendly…definitely.

Johnnie, probably having heard enough, interjected, "Well, apparently you gentlemen have been hard at work. It seems you have your case and fully intend to proceed with it. Or is there something that you're offering Mr. Tucker today?"

Attorney Emig jumped in, "If Mr. Tucker will cooperate with us, become a cooperative witness, we will see what we can do toward making a recommendation to the court for leniency."

"Cooperate? Sounds to me like you set this whole thing up. What could he possibly know that you don't already have on tape?" Johnnie asked.

"True, but we have information that there is widespread corruption in the South Bay, and if Mr. Tucker would agree to wear a wire and help us obtain solid evidence on the certain…uh, parties making bribes to city officials throughout the South Bay, then upon the convictions of these parties, we will, of course, see what we could do to help Mr. Tucker."

"And just what makes you think that Mr. Tucker has any information on this widespread corruption?"

While they were slow to answer, Johnnie instinctively caught my eye for a reaction. He could see that I thought these folks were out of their minds and that I had nothing to say to them, but *see you in court!* I leaned over and whispered in Johnnie's ear just to confirm my position.

"No way I'm wearing some wire. We're outta here."

They're just trying to use me to do their dirty work. They don't care about my safety, my future or my family.

Johnnie nodded, cleared his throat, and looked squarely at my accusers.

"Well, you've certainly made your position clear, and we appreciate that, but my client won't be serving as your cooperative witness. When can we expect to receive discovery?"

Those were the magic words that needed to be said then. We needed to see what evidence they had amassed against me.

Johnnie's words signaled to them that we were going to fight; that they could take their nothing-of-an-offer off the table and shove it.

"We'll get you the discovery by the end of this week."

"Well, I don't think there's anything else, gentlemen. I'm sure we'll be hearing from you," Johnnie said.

"Yes, you most certainly will."

My team and I rose from our seats and quickly left the room.

The government had stuck a carrot in front of me and I had refused it. They wanted me to deal, to roll over and help them get an even bigger fish, whoever that might have been. That was the way the game was played. In order for the little fish to preserve its life, it had to deliver a bigger fish. Unfortunately, as a congressman, I was the biggest political fish I knew. And, as for fish in the business world, I wasn't about to put my life or family's life at risk trying to do to someone else what they had done to me.

My attorneys and I remained silent until we stepped out-side the building. We were cautious. We knew this was a federal building with walls that had ears. Everything George Orwell said about omnipresent governmental surveillance in his popular, fictional novel, *1984*, came to reality in March 1994. The concept of a fascist state where every move a person made was detectable by "Big Brother" was never more real and current. Once outside, we all began talking at once. It was now clear that there was going to be a fight—a big one! The U.S. Attorney was not like the County DA. They were well-staffed, well-prepared, and boasted a 98% conviction rate. Their support staff, including the IRS, and the FBI, went for the jugular every time.

"Look, guys, I know what I've heard, but I haven't seen anything yet. They talk about tapes and videos, but I didn't see any. Anybody can read some things from a transcript!" I said.

"Well, we need to talk about the contents of those transcripts right away," Johnnie said. "We're playing at a disadvantage right now. They know who, what, when, and where, and Congressman, only you can answer those questions for us. Let's go to my office and get to work."

CHAPTER FOURTEEN

The Trap

Robin, Mom, and I hopped into the Town Car and edged through heavy traffic toward Johnnie's law office, which was located in the Mid-Wilshire district, just west of downtown L.A. Mark followed us in his car. Once at Johnnie's office, my lawyers, family, and I gathered around a large mahogany conference table. As we sat, I admired the black art that graced the walls. One painting by Ernie Barnes especially caught my eye: a black lawyer making a jailhouse visit to an emaciated client. I guess the point was that despite Johnnie's success of being an attorney to the stars—with plush offices and a Rolls Royce—he would never forget his roots.

A good thing.

Jan popped into the room. "May I get anyone some coffee or water?"

"I'll take some coffee," Mark said.

"Me too, please," Robin added.

"Water for me please," I said.

As soon as Jan left the room, Johnnie cut to the chase. "Well, we all know why we're here, Congressman. We need to get as many details as possible. For starters, where and when did this incriminating conversation take place?"

I sighed. "I had lunch with John Macardican at a restaurant at the Long Beach World Trade Center, just after I became mayor."

"And?" Johnnie asked.

As an attorney myself, I knew that Johnnie was urging me to put all the cards on the table.

"Well, he said he had been my father's friend and that my father strongly favored his project."

"What project?"

"A plant that would burn waste and convert it into energy; it would create electricity and about six hundred jobs—a politician's dream! He was talking state-of-the-art technology and minimal environmental impact."

Johnnie scribbled notes on his legal pad.

"So, he reeled you in with the promise of lots of jobs for your community," Johnnie said.

"Tell me more?"

My mind leaped back to that time, three years ago.

* * * * * *

I had been delayed for my twelve o'clock lunch appointment when a sixteen-wheeler jackknifed on the southbound Long Beach Freeway. After being at a standstill for twenty minutes, I screeched into the World Trade Center parking lot, trying to make up for lost time. I darted into the tall granite and glass building known as 1 World Trade Center Club.

Once inside Long Beach's tallest building, I saw its plush restaurant on the first floor—a well-kept, almost secret space designed and protected for high rollers. It reminded me of when my dad would take my sister, Keta, and me to grand places, saying it was good exposure for us, so we would never be intimidated by such places, or be too impressed by their appearances. This place was impressive. I imagined it as the Donald Trump-kind-of hang out for negotiating deals.

As soon as I stepped into the restaurant, the maître d' greeted me. "May I help you, sir?"

"Yes, I'm here to meet Mr. Macardican."

"Oh yes, the gentleman has been waiting. Come this way."

I eased into the semi-private booth where Macardican sat facing me.

"Sorry I'm late. A truck jackknifed on the freeway."

Macardican extended his hand and smiled nonchalantly. "No problem."

I glanced around the room and noticed waiters standing near a station with small white towels hanging over their wrists. They stood just close enough to be handy, but not too close to invade the customers' privacy.

Macardican motioned with his hand and a clean-cut waiter came forward and laid elegant menus before us—crab cakes with a lobster sauce, salmon almandine, cherries jubilee, and crème brûlée stretched across the pages in subtle colors and texture. The prices were as high as the cuisine seemed exquisite.

"I'm David and I'll be your waiter today. Can I get you gentlemen something to drink?"

I checked my watch and said, "No thank you. I'd better order."

"Have you dined with us before?" the waiter asked.

"No, I have not."

"The food here's excellent. Please order whatever you like," Macardican said.

"I recommend the crab cakes," the waiter interjected.

"Crab cakes it is, and the Caesar salad," I said.

"And I'll have the free-range chicken," Macardican said.

The waiter scooped up our menus and disappeared. I checked my watch again. "I've got to be back at my law office by two to see a client. I'd better use the phone."

Before I could move, Macardican gestured and the waiter brought a phone to our table. Once again, he left us alone. I called my law office, and Wanda, my legal secretary, answered. I gave her the scoop on the freeway incident. "I'll probably be late. Please take care of Mr. Jones until I get there. Thanks." Then I hung up.

The classical music softly playing in the background helped to settle me down from my tense drive. Macardican pushed the phone aside and began to toy with his silverware, polishing his knife with his napkin, as if it were a valuable old coin going to auction. He cocked his head to inspect his handiwork. Since he had set up this lunch invitation through his representative, Bob Gavin, I waited for him to start the conversation.

"Wanda?" Macardican asked, "Is that the secretary I've talked to at your office?"

"Right."

"She's excellent. She's got a pleasant demeanor on the phone."

"Yes," I said.

"She's smart too. She always asks me if you were expecting my call. You never know these days. I could be some crackpot calling."

I nodded. "Yeah, you've got citizens and everybody else calling my law office thinking it's my mayor's office. It goes with the territory of being a part-time mayor."

"Guess your dad must've put up with that a long time?"

"Yeah," I replied.

"How old are you?" Macardican asked.

"I just turned thirty-four two days ago."

"A young, young guy," Macardican said, smiling and shaking his head.

"I guess the citizens finally said, 'It's time we take a *young* lamb to the slaughter,'" I joked.

"I don't know about that. All I know is that your dad was a classy man. The city needed a man like that. And now they trust his son to continue his legacy," Macardican said.

"Yeah, he definitely changed a lot of negative notions about Compton."

"Exactly."

"I'm going to do all I can to continue his work."

"Yeah, I met with your dad a lot. Me and Seymour Green, a wealthy old Jewish guy. We used to go to lunch with your father, maybe once a month. We all liked talking about the potential of Compton. Your dad was my friend."

"Yes, I'd heard your name before, and now it's good to meet my dad's friend. He always wanted to solve Compton's problems. I do too."

"You know, I am so sorry about your father. Throughout all his years on the City Council, I admired him. He was the only one who even tried to help me."

"That was my dad, all right."

"Back in the eighties, the Compton City Council caused me to lose ten million dollars."

"How?" I asked.

There was a long pause. Then he said, "When I asked your father to take a second look at my project, he said he would. He brought it back again for a city vote, but the council turned me down." His hand patted the table. "Your father was a fair and honorable man. Honorable as I've ever met."

Tears swelled inside of me, as Macardican's words spoke the truth about my dad's commitment to helping others. I realized I was still mourning my dad's death and longing for his presence. "Yeah, he was the best," I said.

I wanted to stop talking about my dad for fear that one of those tears welling inside might drip down my cheek. I clenched my teeth hard and kept listening. Macardican kind of reminded me of my dad's close friend, Big Wes, an older man who was easy to talk to. I always said that every day brings something that marks it as good or bad. I thought, coming together with Macardican that day for a sumptuous lunch in an exquisite environment marked it as good. I kept listening.

"But that was another time and this is another time," Macardican said.

"Right," I replied.

"Maybe it's a better time now."

"Yeah...I was glad to sit down and meet with your rep— Bob. He represented your project well."

"Yeah, he believes in the project for the city," Macardican said.

"He gave me some history and I told him I'd keep an open mind until I could hear the whole story from you. So tell me more about this waste-to-energy plant?"

The waiter eased the Caesar salads in front of us with a cosmopolitan gesture. As we began to eat, Macardican broke the silence.

"Well, the project's a plant that burns waste and converts it to electricity. I even have an exclusive contract with Southern California Edison to buy the electricity. We're talking state-of-the-art technology, minimal environmental impact, and about six hundred new jobs!"

Six hundred jobs for the people of Compton. I'll be a hero if I can deliver that many jobs. Wow! My dad would look down from heaven and grin. I kept my cool while the surge of hope stirred deep inside. *This can turn out to be something that a lot of big cities don't have. Compton! A model city!*

* * * * * *

Johnnie's legal pad seemed almost full and he motioned for Jan to bring him another. I breathed deeply and took a pause. Then, she was back and placed the pad near his hand. I continued to tell him my story.

"Then, out of nowhere, Macardican said, 'Mr. Mayor, I would like to donate to your campaign.' "

"Of course, those are the words a politician loves to hear," I said.

"So, he was the one who first brought up the subject of giving money to you?" Johnnie asked.

"That's right and I told him that like any politician, I had campaign debt."

Now as I sat at the conference table prepared to give the rest of the story, Jan stuck her head back through the conference room door.

"Excuse me, boss, Michael Jackson's people are holding for you."

Johnnie reached to pick up the phone.

"Uh, the private line—they're calling from Paris." She paused and added, "The settlement sounds like it's going to take a while."

Johnnie nodded and stood. He paused, then turned back to me apologetically. "Congressman, forgive me, but we're going to have to finish this next week."

I knew that settlement was going to be in the millions and would easily take priority over my case.

"Jan'll set it up. By then we'll have the prosecution's tapes and fill in the details," Johnnie concluded.

"Yes, we'll need some time to digest all of this stuff," Attorney Carl Douglas added.

Mark, my personal attorney, checked his notes. "Some thirty hours of video, and thousands of pages of transcripts. That's the word."

"Well, I guess it's pretty clear that I'm the latest," I said.

"The latest?" Carl asked.

"The latest black politician to be targeted for a takedown," I said.

The room went eerily silent. Even silence felt silent, somewhat like the massive chill of a disturbing horror movie. It felt like sudden sunlight that blinds one's vision and attacks the psyche. I felt the path to freedom narrowing. The unofficial gun sounded, and we were off and running! War had been declared, and there was no turning back.

CHAPTER FIFTEEN

Targeted

The battle I had to fight was made even more difficult because I was hopping on coast-to-coast flights to maintain my responsibilities in Washington D.C. and in the District every week. After what I had seen and heard in L.A., it was almost impossible to focus on congressional work or community issues, and yet I pressed on.

A few days after returning to The Hill, Johnnie called to tell me that a grand jury had been impaneled. The U.S. Attorney's Office followed that news with an all-out assault of subpoenas, interviews, and surveillances. Every check, document, photo, or paper I had ever seen, touched or possessed was subpoenaed. Because I had been a lawyer, a mayor, and a congressman, I had documents at my law offices, campaign offices, mayor's office, banks, congressional offices, and at home. Trying to satisfy the government's request for countless documents, and carry on my extensive congressional duties wore on me heavily.

Every prominent city official in Compton was subpoenaed to testify at the grand jury—city manager, city clerk, ex-director of the Planning Department, the mayor's secretary and, of course, all the city councilpersons. The U.S. Attorney also subpoenaed business executives whose companies did business with the city, my friends, foes, and family.

I was informed that in a room full of elderly, white grand jurors, the prosecutors paraded the witnesses in and out. Testimony could be taken without the benefit of defense counsel to make objections, ask questions, or cross-examine. This was the grand jury process in our American criminal justice system. I was helpless in the hands of what seemed to be a "kangaroo court!"

The grand jury only dug for dirt to bring an indictment. God forbid they consider any evidence that might point to the innocence of the person in question. With the government buying the grand jurors' lunch every day and housing them in close proximity to the U.S. Attorney's office, an indictment seemed to be a foregone conclusion.

The U.S. Attorney's office had taken three years to compile that lethal BRIBURN file on me. *What else can they possibly need?* Still, the U.S. Attorney dug in during that summer of '94 and so did I. My lightweight digging was in an article called, "Witch Hunt"— the government's practice of *targeting* black male politicians for destruction—the new Jim Crow. It reminded me of how black men were thrown into prison disproportionately to white men. It reminded me of photos and drawings of black men hanging from trees, and I never saw a white man hanging from one.

One colossal article published in *GQ Magazine* [circa 1994], entitled "Witch Hunt," asked one question: Is there a conspiracy to target and take down black elected officials by the federal government, including the Justice Department and the FBI? One article led to the next, and I became engrossed with that suggestion of a national atmosphere of "set up and take down," based on race.

As a black man, I could not be exempt. As a hopeful man, it was a bitter pill of reality to swallow. If this was true, it overtook everything my family had taught me: the inspiring notion that if you study hard, get a good education, and want to help others, you could become President of the United States and rise above discrimination.

* * * * * *

I was now back in Johnnie's L.A. office in the same conference room where I had sat venting to my attorneys after my initial meeting with the U.S. attorneys. I knew we were playing catch up and I wanted to explore every theory and share every bit of potentially relevant research.

"Carl, here's the information on political targeting. Check this out:"

According to a *Washington Post* study, the issue was real. "Of four hundred sixty-five publicly known political corruption probes launched between nineteen eighty-three and nineteen eighty-eight, fourteen percent targeted black officials, though blacks accounted for only three percent of all U.S. officeholders."

"We're over four times more likely to be criminally investigated. That's a national scandal!" Mark slapped the desk.

"Wait, there's more." I continued to read. "High-ranking Federal prosecutors, black and white, strongly denounce charges of selective prosecution as blatant lies and insist that justice is applied equally. As the single largest source of corruption case referrals to the Justice Department, more than fifty percent, the FBI plays a central role in this controversy. The problem is described as *"institutional racism."* This fear is based on a range of events, from COINTELPRO to the nineteen sixty-three bombing of Birmingham's Sixteenth Street Baptist Church, which the FBI knew about in advance but did nothing to stop four black girls from being killed; to the public acknowledgment of Director J. Edgar Hoover's racist notions that blacks were inherently inferior and thus unacceptable as agents." [8] I stood, rolled my shoulders, and stretched.

"All of this stuff goes back years," Carl said, looking nervously for coffee that wasn't there.

"Listen to this," I read, "Atlanta lawyer, Hirsch Friedman, a former FBI informant who specialized in providing dirt on low-level organized crime figures, described an unofficial Bureau policy that targeted black officials for prosecution. In sworn testimony, Friedman testified that the policy was called 'Fruhmenschen'. "

"Fru-men-shin. What's that?" Mark asked.

"It says here that it's a German word meaning 'primitive man' and that the purpose of the policy was the routine investigation without probable cause of prominent black elected officials in major metropolitan areas throughout the United States." I shoved the magazine back in my briefcase.

"Hey, let me see that." I handed the magazine to Carl and he started reading.

"Friedman testified that in the Atlanta office of the FBI, agents targeted black politicians on the assumption that black officials were intellectually and socially incapable of governing major governmental organizations and institutions. COINTELPRO, now the discredited brainchild of former FBI director J. Edgar Hoover, was intended to gather damaging information on the Reverend Martin Luther King, Jr., the Black Panther Party, sixteen hundred civil rights workers, a number of other activists, and anyone whom the FBI deemed a threat to the U.S."

"Like Walter Tucker III," Mark interjected.

Carl continued reading, "Some who heard about Fruhmenschen dismissed it as an aging legacy of J. Edgar Hoover. Nevertheless, using Justice Department records, the Transactional Records Access Clearinghouse (TRAC) at Syracuse University, conducted a computerized study of official corruption referrals between nineteen eighty-three and nineteen eighty-four, which showed that its effects are still being felt."

"Hey, that's right during the time Macardican operated as an FBI informant," I said.

Mark looked up with a glint of fear... "Hey lemme see that." He took the article and continued reading it aloud. "At one time or another, many of the nation's prominent elected black leaders have been under investigation, including Congressman Ron Dellums, Mervyn Dymally, John Conyers, Charles Rangel, William Clay III, William Gray, Harold Ford, Floyd Flake, and Mel Reynolds; big-city Mayors Maynard Jackson, Andrew Young, Michael White, Harold Washington, Coleman Young, Tom Bradley, and Marion Barry; Georgia State Legislator Julian Bond; Maryland State Senator Clarence Mitchell III; Federal Judges Alcee Hastings of Florida, Robert Collins of Louisiana and Federal Judge U.W. Clemon of Alabama."

"Man, this is too much bad news to take in on an empty stomach. Let's get something to eat!" Mark said.

As we walked to Tiger Deli across the street, the *GQ* magazine article stuck in my mind. As we ate pastrami on rye, I grabbed the article from Mark and continued reading it aloud.

"For the number of whites investigated to be comparable to the number of black representatives investigated, two hundred four of the four hundred nine white representatives would have had to have been subjected to the same scrutiny during that time. Yet according to Justice Department figures, only fifteen actually were targeted.[9]

"Senator Carol Mosely-Braun, a member of the Congressional Black Caucus, remains adamant. 'Do I believe black officials are unfairly targeted because of their race?' she asks. 'Yes.'

"Mary Sawyer, a professor at Iowa State University, who has studied the treatment of black officials, says, 'The magnitude of the harassment cannot be measured solely in terms of numbers of cases. The debilitating impact on the individual and his or her constituency also must be considered. The higher the level of office or the more outspoken the official, or the greater the influence and power—the higher the incidence of harassment. Harassment weakens movements for social change by dividing leaders from the people and cuts into the influence of black leaders in the formulation of domestic and foreign policy. In short, harassment is a form of discrimination that inhibits and restrains black political development.'"

"Well, at least we all know what we're up against," Carl said.

"Yeah, something big, something systemic; ingrained in the very fiber of our society," Mark said.

I banged the table. "But we will not be defeated!"

"Amen, homeboy. I'm with you no matter what! You know that," Mark said.

Carl, realizing the tension was high, said, "Hey guys, let's meet the same time next week and talk it out. The more we understand the back story, the more Johnnie can build your defense. We've got to see every angle. We need to know everything to fight this battle."

CHAPTER SIXTEEN

Home Again

After the meeting with my attorneys in L.A., I hopped back in the Town Car and headed home. The Tichenor Street home in Compton was the house my dad built and where my immediate family lived. But now, it was the house I returned to for district business.

I tried to wrap my head around all that had just happened and all that was about to come as I peered out my car window and took in the L.A. landscape. Seemed like I had spent half of my life away from L.A. and the rest of it trying to get back. People always questioned why I returned to L.A. after graduating from Georgetown Law School. After all, a Georgetown Law Center graduate could write his own ticket in Washington, D.C. I could have worked for the D.C. government or the federal government. I could have worked on Capitol Hill, or joined one of those big law firms down Connecticut Avenue. But D.C. was not my home. L.A. had the weather, the cutting-edge culture, the fun life I knew. It was where my family and my roots were. It was the place where I always believed my dreams would come true.

* * * * * *

June 1981. After graduating from Georgetown Law School, I had returned to the Tichenor house and found myself on the front end of my biggest battle to date—the California Bar Exam! It was easily known as the toughest Bar in the entire country, and California didn't recognize certification from other states as some states did. Only a handful of applicants passed the California Bar each year. But I was Georgetown Law School trained. I had it in the bag.

Since returning home from law school, I decided it was time to sleep in a new bedroom. My dad had converted our original garage into a large bedroom on the west wing. More importantly, it was far away from everyone else who slept on the east wing. I was now a young man with my own space. It was like having a one-room apartment with access to the Tichenor home. I set up shop and started studying for the California Bar Examination. Just like when I was a boy, living a Spartan life on the east wing with nothing but a desk in my bedroom, I placed a small wooden desk in the middle of my new bedroom and went to work.

I spent the summer of 1981 studying. It was perhaps the weirdest summer I'd ever known. I wasn't quite sure where I was or where I belonged. I was home, but everyone and everything I knew was back in D.C. And everything at home had changed. Everyone I knew from home had grown up and moved out of Compton, or out of California. Just about everyone except my next door neighbor, Lolita Carter.

Lolita, a tiny, 20-year-old with horn-rimmed glasses and a cigarette in her hand, had lived next door to me on Tichenor Street all of my young life. She was the proverbial girl next door; like a little sister to me. Lolita was a couple of grades behind me, and I don't think I had seen her since one of my summers during college. But suddenly, there she was at my front door with a graduation gift, a card, and a bottle of Blue Nun wine in hand. After being totally surprised, I invited her inside.

We sat on bar stools in the family room and opened the wine. I paired it with some smoked oysters and crackers, and we began catching up on old times. Who went where? Who married whom? The typical post-graduate update. Before I knew it, we both had a buzz, and somehow the conversation turned to music.

Lolita had been studying and playing the piano since she was a child, and because her house was next door, I always heard her practicing her chords over the brick wall that separated our properties.

"And yeah, I'm still on that same piano." She laughed.

Suddenly my mind skipped to the possibility that she might be the answer to a silent prayer. Since leaving Washington, I had been cut off from the songwriter I had discovered in me. Maybe, just maybe, Lolita wanted to partner up with me.

"Hey, we still have our piano. Come on and play something for me," I suggested.

We talked and walked between off-white Roman columns, taking a step down into the opulent living room. There, surrounded by my mom's vintage paintings and statues, sat the stately, black Steinway grand that no one played anymore. I had stopped playing at age nine when my interest in basketball took over. Keta had stopped taking piano lessons at age fourteen, even though she had become quite proficient. I always loved hearing her practice Beethoven's *Fur Elise*.

Lolita mounted the piano seat, scooted in close to the keyboard, and let her baby fingers loose across the keys. "This is a little something I've been working on," she said.

Immediately, I could see that she was no longer the little girl struggling to learn the chords. Now there was flow, there was beauty, there was magic. She didn't know it at the time, but in a blink, our new songwriting team was born. In fact, I had been humming a song called *Tonight* ever since I left D.C.

When Lolita finished her song, I laid my cards on the table.

"Hey, you may not believe this, but I've learned to write songs, and I love it," I said.

"Really? And you don't play an instrument?"

"No, but I hear the songs."

"What you got?" Lolita asked.

I began to sing the melody and the lyric to *Tonight*.

Tonight, we're more than strangers passing through

The feeling's true…tonight…

Tonight, we're flying high like angels who

have heaven's view, tonight

Tonight, we'll dance on air

without a care, until we're there—paradise…

We're so in love, so in love

So in love…tonight…

Lolita found the chords and before long, we had the song.

"That's an awesome song. Who inspired that?"

"The girl of my dreams. A lady I know I'm going to meet someday—soon."

"I'll drink to that."

Lolita and I toasted and sipped some more white wine.

"Look, I'm studying this summer to take the California Bar this fall, but when I get some downtime, you wanna do some song-writing?"

"Sounds like a plan!"

For the next few months my routine was set. I studied for the Bar by day and worked on music by night. Lolita had some songs and I had some songs, and together we had a lot of songs. Having a creative outlet made studying for the Bar tolerable. By the end of the summer, we even found a local band willing to play some of our songs. I was on cloud nine. After a while, I was so busy that I managed to forget that all my friends were back east and that, for the first time in a long time, I didn't have a girlfriend. It was a new season, a new day. I was going with the flow, but somehow I could feel love was near.

CHAPTER SEVENTEEN

A Date with Destiny

Wednesday, September 2, 1981, sizzled with the hot, summer heat of Southern California. As I was still studying for the Bar and dabbling in songwriting, I went to drop off a practice tape to a keyboard player who also lived on the west side of Compton. I hopped in my white 1979 BMW and drove to his house.

"Here, man, here's the tape. The song's called *The Magic of Your Eyes.*"

"Alright, we'll check it out and get back with you, man."

As the keyboardist took the tape, my eyes focused in on his young daughter who was clinging to his leg. She was licking on a Big Stick, a popsicle I hadn't had or thought about for years. As I walked outside into the hot September sun, I had this sudden urge to have a Big Stick. Where could I buy one? My mind clicked: *There's a dairy right up this street, on the corner.* I sped up the street, and just as I had remembered, at the end of the block—at the corner of Haskins and Alondra—there was the community dairy. I pulled up close to the cashier's station and waited for the attendant to come to my car window, but the attendant was waiting on a customer at the grill—a young woman whose back was toward me. Her body seemed perfectly shaped.

Wow, look at that! No way in the world she's as fine from the front as she is from the back.

While the attendant cooked up her burger, the young lady turned around and we were face to face. The earth moved, lightning struck. My mind started spinning. It was, on my part, love at first sight. She was the one. She smiled and moved in close for a hug. I couldn't believe it. I felt paralyzed.

"Hi, how have you been? It's been such a long time," she said smiling.

"Great, great," I stammered. "Yes, it's been way too long." *Who is this beautiful woman? And who does she think I am?*

This had to be a classic case of mistaken identity, but I was determined to carry on the charade as long as I could. Whoever she thought I was, I would be. As we continued to gaze into each other's eyes, she could see that I didn't know who she was.

"You don't know who I am, do you?"

"Sure I do…like you said…it's been a long time," I continued, trying to string it along.

"I'm Robin."

"Right…Robin," I said, still struggling to figure out who she was.

"Robin Smith," she said.

My brain was racing. Robin Smith? Robin Smith? Did I know her? Where did I know her from? Please, I need to know this girl, because at any minute she's going to tell me that it's all one big mistake and walk away abruptly. That can't happen!

She stood her ground and continued to search for a connection to my brain.

"I'm Mark's sister," she said.

That still didn't ring a bell. Mark was a common name. Somehow, she persisted.

"I'm Ricky's cousin."

The only person I referred to as Ricky was my own cousin, so I was still clueless.

Finally, she exclaimed, "I'm Nedra's sister!"

That did it. Suddenly it all made sense. Nedra was not a common name. I knew only one Nedra. Nedra Smith. My mind reviewed what she had been trying to tell me: Mark's little sis-ter...Ricky's cousin.

Oh my God, she was talking about Mark Smith, and Eric Smith, my good friend from high school. In that single moment, I knew she was the present manifestation of the 13-year-old girl in pigtails I had seen once when I went with Eric to Mark's house to pick him up to play basketball at a local park.

Now standing before me was the most beautiful young woman I had ever seen. She reminded me of the painting of a strik-ing Afro-Asian woman that hung on our breakfast room wall at Tichenor. She was no longer thirteen and cute, but twenty and beautiful.

"Yes, I know exactly who you are. Robin—Robin <u>Smith</u>," I said.

"Here you go, sweetheart." The attendant handed Robin a bag with greasy spots and the smell of hamburger and fries.

Robin looked at her watch, turned to me and said, "I've got to get back to work."

"Where do you work?"

"City Hall."

I was determined not to let this meeting be in vain.

"Well, I'd like to call you and catch up. May I have your number?"

"Okay," she said, scribbling on a piece of paper she pulled from her purse. She handed it to me and before I knew it she hopped into her little yellow Mercury Comet and drove off. I was in a daze, but not so much that I didn't put that piece of paper securely inside my right pants pocket.

"Now what would you like?" the attendant asked.

"Well, I would like a Big Stick. A Big Stick popsicle."

The woman went to the freezer but returned empty-handed.

"Sorry, we're all out of Big Sticks."

On any other day, at any other time, I would have been disappointed. But not that day. I realized I hadn't driven into that dairy by mistake. I had finally found the girl of my dreams—Robin Smith. *Yes, she could be my wife.*

CHAPTER EIGHTEEN

Dating Robin

How ironic it was that since high school I had spent most of my years back east, meeting the college elite and not-so-elite—the brains and the beauties—only to come home after law school to meet the one who made every other girl a distant memory. She was a Compton girl from a good, middle-class family. Her father, Robert Smith, had worked for over forty years at the Rockwell plant in El Segundo, helping to build aircraft like the B-1 Bomber. Her mother, Pauline, worked as an assistant librarian. Her sister, Nedra, my high school classmate, worked for the Probation Department, and her brother, Mark, was a deputy sheriff, studying to become a lawyer.

Although Robin was the youngest child, she was mature for her age. By senior year in high school, she was interning at the Compton Superior Court. She parlayed that internship into a position with the Compton City Attorney's office. Then, she was promoted into the City Controller's Office and eventually landed at the City Manager's Office. In total, she worked at Compton City Hall for thirteen and one-half years.

From the day we met as adults at the community dairy, we were rarely apart. That night, after studying all afternoon, I called the phone number she gave me.

"Hello."

I could tell right away it was Robin.

"Hi, Robin?" I asked, just to be polite.

"Yes," she said.

"This is Walter."

"Oh, hi! I didn't expect to hear from you so soon."

"Well, we were having such a great conversation today, I wanted to continue it."

"Yes, it was good. I'm glad you called."

Before I knew it, we had been talking on the phone for three hours. I had never talked on the phone to a girl for three hours! Before hanging up, I asked to take her to dinner on Friday night. She agreed. My mind went into overdrive. *Where do I take her? It has to be the best. Something unique. Something to impress. Where? Hmmm. Got it.*

My mother had a membership at the Marina City Club, which featured dinner and dancing. That would be the ticket. That place required a membership card and ID just to get beyond the gate. There would be no need to go anywhere else after dinner. The club's dance floor was right next door to the restaurant. Just outside was a boardwalk with a breathtaking view of the marina, full of beautiful white boats underneath twinkling lights; boats with names like *Star Ruby*, and *Maiden Voyage*.

Our first date at the Marina City Club went even better than planned. I ordered Steak Diane for the two of us, which was prepared tableside with fresh garlic and impressive, shooting flames. And after dinner, we danced to the beat of Earth, Wind and Fire's "Let's Groove Tonight," Kool & The Gang's "Get Down On It," and Rick James' "Super Freak." When the DJ slowed things down, it was Lionel Richie and Diana Ross singing "Endless Love," for our first slow dance together. That classic became our song. I can never forget how it felt to hold Robin in my arms for the very first time. We fit together perfectly.

Near the end of our date, I started anticipating the kiss. *How will it happen? Will it happen?* After Lionel Richie had set the atmosphere, I asked Robin to join me for a walk on the boardwalk. We walked outside to a perfect L.A. evening. A clear moonlit sky with shining stars, and still air. We ambled about, enjoying the view of the docked boats. I noticed a tropical pink hibiscus flower, picked it, and placed it on the side of Robin's hair. She smiled, looking now like a Tahitian princess. She was so poised and so mature to be only twenty.

I stopped walking and grabbed her hands. I leaned back against a gate and pulled her close, but the gate was not fully closed and we fell backward. Before I knew it, Robin fell onto me and we found ourselves in a close embrace, body to body, cheek to cheek. I turned my head slightly and went in slowly for the kiss. If she didn't turn her head or pull away, then I knew all was right. She didn't and everything was more than alright. But just when I was going into second gear, she abruptly pulled away and stood up.

"Wow! I don't know what came over me. We'd better go," she said.

Go? *When I'm in paradise?* "But I thought you were having a great time." I stood up straight and reached for her hand again, but she pulled away again.

"I am, but, well...I told you I have a boyfriend."

There was a moment of deafening silence until I looked her square in the eyes and exposed my thoughts. "Hey, tell him you found a new love."

Robin looked at me as if I were out of my mind. But before she could get out a word, boldness took me over, and I broke out singing:

Tell him that you found a new love

Let him down easy, but leave no uncertainty...

Tell him that you found a new love,

Don't keep me waiting, 'cause my heart is yearning for you...

After a full serenade of my original song I just knew she was mine. To my surprise, she held fast and politely hugged me.

"Thank you so much for the evening, the song, and everything. But I think we'd better go.

Go? I can't believe this!

When we got into the car, Robin reiterated to me that she was committed to the 3-year relationship with her boyfriend who played football at Arizona State University. While she was explaining all this to me, it was like she was speaking to the air.

He can't have you. I'm going to make you mine and it's just a matter of time.

Weeks became months, and months became years.

Who was this young beautiful lady who had captured my heart and blown my mind? She inspired me to write countless poems and songs; she was my muse. She was the woman I wanted to marry—all in good time.

CHAPTER NINETEEN

The Bar

When I didn't pass the Bar exam after four attempts, I was at my wit's end and totally frustrated. I was sure that managing a musical group was my destiny. All my life I had overcome every hurdle with hard work and determination. But not this time. My dad was really concerned and decided it was time to intervene.

"Son, it's time for you to stop partying around town and playing around with music and pass that Bar."

"Hey, I've tried and tried. Look, even if I don't pass the Bar, I can still be successful, manage some musical acts. Barry Gordy did it, and look how that turned out."

"His situation was one in a million. Take it from me, there's nothing in the world like you having your license. It opens doors, even if you never practice law, per se."

"Uh huh."

"Seriously, you didn't go through all that schooling for nothing. That license is the brass ring and after you get it you can do just about anything."

"Yeah, right."

Though I wanted to forego taking another grueling exam, I forced myself to take the Bar a fifth time in the summer of 1983. There I was waiting anxiously for Bar results around Thanksgiving.

One Saturday in November, the thin, white envelope finally came. I never will forget walking straight into my dad's bedroom to share the news with him. He was shaving in his adjoining bathroom.

"Hey, Dad. Well, it finally came."

My dad stepped out of the bathroom to see what was up. I showed him the envelope, and he knew what it was.

"Wish me luck."

I opened the envelope nervously, pulled out the letter and read, "We regret to inform you that…" I just mumbled the rest of the words on the page.

"Damn, not again! I'm so tired of this Bar Exam! Goddamnit!" I exclaimed.

My dad had never heard me curse like that before.

While I wanted him to join in on my rampage, I fully expected him to give me one of his patented pep talks. Instead, he laid some words on me that rocked my world forever. "Son, don't ever use the Lord's name in vain again."

I was stunned by my dad's spiritual comment, as he turned around and quietly walked back into his bathroom. I stood there motionless, confused. This was the man whom I had known all my life. He had lectured me about a lot of things—homework, housework, and spending money. He had yelled at me when he was upset. He had even cuffed my head a couple of times. But lecture me about religion? It had never happened before. It was as mysterious as his quiet walk back into his bathroom. It didn't give me a chance to argue or discuss the matter, only time to think.

The more I thought, the more I noticed the difference in my dad. I noticed that he'd been waking up early Sunday mornings and going to church. Mind you, going to church for a black politician was not novel. In our community, black politicians went to church, but they generally popped in and out of several churches on Sunday mornings. It was all political—maintaining maximum exposure and keeping their political competitors at bay between elections.

No, this church attendance was different. He was going to only one church every Sunday— Enterprise Methodist—a small church in Compton. And he didn't pop in and out—he stayed for the full service. Also, I noticed that almost every night he had started reading some church materials as he lay in bed. I later learned they were Sunday school books. The more I looked, the more I noticed. But the most important thing I noticed was not the change in his church attendance or church reading, but the change in him. I noticed a man who was more meek, more at peace, more patient. He stopped drinking liquor and, once a week, he started fasting from meat.

He started saying, "You know Jesus asked, 'Can anything good come out of Nazareth?' Well, I ask, can anything good come out of Compton?"

Like most people who have family or friends who professed some newfound religion, I kept watching. I kept watching for his old self to show up. It never did. His conversion was the real thing. Whenever we were together, going to the grocery store, or going out to eat, a little more of what he was learning from the

Bible would pour out. He wasn't hitting me over the head with the Bible, but ever so subtly he was witnessing Christ to me.

As I lay in my bed one Saturday night, I realized that I was frustrated; I had no peace. I had spent my whole life making things happen and now, I couldn't make anything happen. I had come to the end of myself, and I was afraid about what the future held.

Earlier that day, my dad had asked me to go to church with him in the morning. Now as I lay in bed that Saturday night, I could hear a small voice inside my head, "Hey, what do you have to lose? Go to church with him." No one else could have had the impact on me like he did. I respected him tremendously. He was a good dentist, a faithful mayor, a loyal husband, guiding father. Most important for me, he was a real friend. And so that night I decided to go with him. It was a decision that changed my life forever.

One Sunday morning at Enterprise Methodist turned into two, two turned into three, and then I was attending church weekly. Like most traditional denominational churches, before the worship service started there was Sunday school. From the very first time I stepped into the church, I attended Sunday school. It was held in the main sanctuary on the back two pews. There were only about twelve attendees, all elderly. So when I sat down on the back pew, I immediately noticed that I was the youngest person there. Sister Willis, a pleasant-looking woman with salt-and-pepper short hair, passed me one of the Sunday school books, as the Sunday school teacher, Brother Brown, stood before us and referred to the book.

"Here you are, young man. This is what we read from," she said.

I took the book and began to read it. Before long, I was reading the lesson plans every week. Soon, I was devouring several lesson plans in my bed every night. Eventually, I became the Sunday school teacher.

Most people can remember the day they accepted Christ as their Savior. I'm not sure of the exact day I gave my life to Christ. I don't remember going to the altar. I just remember that in the fall of 1983 I started going to Sunday school, and the more I learned, the more I repented and believed in Christ. Christ was now in my heart and I knew it. I was saved for all eternity.

As I continued to give more into Sunday school, I gained a whole new attitude about passing the Bar. After Robin attended a Sunday school class with me, she and I agreed it was time for me to become more focused. So, I put my dating life and music interest on hold and attacked the Bar for the sixth time with new fervor and purpose. What my dad said to me when I didn't pass the bar after my fifth attempt kept ringing in my ears.

"Son, it's time for you to pass that Bar. Take it from me, there's nothing in the world like you having your license; it opens many doors…"

I knew my dad was with me, but I could also sense that God was now with me, because He was in me. I was totally convinced that He wanted me to now pass the Bar. So, I began to dig in deeper. My study routine went to another level. I gathered all the old Bar exams and took them under timed conditions, over and over. I read model answers over and over and over until my eyes were blurry. One day, reading those model answers, it hit me; I had an epiphany. *They're not looking for someone whose answers sound like a good law student. They're looking for someone whose answers sound like a lawyer.*

When I wasn't taking practice exams, I was getting my body in shape—sit-ups, push-ups, pull-ups. I looked at the Bar as the ultimate test of spirit, soul, and body. After all, it was a three-day marathon. The Bar was as much a grueling test of your body as it was of your mind. Having to sit there for five, three-hour sessions and maintain an extremely high level of concentration for three days took a great deal of mental and physical discipline. This time, I would be ready. This time, my body wouldn't tire and my mind wouldn't lapse. After three long days of sitting for the Bar exam at the L.A. Airport Hilton Hotel in early 1984, I exhaled. I had done all I could do. I felt good about it, but not cocky. I had run my race, and the rest was out of my hands.

Over the next few months, I kept busy dating Robin. I needed a job to pay for all those social outings, so I took a job working as a substitute school teacher in the Compton Unified School District. There I was on the front line, a substitute teacher at what some segments of society would call the worst public high schools in the state because the buildings were aged, the budgets underfunded, and the students lacked motivation. But I brought my incurable optimism and drive into those classrooms. It wasn't long before my students loved me, despite the fact that I was a strong disciplinarian. The young black minds were soaring, and so were their grades. I had simply passed onto them what my mother had passed onto me—an insatiable love for learning.

At the end of the school year, June 1984, I was lying in bed with the first of several hernia surgeries I would have throughout my life. Writhing there in medium-level pain, I was surprised by a visit from one of my cousins—Van Scott. Mild-mannered Van was the cousin whom I rarely saw because he lived across town. But on that day, he had come to visit me. Apparently, after Van entered the front door of our house, he saw the day's mail which had been dropped through the mail slot onto the floor. He picked it up and spied a letter from the California Bar. He walked into my bedroom and methodically handed the letter to me.

I took it and paused. It looked the same as all the previous letters I had received from the Bar that began with, "We regret to inform you..." This letter was not thicker. It looked as if I should just toss it and save myself the anguish and embarrassment of another failure. Holding the envelope in my left hand, I began to open it slowly with my right index finger. I removed the folded letter, opened it, and read my newfound destiny. It was the most memorable six words I have ever read. "We are happy to inform you..."

I had done it! I had finally passed the California Bar! I immediately thanked God for it, and I wanted to jump up and down. I wanted to go out, dance, and celebrate wildly, but God knew better. He knew the safest place for me was lying restrictively in bed, planning quietly. I could only imagine what the future held.

CHAPTER TWENTY

New Lawyer, New Life

After the euphoria of passing the California State Bar settled, I could finally focus on taking my relationship with Robin to the next level and finding a job.

Everything my dad had said to me about having a law license was true. No sooner had I passed the Bar did I realize I had a lot of options. Since learning about my creative side in law school, I was strongly considering a career in entertainment law. After all, I lived in L.A., the entertainment capital of the world! I could live the lifestyle of the rich and famous. But I had come to realize I had no contacts, no inroads into the entertainment industry. I surmised that the best thing for me to do was to take a job that would fulfill one of my childhood fantasies—to be Perry Mason. Yes, I'd become a defense attorney, a trial lawyer—I'd be that guy who goes to court and fights it out with the prosecutor; the one who digs deeply to find the hidden truth and delivers his client from the jaws of injustice.

The day I was sworn into the California Bar at the Scottish Rites Auditorium was a gorgeous sunny day. I wore a 3-piece gray Herringbone suit that my dad had bought me to celebrate the occasion.

Robin had to work, and so it was just my dad and mom witnessing my milestone. Perhaps it was only fitting that it was just the three of us. These were the two people who had sacrificed the most for my success. Though I had three siblings, that day I felt like an only child; I had my dad and mom all to myself. Right after the swearing in, they handed me a brand-new, brown leather briefcase with my initials engraved on it.

"Now you really look like a Philadelphia lawyer," my dad teased.

Everything was perfect. Right then I vowed that one day when I had children I too would always be there for the highlights in their lives.

Afterward, they took me to The Tower restaurant, which sat on the top floor of the Occidental building at 1150 S. Olive Street. The food was exquisite, paralleled only by the view of L.A. from thirty-two stories high. The three of us sat together at a table by the window, and my parents toasted me for my accomplishments. I tried as hard as I could to make time stand still; I didn't want that moment to end. It was one of those times in life with your parents that you know you'd never forget, and never be able to relive. I also knew the working world was only a breath away. I looked the part, and now I had my license to actually play the part. I was determined to go to work and start earning some money.

It wasn't long before I saw that certain gleam in Dad's eye. He had started brainstorming again. In the past, when I was in college contemplating law school, he had directed me to talk to men like Stan Saunders—a young black man who grew up in Watts and became a Rhodes Scholar, and a successful lawyer. Talks with Stan were informative and just seeing his legal environment inspired me to attend law school. But, this time, there was someone else Dad had in mind.

"Son, I want you to talk to Tommy Thompson."

"Who's he?"

"A friend of mine. A young black judge who's worked his way up the ranks. I believe he can give you some good advice."

It seemed to be only a blink before I was in Judge Thompson's chambers.

"So, what are your plans now that you've passed the bar?" Judge Thompson asked.

"To become a great defense attorney. Of course, join the Public Defender's office first to get some experience," I replied.

"Listen, Walter, you don't want to join the Public Defender's Office. You want to join the *District Attorney's* Office. See, when you do that, you get two things. You get their excellent courtroom training, but also you get to understand how the prosecutors think and operate. Get in the DA's office, but don't stay long. Learn all you can and it will make you a good private defense attorney one day."

Once I shared my conversation with Judge Thompson with my dad, he advised me to interview with Robert Philibosian, the District Attorney of Los Angeles. After that interview with Philibosian and his review of my outstanding resume, I was a shoo-in. In a matter of days, I became a real-life deputy district attorney. Soon, I was making the daily commute into downtown L.A. to attend Deputy DA training. Every morning I had to allow time to fight bumper-to-bumper rush-hour traffic, make my way through overcrowded parking lots, and endure long lines of people being herded slowly through the metal detectors to enter the Criminal Courts Building. Once inside the Criminal Courts Building, I would squeeze into a crowded elevator and hold my breath until I reached the twelfth floor. I was officially a part of the "rat race."

Inside the secure floor of the DA's office, I learned the ropes by pouring over endless manuals, memos, and cases, and by shadowing senior deputies to see exactly how things were done. There was a lot to learn, from the arraignment court in Division 30 on the third floor, to preliminary hearings and misdemeanor cases in municipal court, to the big-time cases in Superior Court on the upper floors.

Just when I got the hang of things, I was sent to one of the branch offices in the suburbs. My first assignment was in Bellflower. It was a small municipal court, which was thankfully not far from my apartment in Paramount. I spent a few months there, and quickly gained a reputation as a burgeoning hot-shot trial lawyer, even if it was only misdemeanor jury trials. I prided myself on not having lost a case. Quickly, I was transferred to the DA's office in Torrance. It was a welcomed step up. Torrance not only had a Superior court, but the city itself was sort of affluent and aesthetic.

It was fun going to lunch in Torrance, where I was assigned to felony cases. I got so good at trying cases that I started believing my own press. Months went by, and it was no surprise when I was notified that I was being transferred back downtown. Yes, I was going back downtown, but this time it wouldn't be for training. This time I would be a part of "Central Trials," a prestigious unit which dealt with many felony cases and some capital cases. I was really on my way. I was going to mix it up with the likes of Johnnie Cochran, Charles Lloyd, and many other renowned defense attorneys. The Criminal Courts Building was like New York City. If you could make it there, you could make it anywhere.

While my professional life was intensifying, so was my personal life. By now, I had been dating Robin for four years. But in the spring of 1985 something seemingly innocuous occurred that changed the course of our relationship forever. Robin, who had been working hard at City Hall and had some vacation days stored up, decided to take a week-long vacation to Hawaii. Because I had just joined the District Attorney's Office, I couldn't join her. Admittedly, I expected Robin to forego her vacation and wait until we could experience Hawaii together. However, she was determined to go and ended up traveling with a girlfriend. That week apart from Robin seemed like a month. It was the first time since we started dating that we had been apart. Upon her return home, I was steaming.

"I just can't believe you went to Hawaii without me!"

"I worked hard for my vacation and I explained to you that I wasn't going to put it off. Besides, we're not married."

"You're right and that's the problem. Either we're going to really be together or we're not."

For four years our relationship had been in a holding pattern due to my need to pass the Bar, but now I knew the time was right. I had a good job, and I had a good car—a sweet, black T-top 1983 Nissan 280Z, which my cousin, Myrna, sold to me. I was twenty-seven years old, and it was time. So in the summer of 1985, I planned a special trip for Robin and me—a road trip in the 280Z to Monterey. I told her that we were going to see the beautiful sights of Northern California.

While we were in Monterey, we saw the sights, the town, the aquarium, the beach. The highlight of the trip, however, was our drive through Carmel's 17-mile drive parallel to Pebble Beach. The view from the cliffs overlooking the Pacific Ocean seemed to spread out forever, as far as eyes could see.

While admiring lookout points throughout the drive, I pulled over to get a better look at one of the gorgeous, white sandy beaches. Once outside the car, Robin and I walked hand in hand through the white sand to the shoreline. We stood there, listening to the waves gently roaring. We were entranced by the breathtaking view of the bonsai trees accenting the seashore. But as beautiful as the scene was, I felt something more beautiful. I planned something bigger.

We cuddled and I saw the perfect place. I placed a tiny box under a large tree branch lying in the sand, dashed off ahead of her, then quickly returned.

"Hey, Rob, come here. Let me show you what I found!" I exclaimed.

"What?" she asked. "You know I don't fool with any bugs or things like that," she said.

"No, no...it's something beautiful...you have to see this," I insisted.

She walked back with me to the spot where the tree branch laid in the sand. I pointed to the spot.

"See, there."

"See what?"

"See, right there?"

"I don't see a thing."

"Right there," I said.

I uncovered the ring box from the sand. Before she could say a word, I held the little black box in front of her and opened it. The marquise-shaped diamond engagement ring sparkled in the sunlight. It was magical.

"Will you marry me?"

"Yes, I will," she whispered.

The sounds of the waves crashing the shoreline played in the background as we kissed.

Funny how just a few words can bring the greatest change in your life. A few months later, on October 5, 1985, Robin and I decided to get married in the spacious family room of the Tichenor house.

As we stood face to face in the living room, dressed in full, white wedding regalia, clasping hands in front of the well-known, local minister, Beverly Crawford, our family, and a host of witnesses, it was once again a few words that created the most special memories and changed our lives forever.

"Will you, Walter Rayford Tucker III, take this woman, Robin Marie Smith, to be your lawfully wedded wife, to love, cherish and respect her till death do you part?"

"I will."

"And will you, Robin Marie Smith, take this man, Walter Rayford Tucker III, to be your lawfully wedded husband, to love, cherish and respect him till death do you part?"

"I will," Robin said.

"By the power vested in me by the Lord Jesus Christ and the State of California, I now pronounce you husband and wife. You may kiss your bride."

We kissed, then floated right from our living room ceremony into a big, lusciously green backyard overlooking a large sparkling blue swimming pool. The sun was shining, music was playing, and champagne was flowing. It was a perfect day. The Tuckers and the Smiths—two middle-class Compton families who had long known and been fond of one another—were joined together. I not only had a new wife, but we had inherited a host of in-laws.

As a city employee for several years, Robin knew and had long admired my dad—the mayor. One day I recall her saying, "You know, I married you because of your dad. He was so smart, loving, and down-to-earth. I figured if this guy is half the man that his dad is, I'll be alright."

Robin also knew that my entire family always rallied to support my dad in his political endeavors. Therefore, while outsiders may not have understood, Robin had no problem in agreeing to delay our honeymoon in order to support my dad's biggest political fundraiser, which unfortunately was booked on the same night. For some women, such a compromise would have caused the marriage to be over before it began. But not Robin. The only thing greater than her practicality was her loyalty. On the 17-mile drive to Pebble Beach, I pretended to find a wedding ring with a precious gem. However, in Robin, I had truly found a gem worth far more than rubies.

Walter and Robin Tucker - Wedding Night.

CHAPTER TWENTY-ONE

Reflections of A Mayor

s usual, I could only stay in L.A. for a few days before I found myself on another coast-to-coast flight back to D.C., back to the Hill. Still, thoughts of my past filled my mind. How did I arrive at the precarious place where I found myself? After dosing off for a while, I opened my eyes long enough to see a flight attendant walking down the aisle.

"Would you like a blanket, sir?" she asked.

"Sure," I said.

I might as well get comfortable, and try to get whatever rest I can.

As soon as I threw the blanket over me, I resumed my sleep and my reflections.

* * * * * *

In my first few months of being the mayor of Compton, I acclimated really fast. In addition to the weekly council meetings, there were police briefings, community events, visits to churches, meetings with constituents, and special projects. Although being the mayor of Compton was a full-time responsibility, it was technically a part-time job with part-time pay— only $600 a month![10] The salary was a throwback to the ancient notion that the mayor was a mere figurehead because the city manager ran things. So, I struggled to practice law and stay afloat financially. Having taken on the responsibilities of my dad's household, I went from paying $1,000 a month in rent for a two-bedroom apartment to paying a $2,000 monthly note for a five-bedroom house, taxes, and the maintenance of the house, the pool, and the acre of land on which they sat.

In my first few months in office, I knew the first thing I had to do was try to bury the hatchet with the city councilpersons who ran against me. I not only extended an olive branch to them, but also decided to put on the first Unity Festival and Summit Conference to unite the African American, Hispanic, and Asian races in Compton. While the majority of the city's residents were African American, the city's population had become increasingly more Hispanic. There was also a handful of white people and Samoans who had lived in Compton for years. The disparity between the cultures was wide. Of course each group, no matter how small, had some unique issues and needed to be heard. The time was ripe for unity

Nevertheless, with the city councilpersons who ran against me for mayor still licking their wounds, it was difficult to get their cooperation whether or not the project was good for the people. Robin and I went to work. We courted the entire city, including the white business owners in the L.A. Business Park, who were usually left out of city events. We knew their vast warehouses benefited from the protection of our police and fire departments and figured that in turn, they might want to show support. With their financial help and the hard work of city employees, the Compton Unity Festival was a success. The annual event aroused new enthusiasm and discussions of things to come all over the city. Neighboring cities like Carson and Long Beach followed suit, proving once again that imitation is the sincerest form of flattery.

During my first few months as mayor, I proposed a new image for our city; one that would overcome its negative images of poverty and gang violence. I openly identified the city's eyesores—potholes, untrimmed trees, trash, speeding cars, and graffiti—and offered solutions to fix them.

"Junior, I'm so glad to see you and the council putting in some speed bumps throughout the neighborhood streets," Momma Harris said.

"You're welcome, Momma. Keep praying for us. There's lots more to be done."

"Mr. Mayor, we can't thank you enough for the new graffiti removal program. People don't think we have pride here in Compton, but we want our buildings looking as good as any," Clarence Reed, president of the local NAACP, said.

"And we're just beginning, Mr. Reed."

"Hey Junior, I see you got that 'eye in the sky helicopter, at night'," Willie Duhon said. "That thing's working."

"Hey, in this fight against crime we need all the help we can get!"

I had only been mayor for nine months when my mom stalked into our library and closed the door behind her. She routinely thumbed through the mail, then looked up.

"I hear Dymally's retiring, and plans to run his daughter for his seat."

"What? The one who's on the Compton School Board?"

She nodded. "But I hear she doesn't live here, though."

I knew my mother was a real resource of information. Her involvement with the block clubs and her posse of local women in the Compton New Image Committee kept her up on the scuttlebutt in the streets. So I believed her about the Dymally insider tip.

This is a once-in-a-lifetime shot for someone from Compton to win that congressional seat. After my dad, then a city councilman, ran for congress in the '70s but lost, I asked him why he never gave it another shot. "Ah, that's a young man's job. It takes time to build up seniority in Congress and get anything done. But we do need someone who's actually from Compton to represent us at the federal level. Maybe one day…when the time is right, but a man has to pick his fights."

Remembering his words, I thought, *The time is right. It's time to pick this fight.*

A week later, I filed for Congress. Three weeks after, I attended Dymally's retirement dinner at the Beverly Wilshire Hotel. Politicians and businessmen from all over the 37th Congressional District flocked into the hotel's ornate-looking Ballroom to pay homage to Dymally and his clout. After pressing my way through the crowd, I talked with all the locals and shook hands with strangers, trying to determine the community's state of mind since my father's death a year earlier.

Suddenly Congressman Dymally walked on stage, stepped up to the podium, and spoke into the mic. He honored all of the heroes and heroines of his district while we waited to hear the news with eager anticipation. Finally, the moment arrived. He turned slightly to his left and took on a more somber demeanor.

"Ladies and gentlemen, as you know, I have spent twelve years in congress. I believe I've done a lot of good. But now it's time to pass the baton. It's time for a young local who has this district's best interest at heart to continue my good works." He faced his audience head-on.

"I am endorsing the only person who knows what our district needs. Knows how to get things done for Compton and the other cities in this district. No one else is better suited to help us continue to thrive in such rough times. I introduce to some and present to others, my daughter, Lynn Dymally."[11] The audience jumped to its feet and applause filled the air.

Lynn Dymally walked on stage and stood by her father's side. Her slightly overweight body was accented by an olive complexion and slick black hair, which was wrapped in a bun. She stared blankly, admiring her father.

This live endorsement was a well-staged warning for anyone who might think of opposing his daughter's candidacy. The Dymally camp stared me down as I looked on. As I moved in to get a closer look, they tried to block me from getting near the stage. I just kept shaking hands, smiling, and networking. Their stares became a dare and projected disdain. I must have looked small and insignificant against the opulence of the head table filled with shining crystal and well-dressed leaders from both Los Angeles and Compton. But I stood tall because I knew who I was. *They can't intimidate me! He can't anoint his daughter as his successor like this is some royal coronation! I am the son of Mayor Walter R. Tucker, Compton's most beloved mayor. I ran and was elected by the people to fill his seat. And now, I am the mayor, the youngest in the city's history; one who hit the ground running and has already made great progress. She's just a school board member who hasn't done anything. The people of Compton deserve the best.*

CHAPTER TWENTY-TWO

A Twist of Fate

From the moment Congressman Dymally endorsed his daughter, his political media group called "Truth In Politics" pressed the pedal to the metal and never let up. They immediately put out a "hit piece" on me citing that I had lied to a judge while working in the District Attorney's Office: WE NEED LAWMAKERS, NOT LAWBREAKERS!

On the other hand, Dymally had set his daughter up right. In the coming weeks, she lost weight and was sporting a new wardrobe of expensive-looking short skirt suits. Her new hairstyle, a loose look that was vastly different from the matronly bun she wore, seemed to give her a more confident attitude. To top that off, her father put together a well-oiled machine to run her campaign.

My law office, located in one of the few modern-looking office buildings in Compton, soon became my campaign headquarters. That building was rumored to be co-owned by Dymally himself. Needless to say, it wasn't long before all our front windows were covered with huge Lynn Dymally signs. The entire backside of the building became her suite of campaign offices, containing computers, pollsters, data analysts, paid phone-callers, speech writers, schedulers, and an endorsement team. How do you run a winning campaign against a legendary name and a juggernaut? Yes, I was up against a giant, but my dad's good name and deeds, and the accelerated job I had done as mayor in my first year would have to outweigh the odds.

Though a lot of local well-knowns joined Lynn's camp after her dad's endorsement, I was glad that I still had my family's support. Also Kris, my dad's faithful media consultant whom I had come to affectionately call "Big Sis," agreed to help me as she had helped him. Then, just as I was praying for an infusion of youth into the campaign, Marcus Mason, a young man born in Compton and raised in the neighboring city of Carson, came aboard.

I remember it like it was yesterday. I was getting off the elevator at City Hall, and I saw this well-dressed, young man getting on. Being in full campaign mode, I engaged him.

"Hey, young man, what's your name?"

"Marcus Mason, I'm an intern in the city attorney's office, Mayor Tucker."

"Sounds good. Well, I don't know if you've heard, but I'm running for congress. Here's one of my cards. Come join the campaign. We need all the young people we can get."

He took my card and I hurried off to my office.

Days later Marcus showed up at my campaign headquarters. I pointed at him in surprise. "Hey, the young man from the city attorney's office."

"I'm here to help. In fact, Mayor Tucker, if you don't have anyone running your campaign yet, I'd like to be your campaign manager."

"Hmmm. Well, actually, I am looking for a campaign manager. What's your experience?"

"I was raised in Compton, and graduated from Arizona State University—played football there. Honestly, I've never run a political campaign, but I'm a hard worker. Football taught me about teamwork and toughness. I promise you, you won't be disappointed."

Because most seasoned campaigners in the district were afraid to go against the Dymally machine, I was pretty much relying on family and close friends to help me run my campaign. So when young Marcus got in my face, and said with confidence, "I can run your campaign," I took a leap of faith and made him my campaign manager on the spot. Besides, I had always been committed to investing in young black men because my father invested in me and a lot of other young black men. Something told me that when I met Marcus on the elevator that day it was fate.

It wasn't until years later that I learned the back story. After Marcus took my business card at City Hall, he went home and had a talk with his mother.

"Hey, Mom, you'll never guess what happened today. I met the mayor. He said he was running for congress and told me he needed my help. What should I do?"

"You should help him."

"How?"

"Run his campaign."

Marcus was just young enough to not have been influenced by the Dymally mystique. In fact, he later told me that the Tucker name was more identifiable and connected to him and his family. He was young, and I was young, and he felt we could relate to one another.

It wasn't long before Marcus brought some more young troops on board. Dave Mahan, his classmate from California State University Dominguez Hills, and Tyrone Bland, his best friend for life. Each day more young people from the community joined the campaign, jumped on the phones, hit the streets, and delivered yard signs.

We became the young, grassroots campaign up against the big, formidable machine, but there were two things the Dymally camp forgot—local people send congressmen to Washington, and you need a spirited candidate to win. It's usually someone who reminds them of their favorite elected official.

Walter runs for Congress, 1992.

Congressional Rally at Tichenor House.

I was much like my father in many ways. He taught me to care about people. Lynn, on the other hand, bragged about walking the halls of Congress with her father when she was a child, yet she was aloof with people. While at countless rallies, town hall meetings, debates, and block club gatherings, I would jump up and speak to people—any people, all people. I would shake hands, and listen to their stories, their needs, and the desires of their hearts; their hopes and dreams. Whatever they had to say, or whatever joke they had to tell, I listened and joked right back. I laughed when they laughed, even though most of the jokes were not that humorous.

Lynn seemed to be wondering why they didn't come to pay homage to her. On the contrary, with Kris steering me in the right direction for maximum media exposure, I seized every opportunity to make a speech, or speak to constituents. I was comfortable with youth and young adults, as well as the seniors; the undecided, and the disenfranchised. I was making headway, but truthfully, because of the Dymally machine's resources, it was a seemingly impossible battle.

I could hear my dad say to me, "*Nothing great comes easy and anything that comes easy is not great.*"

After the sudden death of one of my staunch union supporters from the Long Beach Shipyard, Frank Griffin, I was thinking a lot about establishing a job skills training center. Before he died, Frank made me promise that I would do all I could to establish one in Compton. Therefore, I drove around inspecting my city for a possible site. Eventually, I noticed a large piece of land with boarded-up buildings on Bullis Road, just south of Rosecrans. It was the old Southern California Edison building that sat on about nine acres. I grabbed the car phone and called my secretary at City Hall.

"I need the number for the CEO of Southern California Edison right away!"

A few days later, I was in front of the CEO's desk, making my plea.

"We need a job skills training center for our kids, so we don't have high crime and unemployment. You all have a property in Compton—Rosecrans and Bullis Road—about nine acres, just sitting there collecting weeds."

"Well, Mr. Mayor, how much do you want to pay for it?" the CEO said without blinking.

"Nothing," I said, unflinching. "The city is strapped. But just think of how much you'd get by way of promotion, good will, investment in the community, and skilled minority workers for your labor force."

"It's an idea...let us sleep on it." He looked at me with a disingenuously smile.

"You don't want to sleep on this too long. There are precious lives at stake!"

"Right...we'll get back with you, Mayor Tucker."

Sure you will. I'll have to fight this battle another day.

A few months into the congressional campaign it happened. April 29, 1992. Twelve misguided white jurors in Simi Valley delivered a not guilty verdict on the charges brought against the officers accused of unlawfully beating Rodney King. Before you could say, "Burn, baby, burn," South Central L.A., Compton, and Long Beach erupted in flames. All of my attention immediately turned from campaigning to saving my city from being burned to the ground.

On April 29th I was in the wake of the worst riot in the history of L.A. Mass chaos, violence, fires, and shooting roared on for three days. Though local law enforcement was putting up a good fight against rioters and looters, by the third day I was convinced it was time for more drastic measures. After having been driven around the war-torn area by local Compton PD, frustrated from breathing in smoke, and dodging bullets, and seeing there was seemingly no end to the shooting and looting, something came over me and I went into action.

"Officer, stop the car right there, next to that CNN mobile unit!"

"Yes, sir, Mayor."

"I'm getting out to talk with them."

"We got you covered, Mr. Mayor."

Immediately, I hopped in front of a burned-out car next to the CNN unit and started yelling for emergency assistance.

"You want to cover this terrible story in Compton. Well, cover this. I'm the mayor of Compton, Walter Tucker, and I've got something to say…"

The CNN reporter quickly moved in closer to me and the CNN cameraman followed suit.

"We're live here in the riot-torn city of Compton, and Mayor Walter Tucker is standing in front of a burned-out car yelling…"

"I'm urging Governor Wilson to send the National Guard in here now! Now, before they burn down the whole *damn* city! If this was Beverly Hills, help woulda already been here! Send in the troops…send them in *now*!"

"You heard it right here, live! Against the backdrop of a riot-torn city, Compton's mayor, urging the governor to send in the National Guard to save his city…"

My father used to say, "Son, the squeaky wheel gets the oil." Due largely to that live TV coverage, the National Guard came quickly and began to restore order in the face of growing anarchy. Sure, like every other black person, I was highly upset by the jury's verdict and I wanted to send out a strong message of rebuke to the country. But as the mayor, the official spokesman of the city, I knew I had to be the voice of reason to restore civil order.

Having seen the devastation of property as a young boy after the Watts Riots, I knew that after all the smoke cleared the people really hurt by all the burning and looting were the local black residents—not the people who were the object of the protest. In the long run, the black community suffers because businesses become reluctant to risk rebuilding in such a "volatile area."

Once it was reported that the National Guard was on its way, the Dymally camp began plotting to have them concentrate their attention solely on the protection of Compton's schools. They planned to give Lynn an opportunity to be seen working with the National Guard to save the schools. Kris informed me that she overheard their strategy at the new Lazben Hotel.

"Listen, some of the stores may burn ta hell, but our kids must have a future!" one of the Dymally aides said.

"Yeah, that's the angle we'll take," another aide chimed in.

"We'll have the congressman call the National Guard for a press conference at Kelly Elementary first thing in the morning. Lynn, as the representative for the School Board, you'll voice your concern about the education and safety of our children."

"But I'm not the president of the School Board, John Stewart is."

"No matter, we got Stewart and the board supporting you. They'll all take a backseat and let you take center stage. Let you look, you know—congressional."

But when Governor Pete Wilson came to Compton on that Sunday morning following the riot, he came to see the burned-down shopping centers, not the schools that were left intact. He didn't come to meet with the School Board or the City Council, but with the mayor of the city.

The governor's security detail had called ahead to see if the area was safe and if the mayor would be on hand to walk the governor through the ruins and show him what had to be rebuilt. After an hour of waiting, Governor Wilson's motorcade rolled in. The governor's security came and put me in direct contact with the governor. I showed him stores ravaged by fire and looting— charred TVs, chairs, stoves, and washing machines lay in the alleyways next to these stores. We cruised by meat markets where steaks and chicken parts lay in the streets and flies had begun to swarm. Shattered glass could be heard crunching into the tires of our car, and broken windows proved that businesses had been destroyed and lives had been forever changed. After all the smoke was cleared, Compton had suffered an estimated $100 million in damage; nearly 200 buildings were vandalized and more than 130 separate arson fires were reported.[12]

Discussing damage of the LA Riots – May. 1992

Well, if I was in disfavor with the Dymally camp before, I certainly seemed to be hated even more. My team had learned to spy on the opposition.

"Tucker's using this riot to get publicity for his congressional campaign. Dirty dog!"

They were accusing me of the very thing they had attempted to do but failed. Dymally and all of the City Council complained that I was hogging the show. Was this a show to them? This was a tragedy—one I hoped our city would never see again. And if I had anything to do with it, it wouldn't. We had to get down to education and creating jobs. The sight of soot and rubble and the smell of smoke were all around us, showing what devastating damage a riot can do.

Congressman Dymally also showed up in the riot-torn streets that morning for the first time to walk with the governor through the ruins. Riot or no riot, Governor Wilson was a Republican, and the congressman was a Democrat. It was an election year and the governor didn't allow the congressman to get too close to him for photo ops.

Nevertheless, Lynn Dymally showed up and tried to stay close to her father, while he was attempting to stay close to the governor and me. At one point, Lynn ventured away slightly and had a little skirmish with Councilwoman Pat Moore about who was going to walk nearest to the governor. This skirmish didn't win Lynn any brownie points with the crowd looking on.

Later that afternoon, Kris informed me that the governor wanted me to meet him at Compton's Lazben Hotel. His security detail had secured a room on the top floor. After clearing security, I approached the governor and he extended his hand.

"Mayor Tucker, thank you for the tour of the damaged area. I have declared a state of emergency and I think I will be able to help Compton rebuild, but there is another meeting I'd like you to make—someone else I'd like you to meet," Governor Wilson said.

"Just tell me when, where and who?" I replied.

Tomorrow at 10:00 a.m. at my L.A. office downtown. Here's my card. Oh, and the meeting will be with the president.

The president? President Bush?

"Yes, President George Bush."

"I'll be there."

Suddenly there was a knock on the door. When the governor's security opened the door, I could see Lynn, her father, and the rest of the City Council trying to enter, but the governor's security blocked their admission. Dymally threw a cursing tantrum. Lynn and the council were livid. Once again, their attention focused on me.

"That damned Tucker!"

They accused me of being the reason security hadn't let them through. I had nothing to do with it.

Later that day, I got a call back from the Edison CEO.

"Mr. Mayor, you were right. Let's get that skills center idea of yours rolling."

"Sounds great."

"I'll have my secretary contact you for a planning meeting next week."

Suddenly, things were looking up.

Everything happens in God's perfect timing.

CHAPTER TWENTY-THREE

Rising Star

T he following day, there I was, standing in the presence of the most powerful man in the world—the president of the United States!

"Well, Mayor Tucker, I understand Governor Wilson has declared a state of emergency because you really got a mess on your hands—a lot of damage."

"Yes, sir, that's right. Now we need your help to get F.E.M.A. to release funds for the rebuild."

Mayor Tucker asks President George H.W. Bush and Governor Pete Wilson for Federal Assistance after the LA Riot

"Mayor Tucker, I'm sure you didn't know this, but when I was in the service during World War II, Barbara and I lived in Compton."

"Really? Where?"

"Right there on Santa Fe Ave, just north of Alondra."

"You're talking about Santa Fe Gardens."

"They didn't call it that then. It was military housing, but those were some of the best years of our lives—right in Compton. You'll have your emergency funds. Now, let's take some photos," President Bush said. The photographer standing by took some candid shots of President Bush, Governor Wilson, and me.

Who would have ever guessed that George Herbert Walker Bush had a soft spot in his heart for Compton? I know I'm being set up for a political photo op, but you think I care? We need that rebuild money and he needs some photos showing that he's taking care of the nation's cities. Like they say, politics makes strange bedfellows.

The next day that photo of me lobbying the president and the governor hit the papers and instantly I was catapulted onto the national stage. More importantly, the citizens of Compton took notice. Compton was no longer alone and unsupported.

"Now that's what we need at a time like this. A mayor who knows people in high places," Momma Harris said while entering the next City Council meeting.

"Yeah, if Compton is going to rise from the ashes, we gonna need some strong and proven leadership," Willie Duhon leaned over and whispered to her.

The Mayor and the President strike a bond leading to Compton's recovery.

This windfall of favor on me seemed to infuriate my opponents to no end. Some days later, things heated up even further. Someone in Dymally's camp took pictures of me getting into my city car in a location where my congressional campaign signs could be seen nearby. They took the photographs to the City Council, and the council accused me of using my city car to run my congressional campaign, which I wasn't. But the majority of the council, supportive of Lynn Dymally, voted to take away my car. I remained unflappable and pressed on to rebuild the city.

In the next few months, I convinced the city to move rapidly to repair the streets, curb gang violence, and step up community policing. Compton residents heard my voice at city council meetings.

"How can we curb juvenile delinquency without including the youth in the process?" I asked. "We need to establish a Compton Youth Commission, a new youth center, and develop more alternatives for our youth."

The Compton Youth Commission was born, even if the council did start splinter groups to dilute its impact and compete with the press it was getting.

I had done well in elevating pride and raising hope. I fought for funds and got them. More Asset Forfeiture Money for our local police department showed up. More money for parks and playground improvements were on the way. More money for street and infrastructure improvements. More money for our Small Business Loan Program. I was fast becoming the people's hometown hero that my father had been.

Notwithstanding all this, every candidate's forum, town hall meeting, and precinct walk was highly contested by the Dymally camp. The intensity of their approach was something like a rabid dog. By that time Keta's husband, Richard Brown—a politically astute man—had joined the campaign. He couldn't help but engage in fiery political debate with the opposition. Unfortunately, Richard didn't realize that you can't reason with unreasonable people. Lynn's campaign reflected the spirit of her father. To him, it was a given that the 37th Congressional District should stay under Dymally control. To Richard, such an opinion was an affront to those of us who wanted a "grass-roots-run" city. One heated campaign night, such debate almost reached a fist fight between our two camps. Thank God Keta was able to pull Richard away from the fray before someone got hurt or arrested.

As we got close to Election Day, I got a call from a very surprising source.

"Hello, Mayor Tucker?"

"Yes."

"This is Congresswoman Waters. I'd like to meet with you."

Wow, Maxine Waters! Renowned in Los Angeles and throughout the nation as a fighter for the rights of the oppressed and underrepresented. I didn't know what the meeting was about, but what local black politician would pass up an opportunity to meet with her!

In a matter of days, I was in her living room seated on the edge of my chair, anticipating her every word.

"Mayor Tucker, I'm aware of your family legacy and I've been watching your campaign for Congress with interest." She took a beat. "I'd like to list you in my Democratic Voter's Guide as my recommendation for Congress in the 37th Congressional District for the upcoming June Primary Election? Are you in agreement?"

Am I in agreement! I could have hit the floor!

"Most of us black Democrats have common political interests. As long as you support the rights of women, our people, and the poor, you will have my support."

In a flash, I speculated as to her reasons for wanting to endorse me over her congressional colleague's daughter – Lynn Dymally. I surmised that perhaps there was "bad blood" between her and Dymally, or maybe she just felt she'd have more leverage with me than she would with Lynn. Either way, I didn't ponder the matter long.

"Yes, sounds great," I replied.

"Alright, I'll need your headshot right away for the mailer."

Wow! The Maxine Waters Voter Guides mailed out before every election were legendary. They carried weight with staunch

Democratic constituents. Voters would even carry them to the polls and use them inside the polling booth to vote. Things were looking up.

My father would often say, "If you take the initiative to do something good, somewhere along the way someone will see what you're trying to do, and help you."

Finally, the day of the primary election had arrived. It was D-day because everyone knew that whoever won the Democratic Primary would be the congressperson elect in such a heavily Democratic Congressional District. On the night of June 2, 1992, I was in a small Lazben hotel room surrounded by family and mostly young, inexperienced campaign workers. We knew we had been outspent and outmanned in our David and Goliath fight. The "X factor," however, was my Lord Jesus Christ.

On election night, Marcus came in like a quarterback and revved up our tired troops. He manned the phones and gave assignments as he had done the entire campaign. He called every twenty minutes for precinct updates from the County Recorder's office. I liked the feel of my troops because we cared about one another and we were quick to pray. But at nine o'clock, we were behind in the count. At that moment, we convinced ourselves that we had nothing to fear.

"Can they beat us?" Marcus called.

"No, they can't!" the team yelled back.

In the luxury suite above us, Congressman Dymally and Lynn were probably chatting away, eating sumptuous hors d'oeuvres, and claiming victory. Everything was going their way. Lynn Dymally was pulling away, and my insides were knotting up.

With 50% of the votes counted, it was Dymally, 14,891, Tucker, 13,288. Though we were only a little over a thousand votes behind, experience had taught me that it's very difficult to catch up once the opponent shows a pattern of winning from precinct to precinct. Some of our team's faces dropped in despair.

A man I didn't recognize, standing in the corner with a cap pulled low over his head said, "Dymally never rests till he crushes his enemies." I didn't know who he was.

But there was one thing I knew: I would never fear him, even though some of my workers said they were afraid he would crush them if we lost. They had put their lives all on the line to support me and the future of their businesses and their careers were at stake.

What's holding up those election returns?

Suddenly, I recalled something my mother shared with me when I was a young boy.

"Remember, son, a watched pot never boils."

These words of wisdom had helped me overcome my impatience at various times in my life. That phrase simply meant, fixating on what you're waiting for, but can't control seems to make time move more slowly. But by refocusing on what you can control, time will pass before you know it. History had shown me that in the moment of despair, words of courage can shape destiny. Therefore, I seized the moment.

"Listen up, everybody! Those of you who've worked this campaign, just know that we've come this far by faith and prayer, and we're not even considering defeat."

The small group of loyal supporters cheered half-heartedly.

"So it's time to pray."

We joined hands and I prayed for victory, not defeat. I prayed for power, not weakness. I prayed for the opportunity to do right by our city, our people, our God.

"Father, we give you all the praise. You promised us victory and we expect it! Right now things aren't looking that great, but we know You can do anything but fail. Turn the tide, Lord, turn the tide! So that we can inherit your promises and serve your people. We thank You for your grace and mercy, in Jesus' name. Amen."

Then, I was no longer anxiously waiting for Marcus to relay the next count from the county recorder's office. It was all in God's hands.

At midnight, Marcus grabbed the phone and dialed in for the latest congressional count.

"Hey, everybody! Listen! We've closed the gap. We're within a thousand votes!"

Our campaign workers erupted into cheers. I imagined Mervyn Dymally upstairs, barking out commands to his staff like a general who sees the battle in jeopardy, *"Damn it, I said no ice in my drink! Can't you get anything right?"*

Lynn had to be in severe denial, *"This can't be happening! This is not happening!"*

At two in the morning, Marcus called again. He raised his hand for silence. A hush came across the room.

"With ninety percent of the vote counted...Dymally, fifteen thousand six hundred twenty-four...Tucker, sixteen thousand seven hundred fifty-seven." He slammed the phone down.

"We're ahead! We pulled ahead!" Marcus shouted.

Hysterical jubilation broke loose. A powerful wind was shaping my destiny. It was, without a doubt, the most exhilarating experience of my life. It was the stuff of which dreams are made. All we had to do now was keep a steady pace and hold on.

At 4:00 a.m., with 99% of the vote counted, the pot was now boiling over. I had won the nomination with 39 percent of the vote (22,536) over Dymally's 37 percent (21,433).[13]

"Congratulations, Congressman!" Kris said with a huge smile as she hugged me.

"Congratulations to you, 'Big Sis!' You just earned yourself a job on my congressional staff!"

"Oh, in that case, let me hug you again, and kiss you!"

We hugged, and both laughed. Then, my small group of loyal soldiers and I rushed downstairs to the lobby. As we were standing in lobby celebrating, Mervyn Dymally marched out of the elevator and entered the lobby. He threw his shoulders back, marched across the lobby, and stood directly in front of me. Dymally reached out his hand and spoke casually in his Caribbean accent.

"Congratulations, Mr. Congressman-Elect, One helluva victory!"

Instinctively I took his hand and we engaged in a brief handshake.

"Thank you," I replied as he pivoted and walked away.

Congressman Dymally had class; he knew how to play the game. I looked around to see if I could spot Lynn, but she was nowhere to be found. Then, I looked to see if I could spot the man with the pulled-down cap who had been in the hotel room with my supporters. I found no trace of him either, yet I remembered his words: *Dymally never rests until he crushes his enemies.*

That night, I was determined to bask only in the elation of victory. My dream had become a reality, and my political future lay confidently before me. I had accomplished something that neither my dad nor any of our local black elected officials had ever accomplished. Yes, the 37th District already had an African-American congressman in Dymally, but not one "straight outta Compton." No, there was no time for fear. It was time for celebration.

CHAPTER TWENTY-FOUR

Indicted

When The House recessed at the start of the summer, 1994, I hopped on another flight back to L.A. After I left the airplane and stepped outside the terminal, I spotted the black Town Car. It pulled up to the curb, I hopped in, and was off to my district office to respond to the needs of my constituents and fend off my ongoing legal problems. In the middle of the government serving me with subpoenas, public speculation, and a series of newspaper articles fanning the flame of controversy, I did what all politicians do in an election year—I campaigned. Kris did her best to feed the media positive information about my community accomplishments in spite of the legal scrutiny I was under. Audrey and Kris coordinated my schedule so that every appointment would produce maximum exposure and votes.

It was nearing the June 1994 primary, and the newspapers projected a hitch-free election for me. Yet, I did have an opponent: an unknown named Lew Prulistsky. *The Daily Breeze* described me as "an incumbent, an ordained minister, the political progeny of a pioneering Compton family, who has built-in clout, and appears to have few obstacles confronting him in his re-election."

Now the challenge was to stay focused on my re-election while under the glaring spotlight of the law. I was quoted as saying, "I'm not shrinking...I believe, as always, that God is on my side."

Political pundits put their money on me, saying the probe was a hurdle I could leap over, especially because authorities were unlikely to make a decision on filing charges before the June 7th primary. Their prediction stood. I did win the Democratic primary by 84% of the vote.[14] The news of the investigation didn't harm my bid for re-election.

I was quoted, saying, "In a twisted way, this controversial press has helped my campaign. My constituency is sensitive to my plight. The amount of community support has been very inspiring to me."

But on my way to another landslide victory in the general election, the news of the pending indictment hit every paper, certainly those read by the constituents of the 37th Congressional District.

August 11, 1994, *The Daily Breeze* in Torrance, California reported:

"REP. TUCKER REPORTEDLY TO BE CHARGED WITH CORRUPTION"
(Indictment alleges bribes taken while mayor of Compton).

The Long Beach Press Telegram headlined:

"TUCKER BRIBERY CHARGES EXPECTED TODAY," August 11, 1994.

The Los Angeles Times reported:

"REP. TUCKER TO BE INDICTED SOURCES SAY."

The news broke first on KNBC-TV, which reported that the indictment would allege that Tucker, D-Compton, violated the Hobbs Act, which makes it a felony to affect interstate commerce by extortion or bribe-taking.

It was widely held that KNBC-TV easily scooped the print media because of an apparent relationship between KNBC-TV reporter Manny Madrano and Assistant U.S. Attorney Steve Madison. The U.S. Attorney's Office was notorious for carefully and cleverly leaking information to the media. This was the first in what was to be many mysterious leaks concerning my case.

The *LA Times* reported, "U.S. Atty. Nora Manella said she could not discuss the case or the possibility of indictments. She confirmed that she expects to hold a two p.m. news conference today, but would not disclose the topic."

"We can't confirm or deny any reports of anticipated indictments," she said.

By Friday, August 12, 1994, it was official. The U.S. Attorney's cat-and-mouse media game gave way to massive headlines:

The *Los Angeles Times*: "REP. TUCKER IS INDICTED! DENIES BRIBERY CHARGES." The *Wall Street Journal*: "REP. WALTER TUCKER INDICTED ON CHARGES OF TAKING BRIBES." The *Long Beach Press Telegram*: "U.S. REP. TUCKER INDICTED. OFFICIAL DENIES FRAUD EXTORTION CHARGES."

For better or worse, finally, there were details. "A federal grand jury Thursday returned a ten-count indictment against Rep. Walter R. Tucker III, charging him with seven counts of soliciting and accepting thirty thousand dollars in bribes in violation of eighteen U.S.C. Section nineteen fifty-one, one count of demanding another two-hundred-fifty-thousand-dollar bribe, and two counts of filing false tax returns, in violation of twenty-six U.S.C. Section seventy-two o six, subsection one, while serving as mayor of Compton," The *LA Times* reported.[15]

It was further reported that I issued a statement from my Washington office, proclaiming my innocence. "I unequivocally and categorically deny all charges that have been brought against me. I have complete faith in God, who is my shield and my defense. He has brought me through many trials of life, and I trust He will bring me through this one. I will not allow this matter to impede the important work that I am doing in the U.S. Congress."[16]

U.S. Attorney Nora Manella said that I'd accepted bribes from people I believed represented Compton Energy Systems (CES) Inc., a business seeking to build a solid waste incinerator at Greenleaf and Central Avenues in Compton. John Macardican, the applicant for CES, described the incinerator as a $225 million, 214,000 square-foot facility that would have generated 600 jobs for the recession-weary city.

U.S. Attorneys: John Potter, Nora Manella, and Steve Madison

According to the indictment, I received the first bribe, $2,000 in cash, from Macardican in June 1991. I was accused of taking an additional $1,000 in cash and a $1,000 check from him the following month. It was further alleged that in August 1991, I received another $1,000 cash payment from Macardican and the following month, I allegedly demanded $250,000 from another undercover government agent. The indictment listed four other payments: $1,000 in November, 1991, $4,000 in February, 1992, $10,000 in March, 1992, and $10,000 in July, 1992. I was accused of lying when I said my 1991 income was $41,924, and my 1992 income was $38,662. During a news conference, U.S. Attorney Manella said the undeclared income included, but was not limited to, the bribe money.

The experts agreed that the indictment wouldn't alter my job tenure at that time. However, a conviction was another story. I was scheduled to be arraigned on the charges on August 22. Johnnie, who was considering getting involved with the O.J. Simpson murder case, called my case "a vicious sting," and vowed to take my matter to trial.

The LA Times reported: "If convicted, the thirty-seven-year-old minister faces a maximum of twenty years in federal prison on each extortion charge and three years in prison on each tax charge. However, federal guidelines dictate a sentence considerably shorter."

Naturally, the indictment brought against a United States Representative constantly fueled the media coverage throughout the summer. Comments by the black press suggested that the tell-tale signs of another "sting" against a black leader were evident.

"He represents what we believe to be the highest hopes of our community," Reverend Lonnie Dawson, a pastor at New Mount Calvary Baptist Church in South Central Los Angeles, said.

I was confident that the work I was doing to break the cycle of poverty, violence and bad press for the people of my congressional district could not be stopped.

Whenever I would begin to sag, all the Olympian trappings of Washington not only reminded me of our country's great history, but of the great opportunity I had been given to serve, to somehow make a difference.

Nothing was a greater reminder and encouragement to me than serving in the Clinton administration. For the first two years of that Democratic president's first term, there was a Democratic House and Senate. It was the first time one party controlled the executive and legislative branches in twenty years. The president essentially enjoyed carte blanche to make public policy. Everyone in the Democratic Party was stoked; all of us were feeding off each other's euphoria. We were a part of a unique time and place in American political history.

All while I was studying Political Science at Princeton and U.S.C., I had no idea that one day I would actually be one of only 435 United States Representatives in the entire country. When I was a little boy watching *Mr. Smith Goes to Washington*, I wanted to be Mr. Smith. Now I was Mr. Smith. I had taken my place under that August Capitol Dome of America's lawmakers.

* * * * * *

President Bill Clinton presided over the longest period of peacetime economic expansion and I was a part of it. When President Clinton took office, he inherited a huge national debt of over $200 billion, but through his fiscal conservatism he continued to reduce the deficit. By the time he left office in 2000, there was a budget surplus of $236 billion.[17] This was accomplished because there was something special about his leadership. After he was elected to office, he never stopped campaigning; he never stopped wooing the American public to support his ideas and programs. He was a laid-back, likable character that was totally approachable by anyone he needed to approach.

One day I was late for President Clinton's briefing with the freshman congressmen of the 103rd Congress. Public Works and Transportation hearings made me late, and I broke my neck to make up the time in my cross-town trek. I was uptight and out of breath by the time I made it through White House security. I was alarmed to see that the meeting had concluded as I found myself standing alone in the largest room in the White House—the East Room. As I turned to make my exit, there he was right in my face—President William Jefferson Clinton! My heart started pounding as my hand automatically extended to shake his.

"Congressman Walter Tucker from Compton, California, Mr. President. My deepest apologies for missing the briefing. I was stuck in committee and the crosstown traffic was terrible."

"Not a problem, Congressman, my Chief of Staff can send you a summary." His slow, southern, easy voice was comforting.

Before I could say another word, I fully realized that we were the only two people in the room. Secret Service was just beyond the door. President Clinton motioned to them and immediately a gentleman with a camera appeared.

"Since you made it all this way, let's at least take a picture," President Clinton said.

I grinned, adjusted my posture, and the photographer snapped that photograph, which was later sent to me, memorializing that unforgettable moment in time. That special photo of President Clinton and me standing together in the East Room of the White House was fitted in an exquisite mahogany frame that matched my congressional desk and hung on my office wall.

Moments alone with President Bill Clinton – White House, East Room

Later, when my mother met him, she said, "He looked me straight in the eyes as if I were the most important person in the world. His eyes never wandered as he said, 'Your son's doing a good job in congress.'" She never forgot that.

Speaking of something someone will never forget, my wife, Robin, will never forget that at the annual Black Caucus Legislative Conference in 1994 she had the honor of praying for President Clinton.

"Father, in the name of Jesus, bless our president. Give him the wisdom to lead, the humility to serve, and the compassion to put others first. Bless his family and his physical body. Show him how to build bridges and not fences, so the things that need to get done in Washington will get done."

President Clinton's political mastery and my political enthusiasm were never more prominent than at the yearly State of the Union Address—the biggest political event of the year. Everyone who was anyone, politically, was under one roof. Everyone gathered to await the triumphant entrance of the president into the House Chambers. Members of the president's cabinet, Supreme Court Justices, members of the U.S. Senate and members of The House were all at the same place at the same time. The only person missing was one lone member of the president's cabinet, whose name was randomly drawn minutes before the ceremony began. That top-secret protocol was done to ensure that should a disaster occur, incapacitating the line of presidential succession, the designated survivor would seamlessly run the country.

With great poise, President Clinton highlighted his accomplishments to the nation. He reminded us that with support from his Democratic Congress, he was able to pass Welfare Reform, the North American Free Trade Agreement, the Brady Bill, the Family Medical Leave Act, and the Omnibus Budget Reconciliation Act, which helped us balance the budget. Of course, President Clinton was not without his detractors and controversies—Whitewater, Troopergate, the White House FBI Files controversy and, of course, the Monica Lewinsky scandal. He was still a great president, caring and committed enough to positively impact the world.

* * * * * *

Now as I reflected on that glorious time in history, I gained great confidence in knowing that if Bill Clinton could rise above his problems, if he could keep his eye on the prize and continue to serve his country in the face of attacks and controversy, so could I.

CHAPTER TWENTY-FIVE

Fallout

With an indictment looming over my head, I had to stay in L.A. for my arraignment on August 22, 1994. When driving from Compton, it made little sense to take the traffic-jammed 110 Freeway during morning rush-hour to downtown. So Tyrone maneuvered the Town Car north on Central Avenue. As our black sedan proceeded up Central Avenue, there was always the reminder of the two sides of L.A. The one with closed-up businesses, struggling single families, and street walkers on the east side, and the one with brand-new high rises, flashy, new expensive cars, and celebrities on the west side. Rich or poor, powerful or powerless, it was only a matter of time before both sides of the tracks would meet in downtown Los Angeles for different reasons.

Downtown became the great equalizer, though. The rich and famous, the violent and infamous, would invariably occupy the same space at the Criminal Courts Building—210 West Temple Street. All the state cases ended up there. But mine was a federal case, and we headed to the United States Courthouse in the Edward R. Roybal Federal Building at 255 East Temple Street. That was where the big dogs played, where power ruled, and where federal prosecutors' careers were made.

We pulled up in front of the Federal Courthouse where a horde of reporters waited. Tyrone opened the street-side door. "I got you, Congressman."

As soon as our feet hit the ground, reporters swarmed us like starving locusts on ripe grain. I grabbed Robin's arm and she grabbed my mom's, and together we pushed our way through the pack. Finally, we reached the security checkpoint and some semblance of calm overtook us. One by one, my family and I processed through the checkpoint, leaving most of the media behind.

Once inside the arraignment courtroom, I met up with Johnnie and it wasn't long before we were called to stand before the arraignment judge.

"...as to these ten counts, how does the defendant plead, Mr. Cochran?"

"Not guilty, Your Honor," Johnnie answered.

After my brief arraignment, I posted a $10,000 signature bond and was released with restrictions only on international travel. Due to the complexity of my case—which demanded I provide thousands of documents to the government, and watch over forty hours of video and audio tapes—and Johnnie's growing involvement with the O.J. Simpson case, both parties agreed that my trial should be set for February 1, 1995—far beyond the 45-day period guaranteeing me the right to a speedy trial.

Time Magazine ran a blurb covering the story.

The Daily Breeze reported: "TUCKER PROCLAIMS INNOCENCE."

Underneath a photo of Johnnie and a crowd of supporters standing with Robin and me holding a press conference on the federal courthouse steps following my arraignment, *The LA Times* reported: "FORMER MAYOR OF COMPTON ENTERS PLEA OF NOT GUILTY: Says his trust is in Christ his Judge."

Press Conference with Johnnie Cochran on federal courthouse steps following arraignment.

About fifty supporters, including community activist, Danny Bakewell, friends, and local pastors surrounded me on the federal courthouse steps while they rallied, and held up signs: *Tucker is Innocent—Witch Hunt, Stop Racism Now! Leave Tucker Alone.*[18] Supporters and I gathered together and prayed. The energy of the crowd truly encouraged me in the face of my prosecution. Since becoming a U.S. congressman, my relationship with the Lord had grown, and I knew He wouldn't leave me or forsake me. I boldly predicted that God would deliver me.

Tucker's supporters march with him on the federal courthouse steps after his arraignment.

"So many black politicians have been targeted for takedown. But what the FBI and the U.S. Attorney's Office have intended for evil, God will turn around for good. God is able. He is my deliverer."

Kris and my supporters ran interference for me to my car while reporters from every conceivable television and radio station pressed in to get their story and a shot of my face. It wasn't every day that a U.S. Representative was indicted and the media smelled blood. The community groundswell sounded the alarm: "TUCKER TARGETED." The conservative white press, replied, "CHARGE OF BIAS GETS TIRESOME."

Safely in the backseat of my car with Robin and my mother, we sped away from the courthouse and I sighed. My brain began to swirl with what Johnnie had said. "Getting the right judge is key. Someone who's fair; someone who knows the law, and won't be biased. We'd love to have Judge Marshall. She's about the fairest one up there."

God smiled on me. Of all the federal judges in the entire courthouse, the following week, U.S. District Judge Consuelo Marshall became my judge: no hocus pocus, no foul play, no sleight of hand. *Thank God my prayers were answered.*

The clerk may have spun the wheel that selects the defendant's judge, but God did the selecting. I believed that with all my heart. I felt so good about it that I decided to give an interview to the most prominent black newspaper west of the Mississippi, *The Los Angeles Sentinel.* The headline read: "CONGRESSMAN TUCKER DIGS IN, PROMISES TO FIGHT CHARGES."

I was quoted saying, "I've been so moved. It's been incredible. You find out in times like these who you can trust." I acknowledged my wife of ten years and the rest of my family for sticking by me. It was good to know that I could always turn to my wife, mother, sisters, and brother. Their love was priceless. Everything I had spent my whole life chasing paled by comparison.

I found a blurb about me in a section of the *Sentinel Newspaper* entitled, "The People's Pulse." The columnist asked the question, "What are your feelings on the indictment of former Mayor Walter Tucker?"

Ernest Johnson said, "He's not guilty of anything yet. The government will have to bring him to trial. They must prove that he's guilty. A lot of people have been under an indictment, but were later found not guilty."

Piper Alvez offered, "I think it's so sad that our politicians are so vulnerable to certain situations that can entrap them. All of the work accomplished by them can vanish overnight. Let's hope that the charges are not true."

Nelson Brown added, "When I heard the news, I couldn't believe it. I always thought of him as a fair man when he was the mayor of Compton. This is a man you could depend on to be there when you needed him. I hope he isn't guilty of these charges."

"Walter, despite the media's daily feeding frenzy, we got your back," Kris said.

"Thanks, Big Sis."

While the government was resolved to prove me guilty, I was determined to continue the business of providing excellent representation for my constituents. Truthfully, it was a struggle. Every weekend, while making that 5,000-mile trek from D.C. to L.A. and back again, and trying to concentrate on the demands of my district, my mind would invariably slip back to my pending trial.

I was facing my possible political undoing. Still, there was some consolation. My only competition in the November 8th general election came from a Libertarian candidate, Guy Wilson, a political unknown from San Pedro. In short, I was a "shoo-in" to return to congress and there was a lot of work to be done. I had no time to become overwhelmed by the proposition of possible destruction.

I carried on my committee and floor duties on Capitol Hill, as usual. Communications to the constituents in the district were never more regular. Unless some news about the trial registered on the radar screen, I remained focused.

It wasn't long before rumors started circulating that former Compton City Councilwoman, Pat Moore, had made a deal with the feds to save herself from prosecution by testifying against me. One rumor after another suggested that was the case. With no indictment of Pat in sight, it wasn't difficult to conclude that the rumor was probably true.

Soon, the news broke: FORMER COMPTON CITY COUNCILWOMAN TO PLEAD GUILTY TO TWO COUNTS OF EXTORTION. Being an ex-criminal attorney, I knew exactly what that meant. Pat Moore had made a deal.

I knew that if the FBI came to me with an offer to help them bring in a "bigger fish," then it stood to reason they'd dangle a carrot in front of her in exchange for any damaging information she had on me. But one thing I knew for certain, whatever illegal activity she did or didn't do, she didn't do it with me. Yet, I wasn't so naïve that I didn't understand they could have her come into court and swear on a stack of Bibles that she was my co-conspirator, and there would be people who would believe her.

The situation was mind-boggling, but what could I do?

Maybe I should call her, talk to her, and see what she says.

But then I heard the small, quiet voice say, "Ask your wife what she thinks." I was getting used to hearing the voice like that. Heeding that voice let me know my relationship with God was growing.

I talked to Robin about it and she said, "Oh no, you shouldn't talk with her at all." If only I had clearly heard and heeded the voice of God earlier in life. If only I had been more open with my wife about important choices I had to make before I made them, how different my life would have been? I hoped to be able to hear more clearly from God before I made future decisions.

Meanwhile, it was becoming progressively more difficult to get an appointment to work up my case with Johnnie, not to mention to raise enough money to pay his hefty fee. On November 9, 1994, the O.J. Simpson jury was sworn in, and every day thereafter that bizarre murder case captured more and more media attention.

On January 24, 1995, opening statements in the Simpson case began, and Johnnie Cochran was consumed. Notwithstanding the presence of a team of glorified defense attorneys, Robert Shapiro, F. Lee Bailey, Alan Dershowitz, and Robert Kardashian, it was Johnnie's light that was shining more brightly each day, having moved from co-counsel to lead counsel. As CNN, CBS, NBC, ABC, and every media outlet from every place around the world continued to hype the People vs. Simpson case, my star defense attorney was being pulled away, and so were my hopes.

Johnnie called and asked to see me in person at his office. The minute I walked in, I knew I was about to hear something unfavorable.

"Look, baby, I'm jammed up here. Back in August, I thought O.J.'s trial would have been done by now. But, as you know, it's just started, and it's estimated now to last for at least eight months."

Wow! How can I compete with O.J. Simpson for Johnnie's attention? O.J.'s a living legend. Football Icon. American Idol. It's not just how incredibly he ran on the field in college and in the NFL, but once that brother ran through the airport in those Hertz commercials, he broke down decades of racial barriers and won the respect of millions of black man in America.

"Yeah, his case has become bigger than life, and you've become the captain of that huge ship," I replied.

Behind my polite response, my heart sank into a dark place where I had no idea what I was going to do. Fear struck in my chest. *Can I really win this thing without Johnnie? He's the best criminal attorney out there, and my life's on the line!*

"I'm sorry, Congressman, but I really can't devote the proper attention to your case and O.J.'s."

"And I really can't match the kind of money he can pay you…"

"It's not about the money—it's about the cause."

What about my cause? I'm just as important as O.J.!

"I don't know if you know, but earlier in my career I represented Geronimo Pratt, and lost..."

As Johnnie talked, I recalled the 1972 kidnap and murder conviction of Geronimo Pratt, a once high-ranking member of the Black Panther Party who had been one of the first blacks targeted in a COINTELPRO operation. I heard that for over twenty years Johnnie had been preoccupied with righting that wrongful murder conviction of a white woman, Caroline Olsen. Pratt had endured twenty-seven years in prison, eight in solitary confinement.[19] As I listened and reflected I became convinced that Johnnie saw the O.J. case as his long-awaited chance to balance the scales of our suspect criminal justice system.

Johnnie's so determined to right the wrongs against us as a people that, on the one hand, I can't fault him at all. As black people, we have always been the ones on the short end of the criminal justice stick. On the other hand, I don't want to hear this at all. My life, a black life, is on the line and O.J. is a black man who doesn't even identify himself as black. I'm the one who's fought for the rights of black people all my life. I'm the one who deserves your help, Johnnie! Still, no matter how much this hurts, or how insecure I feel, I know this has to be.

Reluctantly I said, "I guess it's for the best, all around."

"Here, here's the name of a guy I recommend. He's an ex-U.S. Attorney and he specializes in cases like yours. Attorney Robert Ramsey."

"Hmmm. Robert Ramsey. You sure he's good?"

I've never heard of Bob Ramsey. I pray he's not passing me off to just anyone.

"He's the guy you need for your case. Oh, and here…here's the balance of your fifty-thousand-dollar retainer back—twenty-five thousand dollars."

"But—"

"Don't worry about it, baby, just use it to secure Bob's services. We understand your situation and wish you the best."

"Well, Johnnie, I hate to lose you, but I understand. You're on a course with destiny, and so am I. Thanks so much for everything. I'll give Ramsey a call."

Johnnie and I shook hands. The die was cast, the mill was in motion. I contacted Attorney Robert Ramsey and scheduled a meeting with him for Saturday when I would be back in the district. Maybe, I thought, this was a sign. We weren't prepared at all to go to trial on February 1st. With a new attorney, there would be a continuance. *Thank God we'll have more time to prepare.*

CHAPTER TWENTY-SIX

Changing Horses

After being re-elected and sworn into the 104th Congress on January 5, 1995, I turned my attention to the most pressing matter of my life—the United States vs. Walter R. Tucker, III. But that was easier said than done. While my personal legal problems remained unchanged, the political realities surrounding me had taken a dramatic turn that demanded my immediate attention. In 1995, the scene in Washington was completely different from just two years earlier when I joined congress. Republicans had now taken control of the House and the Senate for the first time since 1948.[20]

On the Hill, former Democratic committee chairmen were so depressed by their recent dethroning that they didn't talk or think of anything else. They walked around in a stupor as if contemplating whether or not to jump off the Capitol dome and end it all. They had enjoyed their powerful committee chairmanships for more than twenty years, and now they'd come to know powerlessness and anonymity in the glaring lights of the national government.

Nevertheless, their worries were relatively insignificant to me. Theirs was about ego, not freedom. I, on the other hand, was dealing with a matter of life and liberty. I hadn't had twenty years

of harvest and then suddenly winter. No, this was the planting season of my career, but I could see only a cold wind rushing in. I
wasted no time calling Attorney Robert Ramsey's number from my
Washington, D.C. office. After a few rings, he picked up the line.

"Hello, this is Bob Ramsey."

Hmm. Answering his own phone?

"Attorney Ramsey, this is Congressman Walter Tucker. I
was referred to you by Johnnie Cochran."

"Yes, I was expecting your call."

"I'm in Washington now, but I'm coming into L.A. this
weekend. I'd like to meet with you about my indictment."

"That'll be fine. What about Sunday morning?"

"Alright."

Usually, I would be in church on Sunday morning, but I
knew the clock was ticking. With trial scheduled to commence in
the next few weeks, I needed a new lawyer fast. However, like
shopping for someone who would operate on my heart, this was
one of the most important decisions in my life—the right attorney.
Mangled thoughts were meandering through my mind. *Does this guy
know his stuff? Is he as articulate in a courtroom as Johnnie would be? Will
he take the case? If so, at what cost? Will I be able to trust him, or is there
someone else out there who's meant to be my lawyer?*

On Sunday morning, I knocked on the door of the law offices
of Attorney Robert Ramsey at Seventh and Broadway in downtown
Los Angeles. Attorney Ramsey opened the door himself.

"Hello, I'm Walter Tucker."

"Bob Ramsey." We shook hands. "Come on in."

I realized my life was on the line, so, as I entered, I observed every detail. His office space was of modest size and taste—nothing like Johnnie's swanky office and atmosphere.

I know it's Sunday, but shouldn't there be at least one staff person on hand?

"Right this way please." I followed him down a narrow hallway into his rather disheveled private office.

Attorney Robert Ramsey Jr., a collegiate-looking African American, wasn't nearly as tall as I had imagined. The rather short litigant, who might take on the crowned heads of the FBI and IRS, didn't look like a formidable force that could pull off a win. His brown, horn-rimmed glasses, closely-cropped hair, and stingy smile all spelled "second chair" to me. When he opened his mouth, the most proper English I had ever heard from a black man came easing out. I tensed up. Could this short man be forceful enough to take on Los Angeles' monstrous prosecutors? I decided to be open-minded, and I straightened up to relieve the wild tension running through my body.

Attorney Ramsey led me into his small conference room with a round table in the center. U.S. Codes and files were strewn about the room. The clutter aggravated my tension.

"Please, let me move these out your way," he said.

Once I realized Johnnie was no longer my lawyer, I focused my own research on the issue of "entrapment." I knew what issues needed to be addressed, and what concerns needed to be articulated. I tried to appear calm, but my stomach was churning like a car engine. I knew exactly what I needed to hear Attorney Ramsey say.

"Well, congressman, I must say it's an honor to finally meet you, although I'm sorry we have to meet under these unpleasant circumstances."

"Attorney Ramsey—"

"Please, call me Bob."

"Well, Bob, there's already been a lot said and written about me. I'd like to know your take on my case. Then, we can go from there."

"All right. Sounds fair. I only know what I've read in the papers."

"And what, if any, conclusions have you come to from what you've read?"

"Well, it's a classic case of an FBI sting—a setup. There's obviously a huge entrapment issue here—one that must be addressed both as a matter of trial strategy, as well as a matter of law, particularly with respect to jury instructions..."

"Mmmm hmmm." I nodded.

Although I was skeptical, the more Bob Ramsey spoke, the more I could tell he knew his stuff. Still, I had some reservations.

"Let me first tell you a little about me. I prosecuted cases for six years as an assistant U.S. Attorney here in L.A., so I know how they think. I understand that John was handling your case—"

"John? Oh, you mean Johnnie?"

"Right. He is, of course, an excellent attorney. But for the kind of case you're dealing with here, you need someone who has federal criminal trial experience. That's something John doesn't have. He's great in state court, but federal court is a whole different animal with a whole different set of rules. I know the judges and the system. Perhaps most importantly, I'm familiar with your judge, Consuelo Marshall, and I have her respect as a member of the Bar."

"I see."

"Bottom line, you've got a tremendous fight on your hands because you're going against the U.S. Attorney. Now, unlike the District Attorney or the State's Attorney General, I must tell you they go for the jugular. These guys boast a ninety-eight percent conviction rate, and they come with all barrels blazing. They've got the staff, the personnel, subpoena power, and all the resources of the government at their disposal to make your life miserable."

"Okay, now you wanna tell me the good news?"

"I wish I could. Did they offer you anything?"

"Yeah, plead guilty, work undercover for them, and see what goodies I can get them on tape concerning public corruption throughout the South Bay."

"And in exchange?"

"They said they'd see what they could do."

"Which means nothing."

"Right. Except that I need your help."

"That's it?" he asked.

"Yeah, that's it."

"Well…"

"Like you said, they set me up, and I wanna fight. I wanna go to trial."

"Okay, let's talk more about the details of your case."

As I talked and studied my interviewer, a feeling of confidence was rising inside of me. Bob Ramsey was asking the right questions and giving it to me straight. I appreciated that. There was nothing flashy or funny about Bob. He was all business.

After spending almost three hours discussing the law of entrapment, trial strategy, and fees, I finally decided that Bob Ramsey would take my case and be my attorney. There was no time to waste; it was time to set up my defense.

Johnnie says this guy is good and I don't have time to search around and interview countless attorneys. I guess I need to go forward.

"Alright, Bob, let's get the paperwork done and I'll get you a retainer. I think between you, me, and my brother-in-law, Mark Smith, who's also a criminal attorney, we can give these guys a real fight."

"I think so, Congressman."

"Please, call me Walter. We're going to be spending a lot of time together for the next few months."

"I will try, but it's hard not to address a member of congress as 'Congressman.' And yes, I welcome the assistance of your brother-in-law, Mark. I'll be honored to serve as your lead counsel."

"Great." We shook hands, memorializing the fact that Attorney Bob Ramsey was now at the helm of my legal ship that was sailing cautiously into stormy seas.

CHAPTER TWENTY-SEVEN

The Die Is Cast

The attorneys representing both the federal government and me sat at their respective counsel tables. I placed my worn out, black Holy Bible on the table in front of me, and prayed silently. The courtroom was packed with potential jurors. I could feel the tension in the air as we all waited for the arrival of Judge Consuelo Marshall, one of the most respected jurists on the federal bench. As the stately-looking, middle-aged judge stepped into the courtroom, I quickly glanced back at Robin and my mom.

Simultaneously the bailiff shouted, "All rise! The United States District Court, Central District, is now in session, Judge Consuelo Marshall presiding."

No sooner had the packed audience stood, she said, "You may be seated." She paused, then continued. " In the matter of the United States vs. Walter R. Tucker, III, counsel, please state your appearances for the record."

"Steve Madison and John Potter for the government, Your Honor."

"Robert Ramsey, Jr., and Mark Smith for Mr. Tucker who is present, Your Honor."

"Are both parties ready for jury selection?"

"We are, Your Honor," both sides responded concurrently.

"Alright, Madame Clerk, would you please call forth the jurors. Jurors, when you hear your number called, please come forward and be seated in the jury box.

The jury selection process was long and painstaking. One by one, jurors entered the jury box and were subjected to seemingly endless questions by both sides, trying to perceive the prejudices of each juror.

When I was a young boy, my mother often said to me, "Walter, once you've given it your all, you're already a success." That was a principle I found to be generally true in life. Therefore, all during the eight-day jury selection process, I was active. I sat at the defense table telling my attorneys what to ask and when to ask it. However, while I was doing all I could, nothing seemed to be working. It was a fait accompli. The jury pool was, for the most part, white, ultra-conservative, right-wing. It was primarily from the northern counties of California's Central District: San Luis Obispo, Santa Barbara, and Ventura counties—areas hardly empathetic with a black Democrat from Compton.

Mark leaned over and whispered in my ear, "Good Lawd, who kidnapped all the black people?" I bowed my head, shaking it slowly.

In light of some of the jurors' written responses to the court's questionnaire, Bob, Mark, and I agreed we should ask Judge Marshall to approach the bench and have a side bar with her and the government. She thankfully granted our request. Standing at the side bar with the government listening, my attorney pleaded, "Your Honor, many of the white, male jurors seem to have problems with politicians. Several of their answers, both written and verbal, reflect what is tantamount to the 'angry, white, male syndrome.'"

Immediately, U.S. Attorney, Steve Madison, blurted out, "Your Honor, the defense is attempting to make a prima facie case against white, male jurors. Now they wouldn't like it if we summarily dismissed all black male jurors, would they?"

I desperately wanted to say that was a moot point since there were hardly any prospective black male jurors to exclude. Nevertheless, Bob Ramsey answered the bell.

"Your Honor, just look at this answer," showing the judge one of the questionnaires. *I believe politicians should serve two terms: one in office and one in prison.*

"Well, Mr. Ramsey, you can exercise your peremptory challenges and have him excused," Judge Marshall answered in her matter-of-fact manner.

I want the whole panel excused! Look at those jurors. What could be worse!

All of Los Angeles seemed to have tension in the air, including our particular courtroom. Even though my trial was gaining some national press, the media coverage was nothing compared to that of a Superior Court trial across the street at the Criminal Courts Building—the murder trial of Hall of Famer O.J. Simpson. It was in its final stage of jury deliberation. In light of the unprecedented rioting that had occurred just three years before in Los Angeles because of the unpopular acquittal of the four L.A.P.D. officers in the Rodney King case, law enforcement, and the entire court system were on red alert.

Throughout the O.J. Simpson trial, there had been a great deal of speculation as to how much the issue of racism would be a factor in the trial. Most legal pundits from coast to coast downplayed the issue and forecasted the almost certain demise of O.J. Simpson.

"The evidence is insurmountable! O.J. has got to pay! This is not about race, but homicidal brutality!" they contended.

That atmosphere carried shades of March 29, 1992, the eve of the L.A. riots, all over again. Oh, how I remember that day! Shortly before that outburst, I had been elected mayor of Compton. Soon after, the media announced the verdict of the police officers charged in the beating of Rodney King. The all-white, Simi Valley jury found them not guilty on all charges.

To whites, they were heroes upholding the letter of the law. To blacks, they were racist brutes executing street justice in typical fascist fashion, only this time the unmerciful beatings were caught on video. How could two different ethnic groups see the same video, the same facts, so differently?

That kind of intensity and disparity caused the L.A. riots. If O.J. was found guilty, I envisioned another massive riot primarily by blacks and other minorities with grievances. Violence, fires, and hatred would boil over from sheer frustration and anger. On the other hand, I wondered what would happen if he was found not guilty? Whites don't riot over court cases like blacks, I thought. I knew that for every action, there is a reaction. It wouldn't be long before they would change laws and redraw political districts to disenfranchise their opponents into perpetuity. And as to O.J. personally, whites would hunt him down and make him wish he had never been born. Unfortunately, it didn't take long after the start of jury deliberation for me to know the outcome of O.J.'s trial. The jury had reached a verdict. The L.A.P.D. was "riot-ready." Those who had half a brain were staying away from downtown L.A. that day.

As for me, I wished I could have stayed away too; not only from downtown L.A. and the courts, but from this entire ordeal.

But that was not to be. Judge Marshall, having the jury nearly impaneled, was concerned about only the news of O.J.'s verdict interrupting the completion of our jury selection. So she gave the order not to stop the proceedings in the event of O.J.'s verdict, but allow jurors to learn of it at the nearest reasonable break.

On October 3, 1995, the O.J. Simpson verdict came back not guilty on both murder counts. There was no rioting in the streets of L.A. No store fronts afire. But the word spread like wildfire that O.J. had beat the rap. Blacks were openly jubilant, and whites were stunned. The shock lasted what seemed to be only a moment. By the time the amazement wore off, unparalleled resentment and anger set in. It was the beginning of a riot that no one had ever seen before. Instead of exploding, the white community imploded. I called it the "Quiet Riot."

Whites commenced their own brand of protest to vindicate this most grotesque miscarriage of justice. Conservative talk radio proliferated across the nation, and lines burned off the hook as white America went ballistic. Someone had to pay! Our criminal justice system was at the precipice of breakdown, in need of an immediate overhaul. An innocent white woman and man were dead and arguably, for the first time in American history, white Americans felt the frustration of being left stingingly unsatisfied with the American criminal justice system. It was a shock to their system, but they were feeling only a small degree of the devastation blacks had felt for over a hundred years. It was an experience so common to black America that our collective conscience had become seared, left without feeling.

But my concern was not for O.J. Simpson, but for Walter R. Tucker, III. I was praying for a jury of my peers. Robin and I discussed the situation during a court recess.

"Honey, I'm really concerned. The few black jurors who have found their way into the jury box have all been dismissed by the U.S. Attorney for no reason."

"Baby, I wish there was something we could do, but the law gives them several 'peremptory challenges,' which means they can kick black jurors off without any explanation."

"What kind of mess—"

"They don't want any jurors who will see this case as entrapment!"

"How did they get so many challenges?"

"Both sides have the same number of challenges. The problem is the jury pool is overwhelmingly white."

"But if we can get a couple of blacks on the jury, don't we have a chance of getting a hung jury?"

"We'll be doing good if we can get even one black on this jury."

"We have to just keep praying."

Unfortunately, when the prosecution didn't kick off prospective black jurors, one or two of them had legitimate personal hardships, and couldn't remain for the expected length of the trial. After using every peremptory challenge available to our side to get rid of the jurors most prejudicial to a black politician, twelve jurors and four alternates were finally seated on Thursday, September 21.

"Madame Clerk, please swear in the jury," Judge Marshall ordered.

When all the dust settled, I ended up with only one black woman on the entire jury, and there were only a couple of jurors who lived in L.A. County. Whoever said that we are entitled to a jury of our peers lied. This was not a jury of my peers! This was a jury of white, conservative Republicans who lived so far north of

L.A. that they had no black neighbors, co-workers or friends. Score a big one for the prosecution: Government 1, Defense 0.

I suddenly realized why prosecutors seek out federal charges to file against black politicians. Those charges take a black defendant out of the state court system and put him squarely into a federal district which is so geographically vast that the jury pool looks nothing like him. No, this was not a jury of my peers. To keep my wife from stressing, I maintained a calm and collected exterior, but deep inside I felt the chances of proving my innocence had just narrowed.

I was convinced then that this was a jury that would tend to believe the prosecutors and the FBI agents because they were white authority figures. I believed these were people who scoffed at the notion that black politicians have been "targeted" simply because they were black. I could hear them immediately charging that someone was playing the "race card." Surely this was not a jury of my peers! This was a post-O.J. lynch mob, and I happened to be the black face that was in the wrong place at the wrong time with the wrong people.

There was no way that O.J. would have ever been acquitted without a jury of his peers. Many whites lambasted his black jury's verdict. But where were their criticisms of our Justice System when four Los Angeles police officers were acquitted of brutally beating Rodney King? Where was their outcry when Judge Joyce Karlin sentenced Soon Ja Du to 400 hours of community service and a $500 fine for killing a young black girl, Latasha Harlins, for stealing a bottle of orange juice from her store? Or, for that matter, where were their cries when the late Black Panther Party member, Geronimo Pratt, was wrongly convicted and had to spend twenty-seven years behind bars when he was innocent? Where were their cries during the 60s when countless southern white men bombed, beat, and killed southern black victims only to be acquitted by a jury of their peers?

Without a jury of your peers, the deck is stacked—there can be no true justice. The lack of proper racial representation on one's jury was the same issue the Black Panther Party had addressed in its formation in 1966. And now, years later, with the line of division between blacks and whites being at its height after O.J., my situation initially looked bleak.

"Walter, I don't feel good about this jury at all," Robin said.

"What can I say, Rob? We have to play the hand we've been dealt. We've just got to remain hopeful."

Once my predominately white jury was sequestered in the jury room, the first communication they received from the court was O.J.'s verdict.

God, talk about bad timing!

When the news of O.J.'s verdict finally reached my jury in the jury room, Wanda Flagg, the lone black juror, was there. I would later learn what she told a reporter about the incident.

I heard she said that they were all sitting there, and suddenly the bailiff came in and told them that O.J. was not guilty. I heard she began jumping for joy inside. I heard that she tried to contain herself, but a huge smile came over her face, and for a few moments she began to rock back and forth with intense satisfaction. I heard that when she began to refocus on the faces of her fellow jurors, she saw that they were motionless and seething. It was as if they were all at a funeral and despised the fact that she was not crying. I heard that she knew then that sitting on that jury would be one of the great trials of her life.

After my jury was impaneled, Marcus called me from the Hill.

"Hey Boss, I heard about your jury and of course every-body's heard about O.J.'s verdict. Are you all alright out there?"

"Yeah, we're hanging in there. As you know, we've been in some tough spots before and this is just another one."

"I heard that. We're holding everything down here. Just call if you need us."

"Will do. Thanks, Marcus."

As the days went by, it became clear to me that it wasn't just the white jurors on my case who had become upset by the O.J. Simpson verdict. Throughout the country, there were shock waves. The Quiet Riot had begun. It was reported that everywhere blacks went, whites were sneering and flashing dirty looks. The campaign to make O.J. pay civilly was already underway. Yes, somebody had to pay for all this injustice. Somebody had to foot the bill for all this anger.

In the succeeding months, the white backlash would be ap-parent. The phones on talk radio were ringing off the hooks. There would be a rise in hate crimes, the burning of black churches, and increased convictions and incarceration of black males and fe-males. Affirmative Action would come under its most serious attack. Somebody had to pay. This time blacks had gone too far. Black jurors had freed a black man who whites were convinced brutally killed a white man and a white woman. Somebody had to pay. Unfortunately for me, my case was up next.

Since my initial indictment, the government had added two more counts of bribery based on accusations from Murcole Dis-posal, Inc., Compton's residential rubbish hauler. It was agreed that Mark would defend me as to those counts. At thirty-eight years old, having now pleaded not guilty to nine counts of bribery, one count of demanding $250,000, and two counts of filing false tax returns while I was the mayor of Compton, I faced ten years in prison on each bribery count and expulsion from Congress. Opening statements were to begin Friday, September 22, but didn't actually commence until Wednesday, October 4, 1995—one day before my wedding anniversary. In the meantime, another series of articles on my plight appeared in *The New York Times*, on Monday, September 25, 1995, by Kenneth B. Noble.

"The case has attracted not only local, but national attention because of what some blacks see as a pattern of the predominantly white federal law enforcement establishment spending time and money prosecuting cases against blacks that it might not have pursued against white leaders," Noble wrote.

"Historically, African Americans have had reason to question the criminal justice system, so it is always reasonable to at least raise the racism issue," said Leo Terrell, a black civil rights lawyer in Beverly Hills.

Royce Esters, president of the Compton chapter of the NAACP, agreed, "They are targeting Compton because there are a lot of black people here. Every time there is a black person in a high place, they try to get them."

A reporter called me and asked me about the issue of targeting due to racism, and I responded, "I think the case will show that I have been targeted, and I am obviously an African American. Based on the information I have, the city of Compton has been targeted a lot over the past several years, and during that time the city was under black leadership."

I was ready to face that jury with my head held high, come what may.

CHAPTER TWENTY-EIGHT

Elementary

Once again, I boarded another American Airlines flight back to Washington, D.C. to handle the nation's business while waiting for the trial to start. After takeoff, I reclined my seat and tried to settle down. Suddenly, a spirited flight attendant stood in front of me again.

"Sir, you have your choice today of beef burgundy, citrus salmon, or chicken Florentine?"

"The chicken, please."

Several minutes later, the flight attendant reappeared with my dinner. "Sir, your Chicken Florentine. Are you sure I can't get you some wine, a cocktail?"

"No thanks. This is fine."

She placed the chicken plate on my tray table and departed. I stared at it.

I don't know why I ordered this. I have no appetite for anything but answers.

Minutes later the flight attendant returned to check on me.

"Oh, my, you've hardly touched your dinner. Are you done?"

I nodded and she removed my plate.

"You sure there's nothing I can get you? Some seltzer water?"

I waved her off and she went on her way.

Suddenly, I found myself staring blankly out the window, as a blackening sky gathered

over the plane's widespread wing that cut through the air. There I was, sitting in business class, 30,000 miles in the air with my mind winding back to the beginning. Seeing all of the stars up there, I could only think about how far I had come; about the race I had already run.

* * * * * *

When I was four, my mother who felt she wanted to return to the working world, enrolled me in Kindergarten early. At that time, we lived at 2107 W. 158th Street in Compton and the school I attended was Bursch Elementary. In the first grade, Mom placed Keta and me in St. Albert the Great Elementary School. Our family wasn't Catholic, but my mother was convinced the Catholics offered the best education. One thing I learned very early on, the nuns had the right to rap you on the knuckles with a ruler for misbehavior or incomplete assignments. After the ruler hit my balled right fist a couple of times, I quickly became a model citizen and an excellent student. I was the reigning, weekly Spelling Bee champion, but one day my teacher changed things up on me and presented us with a Math Bee. Oh, how the mighty had fallen! I was devastated by my loss. When I got home, my mom noticed I was sulking.

"Walter, what happened?"

"I got second place because they didn't have a Spelling Bee— they had a Math Bee."

Mom lifted my head and looked in my eyes, and said, "Everything's going to be just fine. Remember, the cream always rises to the top."

I nodded and she wrapped her loving arms around me.

"Now, we just have to put some time into these math problems, just like we did with spelling, and you'll be fine. You'll see."

By next Friday, I returned home from school with the champion's ribbon for math pinned on my shirt. I learned then that no matter the subject, hard work always prevailed. My mom had "brainwashed" me to believe that hard work would one day get me admitted into an Ivy League University long before I knew what "Ivy League" meant.

Mom also convinced me that I would one day be a lawyer. She used to speak it over me all the time when I was a young boy. As the story goes, one of our neighbors, a little girl about my age named Loretta, had a reputation of having a "snotty nose" while she played in the street. When the neighborhood children saw it, they'd scream and run away from her. One such day my mom and grandmother observed me rushing in and getting tissue and rushing in the street and gave it to Loretta.

"That child's going to be a minister one day," Grandmother said.

"No, Mother, I think he'll be a lawyer," My mother said.

"Mark my words. He has a caring heart. It's born in him."

Time would prove that they were both right.

By the time I was in third grade, my mom convinced my dad to send my older sister, Keta, and me to a private Montessori school in Redondo Beach. I didn't learn until years later that the philosophy of the school's founder, Marie Montessori, was to allow the child to "discover himself," exactly opposite of the rigidity I came from in my recent Catholic school experience.

In many ways, Keta and I did discover ourselves while attending the Montessori school. We were allowed to spend time on the things we liked the most. I got totally wrapped up in geography. At age seven, I knew all the countries of the world, their capitals, rivers, and flags. It was at Montessori that Keta and I came up with our first play based on the TV series, *The Man from U.N.C.L.E.* Little did I know that the theater-bug had been planted in me by my mother's love of writing stories and theater, and would bear fruit many years later.

Not only was that fun, but being in the same class with my sister, a year older than me, was the best. But the Montessori experience was not without its struggles. The biggest struggle was cultural. Keta and I were the only blacks in our class, and just about the only blacks in the entire school. One day, I was sick and stayed home. I sent word through my sister that no one was to sit in my seat. Well, Phillip Thomas, one of my white classmates, contemptuously disregarded my notice, violating the unwritten elementary school code. You just didn't take another kid's seat, no matter where he or she was. Our desk was our only personal possession. The bottom line—that was a matter of respect. Keta brought home Phillip's defiant answer to my request. He would sit where he pleased.

The next day, I walked over to Phillip's desk. "Why'd you sit in my seat, Phillip?"

"I didn't see your name written on it!" He growled.

"It wasn't your seat, and I'm tired of you doing that," I argued.

"And what you gonna do about it?" He stared.

"I'ma teach you not to sit in my seat," I fired back.

"I'll be waiting."

"See ya after school in the sandbox."

During the day, word hit the grapevine that Phillip Thomas and four other white boys were going to teach me, the smart-mouthed black boy, a real-life lesson. School ended at 3:00 p.m., and at 3:05, the cheering squad gathered around the sandbox to bear witness to my massacre. It was the old western movie, *High Noon*, replayed. I stood alone at one end of the sandbox, as Phillip slowly walked onto the playground toward me. I took my stance at the other end. With the intensity of two gunslingers, we stared each other down.

"I told you I'ma teach you a lesson," I said.

"Nah, today *we're* gonna teach you a lesson," he shot back.

Phillip looked over his shoulder and signaled his crew to come forward. Four of his buddies stepped from the crowd and stood alongside him.

"Oh, so that's how you're playing it, huh? Well, I got back up too!"

Keta had heard what Phillip planned and she declared she wouldn't let me face them alone. Her furor surprisingly enticed the assistance of our white friend, Susan Radle. The two of them stepped forward from the crowd and stood alongside me.

"Man, you gotta be kiddin'. All you got is a couple of skinny girls! You better walk away while you still can!" Phillip chided. "Or apologize right now and save yourself."

"You're the one who'll wish you had walked away. Let's do it!"

It was three against five, so we knew we would have to take the battle to them. Between school, homework, house chores, and mom snatching us up for Jack and Jill activities or some other cul-ture-building session, Keta and I didn't get much practice in fighting. But somehow we found the time to plop ourselves in front of the TV and watch a little bit of professional wrestling. Every chance we got, we were watching the wrestlers' moves and practicing what they did. Suffice it to say, at ten and nine years old, Keta and I were lean, mean, fighting machines! Unfortunately, we had no clue about Susan. She was the smallest kid out there, and we had no idea if she had any fight in her. She didn't look like it. Nevertheless, this was no time to be picky about our allies.

"Alright, we're going tag-team rules," I said.

Everyone knew this meant one fighter from each side in the ring at a time, until a fighter can reach back to his or her corner, tag his or her teammate, getting them to come in and replace them.

Phillip and his crew nodded to my call.

A lanky, sandy-haired kid stepped into the center of the sand box and threw down a handkerchief, and said, "Let the fight begin!"

I was out of my corner in a flash and all over Phillip. Before he knew it, I had him in a headlock. Then I took him, flipped him on the ground and had him pinned. Although he was unable to get back to his corner, one of his teammates, John, jumped into the sandbox and kneed me in my back. I was momentarily dazed until Keta jumped to my rescue. She took on John and slipped him into a Full Nelson. Then when he cried "Uncle," Keta swung him around the sandbox until he whirled out onto the ground. With a skinned knee, he ran away. It was now three against four.

Phillip, still exhausted from me pinning him down, ran to his corner and tagged Bobby, another one of his teammates. I grabbed Bobby in a headlock, but he slipped out, bent low, and managed to pull my feet from under me. I hit the sand hard and it momentarily knocked the wind out of me. Fortunately, when I landed, I was close to my corner. I looked up in a daze and all I could see was little Susan with her hand outstretched. I tagged her desperately.

Susan entered the ring like the Tasmanian devil from the Road Runner cartoon.

"Hiiii-yah! Hiii-yah!"

Bobby was staggering from a barrage of Karate chops, followed by a leg sweep, and suddenly his back hit the ground with a loud thud.

"Owww!" he cried out.

He tried to crawl back to his corner for a tag, but Susan was all over him like ants on a cookie crumb. Finally, she lifted him up, turned him around, and kicked him hard in the butt and out of the sandbox. Phillip and his two other teammates, witnessing Bobby's embarrassment, jumped into the sandbox and descended on Susan. Keta and I jumped in and it was a full-scale, three-against-three brawl. After a flurry of Karate chops and a series of quick flips to the ground, Keta, Susan, and I held Phillip and his remaining two teammates' heads in the sand until they managed to cry out, "Uncle!" Nobody was ever going to sit in my seat again.

Yes, I was used to being outnumbered and outgunned. However, unlike the showdown at the sandbox, I didn't quite know what I was up against with the FBI's hammer hanging over my head. Nevertheless, I knew I would fight to the end.

After spending the fourth, fifth, and sixth grade at the Montessori school, where my enemies became spend-the-night buddies, it was time for a change; a change from my Montessori buddies and the school's free routine; a change from being in the same classroom with my sister. I would surely miss the idealistic atmosphere, the smell of the nearby Pacific Ocean, the science fairs, outings, and plays. It was time for a change.

I didn't understand it then, but later, I came to understand that it was time for my younger brother, Kenneth, and my younger sister, Camille, to get a solid private school preparation. It was time for Keta and me to leave private school for public school, freeing up some money for the younger ones, and allowing Keta and me to know our community, and to learn from our heritage.

CHAPTER TWENTY-NINE

Junior High

In a matter of days, I headed back to L.A. again to meet with my attorneys. After another long, five-hour, Friday flight from D.C. to L.A., I stood on the curb with luggage in hand searching for the black Lincoln Town Car. Tyrone quickly pulled up in front of me, grabbed my bags, and I ducked into the backseat.

"How you doing, Congressman?"

"Let's hit Tichenor," I said in a low, tired voice with my head propped up by my right hand.

"You got it, boss!"

Hearing nothing else from me, Tyrone quickly turned down the radio and limited his conversation. He knew I had another full weekend scheduled—a luncheon with community- based organizations and local officials, a fundraising dinner, church hopping on Sunday, and then back to D.C. on Monday.

The Tichenor house, though different now, waited for me, as we pulled into the horseshoe-shaped driveway with memories and worries floating through my brain. At the end of the driveway was a basketball court where many boyhood battles had been won and lost. The rim was not regulation height, so dunking the ball built confidence for my 6'1" height. I knew I would never play college or pro ball, but on that court, I was the king of the world.

I loved sports, but they always took a backseat to my studies and speech team.

Once inside our house, I propped my feet on an ottoman to watch CNN. Instead of focusing on the reporter's questions, I was asking myself questions. How much of my back story is my lawyer going to need to know? How much is relevant to me legally? Then again, how much of it is relevant to me personally? My thoughts reverted to my junior high school—Walton Jr. High School, fall 1968.

* * * * * *

In 1966 Stokely Carmichael had coined the phrase, "Black Power," and subsequently a political, cultural and fashion revolution had taken place among blacks in America. Nevertheless, having spent the past three years at a white, private school in Redondo Beach, California without any black friends, I was culturally out of touch. While my new public school classmates were styling "Afros" and bell-bottoms, I wore a close-cropped haircut, a turtleneck sweater, and straight-legged pants. Everyone seemed to be groovin' to James Brown's funky beat that told us to "Say It Loud, I'm Black and I'm Proud," but I didn't know how to dance. Yes, I was a square trying to fit into a round hole, but my mother wouldn't budge from the "clean-cut, college-bound young man" image that must have been seared into her brain.

"Don't follow the crowd; be a leader," she said.

As "the leader" passed down the crowded hallways searching for his classes, he felt emotionally and socially disconnected. I didn't know anybody and everybody seemed to be bumping into me, a kind of new-kid initiation. I found it difficult to make new friends and to get involved with extracurricular activities, even though there was a myriad of activities for me to join.

Instead of the freestyle of the Montessori sandbox, I now had gym class—a whole hour every day devoted to organized, physical fitness. Every day the entire class of about forty boys would go into the locker room, change into gym clothes, and hurriedly file out of the locker room in alphabetical order to make roll call on time. We stood on rows of white numbers painted on the asphalt, waiting to participate in the physical routine given by our gym teacher, Mr. Spicer.

Mr. Spicer was also the football coach, and his reputation for toughness preceded him. Sporting dark sunglasses, a thick mustache, gym shorts, and wearing a whistle around his neck, he barked out commands like a veteran drill sergeant.

"Come on, men. Let's move it, move it, move it!"

He could tell that I wasn't one of his prospects for the gridiron, as I was lanky and thin, but he drove everybody equally hard.

It seemed as if every day when we stood for roll call, there was always this same guy, Danny Williams, who would be loud talking and acting up before Mr. Spicer came and took roll. Typically, Danny would show up late and speed through the rows to get to his spot on time. Although Danny was as thin as I was, nobody took him on. He had the reputation of being "a wild card." One day, Danny recklessly blew through the rows, but this time, he ran into me. I guess I had just been so tired of being pushed around in that school that I reacted before I thought about to whom I was reacting. Before anyone could say "Don't do it!" I shouted at Danny, "What's your problem, man?"

In a blink, he was in my face, and we pushed each other backward. We got in fighting stances and started bobbing and weaving. Danny's first punch came in a flash and landed hard on my nose. Blood gushed out. By that time, Mr. Spicer arrived and rushed me to a sink inside the gym, and I felt the cold water dosing my face and hands. Someone pressed a gym towel to my nose and the bleeding finally stopped. My first and last fight in public school was embarrassing. Thankfully, it was over before it began. But the word went out through the school grapevine that the new "brain-iac" boy got his butt kicked. Keta heard what happened, and wanted to know if I needed her help, but I assured her I was okay. I didn't tell my mom because she would have made a big deal of it. I may have gotten a bloody nose, but in a weird way, I felt good because I stood up to someone no one else would.

One day, my speech teacher, Mrs. Charles, asked me to join the Speech Team. This classy middle-aged woman with great elo-cution insisted that I participate in an inter-school speech competition sponsored by the Rotary. I was totally reluctant until I heard that the participants got to leave campus and go to a lunch-eon at City Hall. *Time away from class? Free lunch? Count me in!*

I can't remember the title of my speech or even what I talked about. All I know is that I was the only seventh grader com-peting, and I took third place. *Wow, third place!* I received a certificate and got my picture in the local paper. I was a star, even if a geeky one. As usual, my mother had made me wear a turtleneck sweater and straight-legged pants. This time the turtleneck was red, gray, and gold plaid. I never will forget that hideous turtleneck. It had a zipper on the side of the neck. *A turtleneck with a zipper!* I never wore one like that before or since. I guess I was just about as unique as that sweater. I stood out and I hated it.

My mother said, "You're dressed for success."

What did she know? She made me a lamb for the schoolyard slaughter.

I didn't argue too much because my distaste for my ward-robe was overcome by my excitement to speak. That was my humble beginning of a life-long love of public speaking. From that day forward, I employed the art of public speaking over and over again: as a teacher, a lawyer and, of course, a politician. Each of those professions had one thing in common—public speaking. Little did I know that one day I would enjoy the greatest honor—to speak for God.

As the months went by in junior high, peer pressure was mounting. How long was I going to remain the brainiac who couldn't do the things the other kids got to do? For example, although my mom allowed me to walk home from school, I wasn't allowed to stop anywhere along the way. Mom told me explicitly to never stop at the store at the corner of Wilmington and Greenleaf because fights often broke out while kids were waiting in line to go inside and buy their candy fix.

One day, I got daring and stood in the store line and, unbeknownst to me, my mom cruised by the store in her white Chrysler on her way home. When I got home, I didn't know what hit me. She descended upon me like a hawk swooping down on its prey. In her hand was the "TGB" —the thin, gold belt—and she quickly wielded it all over my body while she screamed with each lash, "Didn't, I, tell, you…never to go in there!" I covered up and dodged as best as I could from that Tasmanian devil, but she got her licks in and her point was made. Even as an adult, I never entered that store again.

After I licked my wounds from that beating, something down inside me said, "Never again!" Not that I would never again mess up, but I was now thirteen years old and taller than my mom, and I secretly vowed I would never again take another "momma beating." Well, it wasn't long before that vow was tested. I can't exactly remember what I did or didn't do on this occasion. All I know is that I provoked my mom's wrath and she went to her bedroom to retrieve "TGB" again. This time, however, I ran outside to our spacious backyard. Mom charged toward me like a bull seeing red, but unlike times before where I stood there and took it, I ran for my life. She chased me around the backyard three times, and finally, breathing heavily she said, "Don't worry, you got to come inside, sometime…"

She was so right and I was scared. I stayed out in the backyard for about three hours and I finally crept inside, looking around every corner. To my surprise, she had retired to her room and had fallen asleep in her bed. Not only had I dodged a whipping that day, but I never got another whipping from my mother.

The three years at Walton Jr. High went by in a blur. I blinked and graduation day had arrived—June 1971. I had come far since that first disconnected day at school, and from that first surprising speech competition. I was set to graduate in the top five of my class with honors. The principal called my name, and behind four other students, I walked up to the podium wearing a navy blue suit, two-toned brown shoes, and showing off my growing Afro. I received a certificate for academic excellence. I couldn't wait to show it to my dad.

"Hey, Dad, look at this. I did it. Top five!" I said, excitedly.

Being the "go-getter" that he was, he replied, "That's good, but you let a couple of girls beat you." He shrugged and walked away.

I shrank as small as a speck of dust. I had been riding high on my public recognition, and he shot me down like a plane flying over enemy territory. I couldn't understand it at the time, but later I would come to the conclusion that he was pouring out what had been poured into him. After my dad's father died when my dad was 27 years old, his older brother, Booker, became a type of father to him. Uncle Booker had a gruff, hard exterior, probably because his father, Nye, was a strict disciplinarian and expected nothing less than excellence. I surmise that my great-grandfather, Walter, who had escaped slavery and was tough on his son, Nye, was the one who set the family standard of discipline. But Uncle Booker did have a softness at his core. This was probably because of his mother, Carrie, who was known as one of the sweetest and most diplomatic persons one could ever meet. My dad was loving like his mom, Carrie, but at times when he figured someone needed a push toward greatness, the gruff and tough spirit of my grandfather, Nye, and my uncle Booker, would surface.

Yes, that was my dad, the man who was larger than life to me. Being a professional man, a dentist, he was my standard of success. During my junior high school years, he had also become a member of the Compton Unified School Board. It was his approval I needed. In the moment of my shock and hurt, a different emotion rose up in me, a raw emotion. Anger! I'd show him!

From that moment on, I was on a mission. Junior High School was over. I had a clean slate. I was determined to be the best. I never wanted to see another "B." I was going to be number one, not just one in the top five. If I could carry out my mom's weekly schedules taped to my bedroom wall for years, surely I could study hard enough and regularly enough to be number one in high school. Besides, I now understood the way the game was played in public school. It was all about giving back to the teacher what he or she wanted to hear—whether you believed it or not.

In the fall of 1971, I entered Compton High School with great expectations. The former college-turned-high-school, located just three blocks away from our house, was known for its great athletes and sports teams: Olympians, CIF Champions, and Super Bowl Champions abounded. But each morning I walked to Compton High from Tichenor Street, I imagined I was carving out new paths. Amidst its rich history, I was determined to make some unprecedented accomplishments.

* * * * * *

Now, twenty-four years later, the Tichenor house was totally different. No crowds, parties or fanfare. It was now a place of safety. I was definitely seeking refuge, dozing in front of the TV, drifting in and out of yesteryear, when my mother came into the room. She shook me gently on my shoulder.

"Walter, you need to get some rest if you're going to be fresh for your meeting tomorrow with your staff."

I turned off the TV. The weekly routine from L.A. to D.C. and back again was exhausting. Nevertheless, with the legal "sword of Damocles" hanging over my head, there was no time to be exhausted. The months ahead were critical to my entire life and I knew it. My mind was energized and enervated all at the same time. I was determined not to allow the government to force me out of office without a fight. Tomorrow I would get more information from my attorneys and the next day I would hop on another plane back to D.C. I missed my wife and kids and couldn't wait to see them. I even missed the intense beat of Capitol Hill. My colleagues on the Hill knew I was going through a storm, but I had no shoulders to cry on. Every congressman had more than his share of problems. Like them, I had to keep up appearances and continue to do my job.

CHAPTER THIRTY

Tichenor Street

Those long coast-to-coast trips gave me time for reflections that kept me sane. They reminded me that I was not a perfect person, but someone who truly cared about his community and constituency. Someone who wanted to create new tech jobs, lower the tide of violence, and provide quality healthcare and education for all the citizens of the 37th Congressional District. Tyrone was right on time to pick me up at LAX. Again, he could see I wasn't in a talkative mood. He drove in silence toward Tichenor Street.

We made good time, pulling into the driveway in twenty minutes. Tyrone put the Town Car in park, and we carried the bags into the house. It seemed like I had lived in every bedroom of that big house. When I was in high school, I lived in the east wing in one of the smallest bedrooms. That tiny space suited me just fine. I had a twin bunk bed, a dresser with six drawers, a small matching desk, an oak-grained bookcase filled with lots of school books, and a swivel chair—no boom box, no TV, no electronics. My weekly schedule was the only ornament on my wall. I believed the Spartan existence was just what I needed to get me where I wanted to go.

Don't get me wrong, I wasn't totally boring. I just knew this was the time when I would either sacrifice for the Ivy League and where it could take me, or end up like far too many young black men in my city: hanging out at the corner liquor store, getting shot, or getting into drugs. I believed I was destined to impact and empower those men to become the best version of themselves.

Every week, I would trek to Jimmy's Record Shop on East Alondra Boulevard to see who was moving up the music charts for 45s, albums, and 8-tracks. The Isley Brothers and James Brown were my up-tempo favorites. On the slow side, I loved the Dells, the Stylistics, and the Delfonics.

Now inside the foyer of the Tichenor house with bag in hand, seeing that huge family room with its terrazzo floors, I remembered how my dad once allowed us to throw a Sweet 16 party for Keta in December 1971.

* * * * * *

While we were joyful about Keta's party, Dad was leery that some kids might get out of order. For that reason, Sheriff John, the rotund security guard in gray uniform, came on loan from Dad's doctors' building. We joked that if there was an incident, Sheriff John could never run fast enough to catch the culprit. Unfortunately, the only incident at the party involved me.

The party had really started getting good when one of my buddies pulled me aside and said, "Hey, Tuck, this is really a cool party, man, but, uh, can you get that light out of our eyes?"

"What light?" I asked.

"Over there. That light. It's killin' the vibe, brother!"

I had been so busy running around making sure that all the musical selections and refreshments were right, that I hadn't even noticed the light. It was a bright light beaming from the kitchen into the family room where young couples were trying to move in close to each other as The Chi-Lites sang *Have You Seen Her.* I rushed and turned off the light. A few minutes later, I noticed that same light was on again. I marched into the kitchen and switched it off again. My dad marched in right behind me. "Who turned that light off?"

Inside the kitchen, Keta and a couple of her friends looked dumbfounded as they shrugged.

Unwittingly I said, "I did."

In a second my dad's open hand landed on the side of my head...*POWWW!* I was stunned. *What the hell happened?*

"I turned that light on and I meant for it to stay on!" he yelled at me.

Just as quickly as he had hit me, he walked away, leaving me in the middle of the kitchen, embarrassed, hurting, and speechless. I'm not sure what hurt more—the side of my head or my bruised ego. Growing up, my dad had never hit me; it was my mom who had been the enforcer. But there I was, the host of the year's most jamming high school party, cuffed upside the head by his dad. What really hurt the most was that I felt it was so undeserving.

Looking back on it, I realize my dad must have assumed I knew he had turned on the light. He must have thought I was rebelling against his authority. Although I was growing up into manhood, I never even thought about saying or doing one disrespectful thing to my father. Obviously, it didn't matter what I thought. The only thing that mattered was that my dad felt disrespected and he reacted.

It was the biggest social night of my young life and my biggest public embarrassment. Only a few people in the kitchen saw what happened. Nevertheless, I was unable to shake it off. I was like the proverbial performer who had just suffered tragedy, but was obligated to go out on stage and smile as if nothing bad had happened. It was a farce, a sham. It was too difficult to do.

While Sly and the Family Stone pounded out *Family Affair* in the background, I stepped from the kitchen down the hall, passed the party to find a sanctuary—my bedroom. I stayed in there, tears rolling down my face until Keta eased in.

"Walter, are you alright? I heard what happened."

Barely able to catch my breath from fighting back the tears, I managed to speak without sniffling.

"I...I...didn't know...didn't know he turned on the light," I said, breaking into tears.

Keta pulled me close and squeezed me. "Listen, it's over now. This is our party, and we can't let anything ruin it. You and I worked too hard to let anything ruin it."

Just then, my mother swept into the room.

"Are you alright in here?" she asked, putting her arms around both Keta and me. There was only silence and watery eyes.

"Sometimes, people do get misjudged," my mom said. "I think that's what happened to you. I know you're strong enough to go out there and see that your friends have a good time. We'll discuss this with your father tomorrow. See if we can't make sense out of what happened," she said.

She dampened a towel in my bathroom and dabbed it on my eyes. "Now, go show 'em what you're made of." She dabbed the towel over my eyes again and gave me a pat on the back.

Nobody could encourage me like my mom. Sometimes, when I was feeling low, I was annoyed by her pep talks. But at that moment, I appreciated the pep talk because it was working. I took a few minutes to collect myself, and I decided to make the best of what had become a bad evening.

After James Brown shouted, *Make It Funky*, all was forgotten. The party was in high gear and everyone was having a great time—even me. Before we knew it, Sheriff John blew his whistle and gave the all-time memorable line, "Alright, party's over. You don't have to go home, but you can't stay here!"

Our friends started filing out, grumbling. But deep inside, everyone was excited that they had made it to the party of the year at the Tuckers' house on Tichenor.

* * * * * *

Still in the party spirit as a sophomore, something surreal happened. The people from *Soul Train*, the hottest new dance show on TV, came to Compton High and held auditions for local teens to appear on the show.

My mom said I wasn't a great dancer like Keta, but I tried harder. I practiced for three days straight on our patio until I felt the rhythm.

My good friend, Eric, and I decided to try out and we made it! We and our dates were the talk of the school and the city! We were actually dancing on *Soul Train*! If that wasn't enough, they had a dance contest on the *Soul Train* set, and my partner, Carolyn Hines, and I became one of the *Soul Train* dance contest winners. The camera captured me in my headband and newly-purchased, rust-colored suede and leather outfit. Fringes hung from the bottom of my jacket and from the top of my brown suede moccasin boots, which made for a perfect match. Unfortunately, when I went down to do "the splits," I heard my pants split. No one knew it but me. My embarrassment was easily overshadowed by my elation for winning the dance contest. Carolyn and I were overjoyed to receive a free three-month supply of Afro Sheen hair care products.

The Tichenor house saw me really grow up into a young man. After *Soul Train*, I was no longer the wall flower. But my academic priorities never changed. I was invited to several house parties, but the weekends usually found me studying at my tiny desk. At first, I felt resentful of the sacrifice. But then, Monday morning would come and I would hear that somebody got shot or stabbed at a party over the weekend. I had made the right decision. I vowed to become valedictorian. All the days to graduation, I studied the valedictorians before me, and by 1974, I was determined to be the first valedictorian with a big Afro. I wanted to be the first well-rounded valedictorian. *No more geek.*

* * * * * *

After Tyrone sat the last bag down, he asked, "Anything else you need, Congressman?"

"No, that's it. Remember, tomorrow we've got the Prayer Breakfast at nine, then the Town Hall at eleven, followed by the rally at the Shipyard at three."

"And followed by the One Hundred Black Men's Dinner at seven."

"You got it. See you in the morning at eight."

CHAPTER THIRTY-ONE

High School

Afuer chatting with my mom and the rest of the family who lived at Tichenor Street, they must have known I was jet lagged when I left them talking and went to my bedroom. The stress of the pending trial was wearing me down. Once inside my room, I picked up my old high school yearbook, sat down on the bed, and slowly started turning the pages—my life at Compton High.

* * * * * *

The speech team was my favorite. I kept competing and winning minor awards until I won the Best Original Orator award. During those three years, my name appeared in the *Los Angeles Times'* annual recognition of honor students. My community was proud of me whenever we met at churches, stores or in the streets. Life just seemed to move in a straight line of better and better, and I expected it to continue.

If optimism was my strength, being too trusting was my weakness. In my early high school days, Gus Waters was my best friend. He attended Dominguez High because he lived on the east side of town. Actually, Gus and I had known each other from junior high, but our mothers knew each other from Jack and Jill days, and we became friends—blood brothers. We spent Saturdays, Sundays, and summers together.

If I had a piece of bread, Gus had a half. If I was going to Disneyland, Gus was coming along without having to pay. He was like the brother I never had because my real brother, Kenneth, was seven years younger, and during that time, those years made a big difference.

One day, Gus, who was older than me by a few months, finally got his driver's license. The only person happier than Gus was me. My best friend had a license and his mother had given him a brand-new green Dodge Demon. Just as my bread had been his bread and my money had been his money, I thought his car would be my car. Instead, he started hanging out with some questionable guys from his high school. Perhaps it came from his need to be recognized, but the bottom line was that instead of picking up his best friend, me, he would pick up his new crew. One of those guys was always in trouble with the law. I don't know which was more amazing to me, that he had "dissed" me, or that his new best friend was a questionable character. I thought he was smarter and more loyal than that.

That was my first lesson in betrayal. It hurt and I didn't speak to Gus for years. But, after I became a Christian, I did see him again and I forgave him. Nevertheless, the matter of me being too trusting of others would come back to bite me again.

Despite the break in my friendship with Gus, my goals were still the same: I was still marching toward becoming the first valedictorian of Compton High with a big Afro, and the first Compton High student ever to attend an Ivy League school. My goals were clearly in sight.

My senior year in high school finally arrived—1974. By then, I not only had a driver's license, I even had a car. My parents honored my accomplishments with a green Mustang. It was really Keta's high school graduation gift. However, that fall when she left to attend Fisk University in Nashville, the car didn't make the trip with her. Her loss was my gain. Suddenly, this once high school geek was rolling! My Afro was now full-bloom (probably with the help of all the Afro Sheen I received from Soul Train), and my wardrobe was updated. I was sporting platform shoes, bell bottoms, and cool-colored sunglasses. By the end of my senior year, I was no longer stressing over every grade. I even accepted one "B+" with calmness and humility. It was the only "B" I had received in three years. There was a quiet tension in the air as valedictorian and salutatorian selections were fast-approaching. I was at peace, cruising my ride and playing my music, waiting to hear from Harvard, Princeton, and Yale.

Not many people knew that I was the frontrunner for valedictorian. Many students thought it would be Paul Richards, our student body president. Others thought it would be some of the more scientifically gifted, like William Martin or Alvin English. One day, I was pulled out of class and called into the principal's office. I had no idea what it was about. In my three years of high school, I had never seen the inside of the principal's office. Generally, you were only called in if you were involved in some bad behavior. Nevertheless, I surmised that he was going to give me my class ranking.

Principal Aaron C. Wade ran our high school with an iron fist. He was widely known as a "go-getter." In addition to being a respected educator, he was renowned for becoming the first African-American referee in the NFL. When I walked in the office, he looked straight at me.

"Sit down, son," he said, carefully.

Knowing that he was a no-nonsense guy, I sat down without saying a word.

"Listen, Tucker, this is a bit unusual, but we have a report of a threat against your life."

A threat against my life! He has to be joking. I waited for the punch line. Unfortunately, it never came.

"I guess some punks might be jealous of you, or have something against your father, as a city councilman. It could be a little of both. All I know is we got a call today saying that you were going to be seriously hurt. So, I'm taking you out of your classes for the rest of the day, and having one of your parents come to pick you up while we investigate this."

I was numb. *This can't be happening!* For three years I had attended Compton High without even an argument. And now, so close to the finish line, there was drama. Maybe I was to blame: my need to finally 'come out' and be this visible, cool kid. But the culprits were really those nameless, faceless ones who were more insecure than I was. The ones who readily called me brainiac, nerd, geek, and "privileged." They seemed to charge me with having more advantages than most. I realized I was fortunate to have been raised in a two-parent home and to have a dad who was a successful dentist and now a councilman in the city. However, I was adamant that it was not a crime to be fortunate. The only crime would have been not appreciating and maximizing the opportunities and advantages I'd been given.

Shortly after my sobering talk with Mr. Wade, my mother arrived and took me home. For the next couple of days, two security guards shadowed me around campus, all without incident. The perpetrators of the threat were never caught, and instead of them causing me to shrink back from my zeal for achievement, I became more resolved than ever to soar to higher heights.

Three weeks later, I was summoned to the principal's office again. *Oh no, more bad news?* I walked into Principal Wade's office and stood in front of him holding my breath.

"Sit down, Mr. Tucker. I have some news for you," he said, in his familiar methodical manner.

I immediately sat and took a deep breath. *Another threat?*

"Well, I am happy to announce to you that you are the valedictorian of the class of seventy-four."

I did it! I wanted to run out of there and scream. Three long years of sacrifice had paid off! Outwardly, I remained calm as Mr. Wade briefed me on the upcoming graduation ceremony. He told me that I would be giving the keynote speech. Yes, I was going to make the biggest speech of my life.

"Thank you, Mr. Wade. Thank you."

I floated out of there and down the corridor as if I were high on something. That day was too good to be true. Once the word got out, everyone was surprised to learn that I was the valedictorian. And Elaine Fletcher, the girl who finished ahead of me in junior high school, was the salutatorian. This time, my dad would not be able to say, "You let a girl beat you." If this was a dream, I was determined not to wake up.

Valedictorian, Compton High, Class '74.

And the dream got even better. Just a few weeks later, I finally heard back from my college applications. I had done it again: WELCOME TO PRINCETON UNIVERSITY! I was going to be the first black person from my family to ever go to an Ivy League school, even though my uncle, Sebron Edward Tucker, was the first black athlete and a Hall of Famer at Stanford University, considered the Harvard of the West. I had never heard of a black student from Compton High School going to an Ivy League school. As far as I knew, I would be the first.

Graduation day was perfect. The weather was not too hot or too cold. Our ceremony was held at Ramsar Stadium, on the football field. The main stage and podium were planted right on the 20-yard line, on the south side of the field. I never played high school football, but that day I took center stage in front of a few thousand parents and family members, local officials, and well-wishers.

While rehearsing my speech, my mom and I had always joked about a line she suggested, and I eventually adopted: "Yes, I've come this far with a driving force." She interpreted the "driving force" to be that thin, gold belt she had used to discipline me over the years. That was our inside joke.

There were about 700 of us graduating that hot June day. As I squinted against the glistening California sun, looking out over the sea of humanity, I was thankful. Not only was I thankful for being valedictorian, but I was thankful for being alive. I remembered the fellow student who earlier that year had been shot down in the street right outside of Ramsar Stadium. It was the emergence of gang violence between the Crips and the Bloods. From that time forward, such gang violence would become commonplace in Watts, Compton, and South Central Los Angeles. The Age of Innocence was over.

So, as I ended my speech, I reminded my class, "Because of all that we have endured in the last three years, and in all the years it took us to get to this point, while the future may seem uncertain, with the zeal, and determination we possess, we can do anything! We cannot only dare to dream, we can dare to do!" The crowd of thousands sprang to its feet. Pride and jubilation erupted from the students like an active volcano. Shouts of "'74! '74! '74! '74!" filled the air.

I suppose everyone thinks his or her graduating class is the best, but there was something special about Compton High's class of 1974. Many of my classmates were destined to do great things, and I had never been more proud and excited to be a part of Compton High School. After all the shouting, we graduates walked into the open arms of our loved ones. My family was waiting for me with balloons and big hugs. My mom couldn't hold back her tears. My siblings overtook me with hugs and playful punches. As I surfaced from the sea of congratulations, I came face to face with my dad. He offered me his hand in a matter-of-fact way.

We looked each other square in the eyes, and gripped hands, man-to-man. He said nothing. I guess for him there was nothing to say. For me, it wasn't about what he said; it was about what he didn't say. He made no criticisms, corrections, challenges, or suggestions. It was a moment of silence that spoke volumes. It was a perfect moment. It was a healing moment. The past was swallowed in the present, and with his silent approval, I was now ready to fly.

* * * * * *

I woke up thinking about calling Bob, the man with my legal life in his hands, to find out what other monsters lurked in the darkness of my future. The smell of fresh coffee and the sound of activity in the kitchen next to my bedroom reminded me where I was—home.

"Buenos dias, Vida."

"Buenos dias, Mijo."

After the exchange of greetings, Vida handed me a glass of orange juice, and I was on the phone talking legal strategy with my attorney. Soon after, I turned on C-SPAN and called Marcus to check the current events in Congress and Audrey to get an update on local matters. But, my mind was bogged down with my personal problems. Despite the temporary solace provided by my fond memories, my present predicament remained overwhelming. I glanced at the clock and saw that it was eight o'clock—time to confront the terrifying trial that awaited me.

CHAPTER THIRTY-TWO

Round One

As I fought for my life in the courtroom, Robin was sitting right there with me every day. "Are you sure there's nothing you can do about that jury?" she asked.

"I told you, honey, nothing."

"I just don't like the way they look at us. There's no compassion in their eyes, at all. I would never have let one of them stay on the jury."

"Like I told you, the jury pool was overwhelmingly white, and we simply ran out of peremptory challenges. What can we do?" I shrugged.

"Well, are you going to argue that you were targeted?" she asked.

"Clearly entrapment is our strongest argument. But if you mean are we going to argue that I was targeted for a takedown because I was a black politician, that ship has sailed; that predominantly white jury is just *not* going to hear it."

"I guess you're right," she said.

"Baby, don't stress over this. Tomorrow's a big day. Let's go home and regroup."

Later that night at home, as Robin sat up in bed leaning against the headboard, I laid my head on her lap and she stroked it. "Don't worry, honey. Tomorrow's gonna be fine. God's on our side."

"Have I told you today that I love you?" I asked.

"Today?" she asked, playfully.

"Uh huh."

"No, not today."

"Hmmm. That's at least one problem I can correct...I love you."

I raised up, kissed her, and we hugged.

"Look, I hate to tell you this, but...I gotta go jump on the computer," I said.

"For how long?"

"Wish I knew. Until it's finished."

"What?"

"The opening statement."

"You're going to do an opening statement? Now?"

"Yeah."

"But I thought you said sometimes it's better to wait until the defense puts on its case."

"Yeah, that's true, but in this case, they're about to bury me before we get out of the gate. The more I think about it, the more I'm sure we've gotta come out swingin'."

"Hmm," she sighed.

"If all they hear tomorrow is the government's version of what happened, the jury's mind will close and never open again."

"I guess you're right, but isn't Bob supposed to write and give the opening statement?"

"Yea, but when I talked to him about writing an opening statement at this point, he seemed hesitant—unsure. Something about not quite having gotten the big picture of the case yet."

"You mean to tell me that on the eve of the biggest threat to our lives, where you're facing twenty years in prison, our lawyer doesn't know what the hell the case is about yet?"

Rising up, I looked deeply into Robin's eyes, grabbed her hands, and said, "Honey, calm down."

"This is making me anything but calm!"

I covered her hand in mine. "Look, he knows the case; he just doesn't know it as well as I do." I read the disapproval on Robin's face in spite of her quiet acceptance.

I stepped on the floor. "It's my butt on the line, not his. It's do or die!" I headed toward my computer.

"Alright, do what you gotta do, but please try to get some rest. You're gonna need it."

"I'll have plenty of time for rest after this trial. Right now I need an opening statement!"

It was a long night, a lot longer than I had anticipated. It reminded me of one of those all-nighters I had pulled in my first-year of law school at Georgetown, cramming through the voluminous material of my Contracts class, and hoping for the best. After a few hours, I had pulled together the necessary pieces to the puzzle and laid out a script for Bob to follow. Final argument was one thing—an attorney could summarize, pontificate, and argue his passion. But an opening statement needed to be thorough—a complete outline, a roadmap of what the attorney planned to show.

The dawn's first light peeked through the blinds, telling me that it was time to go to court. I barely had enough time to change into my favorite dark-blue suit, streak out the door, and get into the Town Car. I guess the good news was I had someone else to drive me. Between lack of sleep and a case of nerves, I truly needed a driver. Tyrone maneuvered through rush-hour traffic, taking the surface streets toward downtown to make it to the court by 7:30 a.m.

Now that the O.J. trial was officially over, the media's feeding frenzy turned to its next victim— Congressman Walter Tucker. Media was all present and accounted for as we made our way up the courthouse steps.

"Congressman, any comments?"

"What do you think about the jury?"

It was all I could do to keep an undaunted gait. I wanted so much to answer, but I knew the jury would read my comments, despite the judge's admonition not to read any newspaper articles on this highly publicized case. The last thing I needed was some juror taking offense because I alleged that they were not a jury of my peers.

As quickly as I zoomed past the throng of reporters, I moved through the sterile, concrete hallways and slipped into Judge Marshall's court. All eyes were on me as I measured my steps toward the defense counsel's table. I felt the hubris of the assistant U.S. attorneys from across the room. They were confident, brimming with readiness, and waiting for the kill. Probably visions of promotions and high-paying jobs in the private sector danced through their heads. This was the kind of case by which careers were made.

The prosecutors whispered to one another at their counsel table, then leaned back confidently in their sturdy chairs. Why shouldn't they look smug? High-tech video and audio equipment surrounded them—all with videos of me in compromising positions. One could have thought that we had stepped into a screening room for the Academy of Arts and Sciences. The government had spared no expense. It had set a precedent for high-tech prosecution. That, plus the legion of investigators, witnesses, lawyers, and FBI agents, showed a kind of undeniable invincibility.

Meanwhile, my two attorneys were giving a frantic review of various documents strewn around my black Bible in the center of our counsel table. There was more paperwork in this case than in any case I had ever seen. It was already a "trial by fire." Silently, I hoped that we'd have just a little more time when…

"All rise. The United States District Court, Central District, is now in session, the Honorable Consuelo B. Marshall presiding."

Everyone quickly rose to their feet.

"You may be seated," Judge Marshall stated.

The lead counsel for the government, Steve Madison, and my lead counsel, Bob Ramsey, assumed their positions at their respective podiums.

"Appearances for the record, please."

"Steven Madison, along with John Potter for the government, Your Honor."

"Robert Ramsey, Jr. along with co-counsel Mark Smith for the defense, Your Honor. Mr. Tucker, as you can see, is present in court."

"Alright, unless there are any special requests, we'll bring the jury in for opening statements."

"Nothing from the government, Your Honor."

I nudged Bob.

"Uh, Your Honor…we've been noticing the incredible amount of technical equipment in the courtroom, and we were curious as to whether the government is going to be attempting to use this equipment, video, and audio equipment in their opening statement? If so, Your Honor, we believe it is improper, since it is not yet evidence, nor do we know whether or not it shall ever be evidence. Such use would be highly prejudicial to the defense, Your Honor."

"Mr. Madison?"

"Well, yes, we had planned on using it during the opening, merely as a visual aid, Your Honor. We have more than a confident expectation that all of these tapes will become evidence and therefore, we see no real issue here."

"I'll entertain an offer of proof at sidebar. Counsel may approach."

This was the first of countless trips to the sidebar, as seen on TV a million times. It's that part of the case when the attorneys go to the side of the judge's bench and lend the most argumentative whisper to issues that the court has deemed inappropriate to be heard by the jury, or in open court. It's where all the dirt is discussed; it's where the fly on the wall wants to hear what only flies can hear. Unfortunately for me, the fly heard Madison convincing Judge Marshall that the evidence was reliable and would eventually be admitted. Score another one for the prosecution: Government 2, Home team 0.

After returning to our seats, the judge made it official.

"Alright, based on the offer of proof by the government, I will allow the visual and audio presentation at the appropriate time. Now, Attorney Ramsey, as to the matter of opening statements, I'd like to know if you're planning to make one."

Bob glanced at me and received the non-verbal assurance he was looking for.

"Uh, yes, Your Honor, we do plan to make an opening statement this morning."

"All right then, please bring in the jury."

The jury members marched in, one by one, and took their respective seats. Seven women and five men. One black, two Hispanics—the rest were white. They were conservatively dressed and seemingly hiding a cauldron of emotions behind guarded faces. As I stared at those twelve people taking their seats in the jury box, I thought back to times on Capitol Hill when people of all races marched into my congressional office to see me and seek my help. But that group was not marching in to help me, but to judge me, and the most frightening thing was that they would only know me from what they heard in the courtroom.

Immediately Assistant U.S. Attorney Madison put the question to their minds: "Was Walter Tucker a corrupt politician who betrayed the public trust by soliciting bribes within weeks after his election, or was he merely the victim of a calculated plot by the FBI to entrap him by undercover agents and operatives? This, ladies and gentlemen of the jury, is the central question you must answer."

CHAPTER THIRTY-THREE

Round Two

Assistant U.S. Attorney Madison's stance was that of a soldier; his eyes and jaw were set and his shoulders square, and his back straight. He looked rigid, but assured. He came out blasting, "Ladies and gentlemen of the jury, Walter Tucker broke his promise to the electorate, and sold out his city for money."

Then he lowered the boom, "Most of the evidence will come to you by way of video tapes and audio tapes. Nearly thirty hours of them where you will see and hear then Mayor Walter Tucker demanding and receiving money—payoffs! Our chief witness will be Mr. John Macardican, a San Gabriel Valley businessman who wanted to construct a multi-million dollar waste-to-energy conversion plant in Compton."

Madison never relaxed his eyes or his hard jaw. He never shifted as most lawyers do. His cold eyes bore straight into those of the jury as he spoke, "Mr. Macardican had presented the proposal to the city in the mid-80s, but was turned down when he refused to pay a bribe to city officials. Mr. Macardican reported the bribery attempt to the local FBI, but because the project died, there was no evidence to follow up on." He paused, his face gave way to a little smirk, and he continued, "However, in nineteen eighty-nine, the state legislature mandated that all cities reduce the amount of waste going to landfills. This time, city officials sought out Mr. Macardican, asking that he resubmit his proposal. After conferring with the FBI again, Mr. Macardican agreed to work for them as a 'cooperating witness,' thereby setting into motion a three-year investigation into political corruption in Compton. Mr. Macardican officially began working for the FBI in April of nineteen ninety."

Now Madison leaned forward, rolling a shoulder like a Siberian Husky carrying a sled. "But it wasn't until Walter Tucker, III won a special election to fill a vacancy created by the death of his father that the probe began in earnest. The evidence will show that it was only a few weeks after he was sworn in that the defendant, then Mayor Tucker, approached Mr. Macardican at a fundraiser, and said, 'We've got to talk.'" Madison's shoulder rolled back in place, but the hard squint of his eyes remained.

"And they did meet for lunch shortly thereafter—May thirtieth, nineteen ninety-one to be exact. Mr. Macardican was wearing a wire. During their secretly recorded conversation over lunch, Mayor Tucker told Mr. Macardican that to win approval for his project, Mr. Macardican must start 'letting people know that you support them.' It was then that Mr. Macardican asked Mr. Tucker how he could show his support. The following taped exchange took place."

At that moment, Madison grabbed a transcript and began reading from it:

TUCKER:Well, I guess I'm not unlike any other politician. I just came off a campaign, and I have a debt to retire. What I'm comfortable with is—and again, it depends on how you like to do it—it's probably to your and mine and the project's benefit to have no checks...you know, from you...or what's the name of the company that the project is?

MACARDICAN: Compton Energy Systems.

TUCKER:Yeah, Compton Energy Systems. CES.

MACARDICAN: Absolutely.

TUCKER:Right, yeah, that's right, that's just a deal breaker, you wouldn't want to do that. But I would be comfortable with a check or checks in some other name. That would be comfortable with me.

MACARDICAN: OK.

TUCKER:As I said, I have a relatively considerable debt. It's not that bad, but whatever you can muster, something in the area of, maybe ten grand could help.

MACARDICAN: OK.

Madison continued, "And ladies and gentlemen of the jury, it was OK! During the next ten months, in seven secretly recorded meetings, the defendant received thirty thousand dollars—all but one thousand dollars of it in cash—in exchange for his support of the waste conversion project. In addition to that, in September of nineteen ninety-one, the defendant demanded a two hundred fifty thousand dollars kickback from an undercover FBI agent who was posing as the chief financial backer of the project.

"At one of the video-taped meetings at the CES office in Compton, Mr. Tucker is seen pocketing two thousand dollars in cash, then he stands up, smiles, and shakes Mr. Macardican's hand, and says, 'We'll be friendly, definitely.' It is the same Walter Tucker who, at another point in the recorded conversations with Mr. Macardican, says, 'You did a smart thing this time, and you approached it properly.' "

"The evidence will show he was making reference to the fact that this time, Mr. Macardican chose to make the bribes he had previously refused to make.

What a bunch of crap. That is not what happened.

"Finally, you will hear and see evidence that the defendant took his ill-gotten monies and did not report them to the IRS as income, along with some monies, which he earned legally, thus knowingly and willfully being guilty of tax fraud.

"Ladies and gentleman of the jury, once you have seen and heard the totality of the evidence, you will have absolutely no doubt that the defendant, Walter R. Tucker, III, is guilty of the eight counts of extortion and two counts of filing false federal income tax returns in nineteen ninety-one and nineteen ninety-two. The graphic nature of the videos, one of which showing the defendant stuffing ten thousand dollars in his briefcase, will convince you, beyond a reasonable doubt, that while Walter Tucker took an oath of office, promising to give his faithful service to the residents of Compton, within a matter of weeks he broke his promise and sold them out for money from Compton Energy Systems.

How in the world did I ever get in the middle of all this mess? The video that's always rolling on all our lives can be such a cold, cruel critic, but fails to tell the complete story.

"The defendant is also accused of two counts of extorting money from Murcole Disposal, Inc., the city's waste hauler. The evidence will show that the defendant even tried to trick Murcole officials into doubling their bribe. This defendant talked about money. He talked about what he would be paid when he would be paid, how he would be paid, and how he believed other members of the City Council could be persuaded to vote for the waste-to-energy project.

"The evidence will show that Walter R. Tucker, III was a corrupt politician and a tax cheat who victimized his constituency. After you've heard and seen all the evidence, we expect you to strike a blow for justice and find the defendant guilty on all twelve counts."

Throughout the government's opening, I knew all eyes were glued to me for my reaction. Remaining outwardly void of emotion under such an assault was absolutely one of the most difficult things I ever had to do. Vicious, reframed, ill-gotten, and re-interpreted attacks were being hurled around the courtroom like ancient spears of war. They made me out to be just a step short of a super villain, winning my place in the criminals' "Hall of Infamy" along with the likes of Hitler, Eichmann, Idi Amin, or Genghis Khan. I was being reduced to a callous monster that the righteous government had captured. They had saved the citizens of Compton from a dangerous leader.

As I looked over at Madison, I recalled the countless times I had sat at the prosecutor's table on the right side of the courtroom hurling my own accusations at people perceived to be vicious defendants. The sum total of them didn't seem to equate to the weight of this persecution. My teachings, my character, my care for people, and my spiritual upbringing would not have allowed me to ever be so despicable.

The jurors stirred in their chairs, shifting their body weight in anticipation of our opening statement. In the audience, beyond the court bar, there seemed to be great distress, a kind of restlessness among the crowd that had come out to support me. They knew they weren't allowed to say a word, but they must have known also that their presence would give me moral support. In my heart, I thanked them for coming.

In the packed courtroom, U.S. Attorney Nora Manella and her assistants finally had their moment. They had waited for three years to get me in court, and publicly proclaim me to be a corrupt politician. Now they could breathe their first sigh of relief. On the other side of the courtroom, I sat upright and breathed slowly in and out. I hoped for victory. The very core of me was set on telling my side of the story.

All eyes were now focused on Attorney Bob Ramsey as he shuffled his papers together methodically, and composed himself for his opening. The short, conservatively dressed defense attorney wearing his horn-rimmed glasses approached the podium slowly, much like an elderly law professor about to address his young students on the first day of Criminal Law class. *I pray he brought his A-game today!*

"Good morning, ladies and gentlemen of the jury, I'm Robert Ramsey, Jr., counsel for Mr. Tucker, and this is my opportunity to convey to you what we, the defense, believe the evidence in this case will show. First, the evidence will show that in April of nineteen ninety-one, Mr. Walter R. Tucker, III, at the age of thirty-three, became the youngest mayor in the city of Compton's history. Mr. Tucker was not this sophisticated politician that the government has made him out to be. He was a young, novice politician who, by the way, had just lost his father to cancer. In fact, the evidence will show that it was his father's death during his third term of office that prompted Mr. Tucker to run for mayor, and fill the unexpired term. He did become mayor, having endured a hotly contested election that left him with some campaign debt.

Bob fiddled with his glasses and continued, "The evidence will show that Mr. Tucker was manipulated into accepting cash from Mr. Macardican as part of the government's entrapment plan. Though Mr. Tucker had never met Mr. Macardican previously, he knew he had been a contributor to his father's campaign for mayor. After Mr. Tucker's victory in the mayor's race, it was Mr. Macardican, through an intermediary, who sought out Mr. Tucker and arranged their first lunch meeting."

That's right. That's how it happened!

"Macardican's sole purpose for the meeting was to entrap Mayor Tucker. He is the one who brought up the issue of support and then, for the sake of the confidentiality of his business, he insisted that the support come by way of cash. Mr. Tucker regarded the initial offer as an overture for a political campaign contribution."

Exactly!

"You will hear the testimony of Mr. Tucker and hear the tapes. Based on the tapes, you will not hear Mr. Tucker demanding money in exchange for votes. Rather, it was Mr. Macardican who asked Mr. Tucker to give him cash in order to avoid any attention drawn to his project. The project had been controversial in the mid-eighties largely because of its proposed site. With a new site being proposed, the potential for hundreds of jobs for the community, and conservation in accordance with state mandates, Mr. Tucker initially saw merit in the project.

"At the time of his dealings with Compton Energy Systems, Mr. Tucker was, in effect, wearing two hats: that of a full-time attorney, and that of the part-time mayor. As mayor, Mr. Tucker weighed the company's proposal in terms of what was best for the city. However, as an attorney, he accepted money from the company as a "consultant" inasmuch as it had dealings with the Compton School District. Mr. Macardican had proposed building the waste-to-energy plant on school district property and had asked Mr. Tucker to be his consultant. In Mr. Tucker's mind, there was no conflict of interest because the Compton School Board is a separate entity from the Compton City Council."

Good statement of the facts, Bob. Now just up the charisma a bit. Please make them understand.

"Mr. Tucker exercised bad judgment due to inexperience and age, but it took the government to make this occur. Nevertheless, I reiterate, Mr. Tucker never agreed to do any official act in exchange for money received. He never said, 'If you pay me, I will vote for the project, or if you don't pay me, I won't vote for it.' In short, Mr. Tucker was set up by Mr. Macardican and the FBI."

Right. Tell 'em!

"The evidence will show that Mr. Macardican blamed Mr. Tucker's predecessor, U.S. Rep. Mervyn Dymally, for his project's failure in the eighties. Mr. Macardican says that he refused to pay a bribe to Congressman Dymallly and consequently Mr. Dymally used his influence over the Compton City Council to kill the project. Immediately after, Mr. Macardican became a cooperative witness for the FBI and sought revenge against Compton City Officials. In the eighties Mayor Walter R. Tucker, II was the mayor. When Mr. Macardican couldn't entrap that mayor, the FBI kept Mr. Macardican on the payroll for years until he could get his son."

Now that's the truth!

"Ladies and gentlemen, the evidence will show that the Murcole counts are nothing more than a desperate attempt to besmirch Mr. Tucker's character as mayor. Those two counts have to do with a rate increase, and a contract extension, and not any criminal activity. Walter Tucker acted properly in his official capacity as mayor, and there is no reasonable or concrete evidence to the contrary.

"Finally, the evidence will show there is no direct or reasonable circumstantial evidence that Mr. Tucker willfully reported false income tax reports. Mr. Tucker fully intends on taking the stand, explaining why certain monies were not reported at the time. We, the defense, confidently believe that after you've heard and seen all the evidence in this matter, you'll agree with us that the only real victim in this case has been Mr. Tucker. He's been the victim of a vicious entrapment cleverly set up by our federal government. Mr. Tucker wanted to give this businessman a fair shot, and for that, he was rewarded with entrapment. Thank you very much, ladies and gentlemen." Bob folded his papers and carefully stepped back to his seat.

After Bob finished, I wanted to lean back in my chair and give a sigh of relief. It was, after all, the truth, and just the way I wrote it. However, while all the major points were covered, the delivery was questionable. Bob did well in speaking to me in legal terminology when we were preparing for the trial, but connecting with jurors on an emotional level was a different story.

Bob had been deliberate, perhaps too deliberate. The delivery lacked confidence and charisma. The points were there, but the passion wasn't. Maybe I had made a mistake in feeding him the script. I felt it was six of one hand, half a dozen of the other. Without the text, he was sure to wander off course and shoot from the hip. But maybe he needed that to warm up. I wasn't sure what he needed, but I was sure that this was not the kind of delivery I had hoped for. It was as if reading the script took Bob totally out of his element. The horn-rimmed glasses came off during the reading, and whenever there was a feigned attempt to gain eye contact with the jury, the glasses went back on. The on-and-off ritual was unnerving and the lack of tonal change in Bob's voice was boring.

For certain now, I felt the government's spears piercing my side. I hated to admit it, but round one had gone to them. They had scored first blood. Government 3, Defense 0.

As a trained, top-notch defense attorney, I became more frustrated than the typical defendant. My legal instincts leaped out from every part of my mind. I knew what to do and what should be done, but my hands were tied. To look out and see my lawyer not exhibiting confidence and poise in the biggest and most critical trial of my life was hard for me to swallow. I wanted to die, right then and there. Just die and get it all over with. *What happened to all those years of experience Bob boasted? Surely you can't be an ex-U.S. attorney for six years and not feel comfortable and savvy in the courtroom.*

But no matter how much I criticized Bob in my mind, I knew deep inside that the one I was really angry at was me. I was the one who, because of bad choices, had allowed myself to be in this horrible situation. And, as anyone who has ever gone to trial knows—with or without a Johnnie Cochran—whatever can possibly go wrong usually will.

CHAPTER THIRTY-FOUR

First Blood

As per usual in Judge Marshall's court, everyone was on time and accounted for, because they knew she ran a tight ship. Today was a big day in the trial. The buzz was that Macardican was taking the stand. I opened my Bible and glanced at Psalm 27:

> "*The Lord is my light and my salvation whom shall I fear? The Lord is the strength of my life of whom shall I be afraid?*" (KJV Psalm 27:1)

I felt the intense anticipation in the courtroom rise and the media's feeding frenzy mounting.

"Mr. Madison, your next witness, please."

"The government calls Mr. John Macardican."

Madison looked back toward the courtroom doors and in stepped Kevin Adley, the steadfast special agent in charge of the FBI's investigation, flanked by two other stern agents. After a couple of steps, they slowed and surveyed the room in one sweeping gaze. The agents nodded to Adley, then he returned through the doors and beckoned to someone in the hallway. Seconds later, Adley and another FBI agent stepped into the courtroom escorting a white-haired, middle-aged man. The audience whispered and pointed surreptitiously; they murmured in curiosity.

"Sir, please come forward," Judge Marshall commanded.

Macardican, looking nervous, was called to take the stand before a packed audience. He hesitantly stepped forward with a sheepish grin on his face. It was a shallow grin—the kind painted on a clown's face; the kind that masked fear. People scrutinized Macardican's every move. He seemed to feel their scrutiny. Would he withstand that scrutiny?

Macardican glanced over to the defense counsel's table and we locked eyes. It was like two prize fighters staring each other down in the middle of the ring before the fight. I had promised myself that, as a Christian, I would have no hatred for this man. It was the hardest emotion I ever had to control. Despite all he had done to entrap me, the words of familiar sermons came to mind: "Hold your peace, and let God fight your battle." "Vengeance is my saith the Lord." "Touch not my anointed; do my prophet no harm."

Yes, I had to purify the hatred for John Macardican from my soul. I couldn't allow myself to hate. To do that would be bigger than anything he could ever do to me. I breathed deeply and let go of disgust, anger, fear, and a deep desire for revenge. Suddenly, like a team of wild mustangs, those emotions fled from me. They didn't manifest in profanity or an audible outburst, but in silent and fervent prayer. Macardican could see my lips moving as my eyes focused intensely on him. Maybe he thought I was cursing him under my breath and, at another time, that might have been the case, but not then. He appeared uneasy, and his face turned pale as I continued my silent prayers.

It was as if the entire room faded into darkness and only we two remained, locked into the shadowy light of each other's stare. I didn't believe either of us would ever forget that moment— I knew I wouldn't. Something life-changing was taking place for me, no matter how the case turned out.

"Please raise your right hand. Do you promise to tell the truth, the whole truth, and nothing but the truth, so help you God?"

"I do," Macardican replied.

"You may be seated."

"Please state your name for the record, and spell your last name."

"John Macardican. M-A-C-A-R-D-I-C-A-N."

"All right, Mr. Macardican, make yourself comfortable. Pull that mic up real close to your mouth, please," Judge Marshall said.

The government's script had already been written in its trial memorandum, and I surmised Steve Madison planned on following it to the tee. He began in typical prosecutorial fashion, laying the foundation with the witness's account of his initial encounter with me. Then he followed up with documentary evidence as reinforcement.

The wonderful thing about the FBI stings, as far as the U.S. Attorney's office was concerned, was that there was always corroborative evidence. It made for a good showing and great overkill. The prosecutor could prove the same illicit transaction by eyewitness, audio tape, video tape, and then underscore it by reference to the transcripts.

The history of the project was the natural place to start. The government made sure to have Macardican step down from the witness box and walk over to a huge model of the project for points of reference. From the very outset, they planned to sell the jury on the notion that the Compton Energy Systems' proposed 214,000-square-foot waste-to-energy plant, to be located in the city of Compton, was a real and viable $225 million project that was thwarted only because of "foul play" on my part. I leaned back to listen carefully to their version of the matter.

As we anticipated, Macardican admitted that in the early 1980s, he originally spent $1.8 million on his plan to build a waste conversion plant in Compton next to a Rosecrans Avenue waste transfer station owned by one of his companies.

While the city planning commission had approved the project on that Rosecrans site, shortly thereafter the City Council overturned the planning commission's decision and effectively killed the deal. Naturally, Macardican said his project was the economic savior for the city. He alleged that the only reason his project was not approved by the City Council in the mid-'80s was that he refused to bribe certain Compton officials. Macardican conceded that I was not in public office at that time.

"During that time, who was the mayor?" Madison asked.

"Walter R. Tucker, II, the defendant's father, was the mayor at that time," Macardican answered.

At any rate, Macardican testified that in 1991 he sought to build the plant on another site owned by the Compton Unified School District, located at Central and Greenleaf. That site had always been recommended as an alternative to the Rosecrans site, based on a preliminary study done in the 1980s. Any other site would have required a costly, time-consuming environmental report, Macardican testified.

"We wanted to stay in Compton because I had a contract to deliver energy to Edison as long as we were operating from Compton. So I rented an office near City Hall because that's what the local business people said I should do," Macardican said.

There it is. By his own admission, he needed a local consultant to know how to proceed in Compton.

"And was this office located near the defendant's law office?" Assistant U.S. Attorney Madison asked.

"Yes, we were just a stone's throw away from it," Macardican answered.

See, I wasn't coming after them, they were coming after me!

"You said, 'we'?" Madison asked.

"Oh, yes, the FBI was using one of the suites in the building for its video equipment," Macardican boasted.

So Macardican and the FBI became buddies to take me down. There is the answer right there…entrapment, conspiracy, set up. I comforted myself with their admission.

After walking Macardican through the history of his waste conversion project, Madison played an hour-long audiotape for the jury that had been recorded when Macardican and I first met on May 31, 1991. The history of the project gave the jury more insight as to what Macardican and I were discussing at our lunch date.

As the testimony proceeded, John Macardican never took off his pasted-on, turned-up smile. I imagined how the prosecution had prepared him: *Don't worry, John, this is going to be a walk in the park. Let's nail this guy and strike a blow for every hard-working, white businessman like yourself who can't get a break because some black guy's yellin' discrimination, affirmative action!*

As the minutes ticked by, Macardican got more comfortable and seemed to be visualizing the conclusion: *The Compton city fathers will pay for rejecting my project that's been out there for approval since '84. They'll pay for the millions I lost. Vengeance at last!*

While the tape of our first meeting played, Macardican's smile changed from a grin to a smug resolve.

Of course, the government knew exactly how to focus on the most damaging excerpts of our hour-long recorded dialogue. And after the tape had been played in its entirety, they proceeded to give Macardican every opportunity to expand on those damaging areas by allowing his interpretation of what was being said. The routine had been nursed and rehearsed. Macardican was allowed to state his opinion about what he believed I intended. Such interpretation would further strengthen the government's already intimidating case.

Having to listen to those tapes was no easy thing for me. But in the final analysis, it was not the audiotapes that concerned my lawyers and me. Rather, it was the video tapes that were the most damaging. In the words of the old adage, "A picture is worth a thousand words." Nothing was mentioned about consulting...I looked like an unadulterated villain.

Yes, for most people, seeing is believing. If they saw it on a video, it had to be true. And yet, the Coon/Powell case tried in Simi Valley, concerning the alleged police brutality of Rodney King, put the value of the video tape into serious question. Defense attorneys argued that what the video tape didn't show— King's alleged resistance of arrest—was critical. The prosecution, in that case, argued that the jury should focus on the excessive force graphically portrayed in the video. In the end, however, because of the white conservatives who sat on the jury, the police officers were acquitted.

In my case, there was no physical beating on the video tapes. Just a 33-year-old black man who happened to be a politician receiving cash from his accuser. It was the strongest evidence against me: black and white video showing Macardican counting out cash in his office, setting it in a pile, and then handing the money to me. Then he said, "That, plus the eight thousand we agreed on, should secure your vote."

The video showed me smiling, shaking Macardican's hand and saying, "We'll be friendly, definitely."

"So, Mr. Macardican, this video-taped payment occurred June twenty-sixth, nineteen ninety-one. Two months after the defendant was sworn in as Compton's mayor, correct?" Madison asked.

"Yes, that's right," Macardican answered.

The video of July sixteenth, nineteen ninety-one showed Macardican and me meeting again in Macardican's inner office. With the FBI video cameras rolling, Macardican questioned whether he should have to pay then Councilman Omar Bradley as much as the mayor.

I disagreed, saying, "Everybody has one vote, and you have to make sure you have it...I think I have to be modest and reasonable."

Macardican was shown giving me a purported $1,000 in cash and handing me a $1,000 check, signed by an undercover FBI agent. After pocketing the cash and check, I was heard saying, "It feels good."

That really takes my comments out of context. I meant that it feels good to be helping get an important project to move forward. And it did.

At our next video tape meeting in Macardican's office on August 28, 1991, Macardican counted out $1,000 and gave it to me. I pocketed it. Macardican promised to deliver the next $1,000 "a little quicker."

Video after video, the damning evidence mounted. In the opening statement by Bob, our defense conceded that I had taken the money, but offered that I was the victim of entrapment by an overzealous informant and FBI agents. As Bob Ramsey sat scribbling notes on his legal pad, I hoped that all the visual evidence the prosecution presented hadn't already caused the jury to forget everything he had pointed out to them in his opening statement.

"Looking at the clock, Your Honor, is this an appropriate place to stop for the day?" Madison asked.

"Yes," Judge Marshall replied.

In what seemed like one breath, the session ended.

"Court is adjourned for today. We will resume tomorrow at nine a.m." Judge Marshall rapped her gavel.

I walked over to the welcomed, supportive handshakes of my family and friends after leaving the defense table.

"It's gonna be alright. Hang in there," my mother said.

Though her words were comforting, the somber look in her eyes reminded me that she and my dad had raised me to make better decisions than those I made. I repented for my errors in judgment. I was sorry for all the pain I had caused my family.

Robin's comforting arm wrapped around my shoulder.

"Don't worry. We're praying," she said.

I had gone out of my way to help someone who said they had a close relationship with my dad. I had acted thoughtlessly about advising a man who I thought had a good project for Compton. I acted foolishly to allow a stranger to convince me that he didn't want anyone to know he was paying for my advice because it could undermine his great project. I repented in the deepest part of my soul. But I also knew that I would fight for the part of me that was innocent, decent, and loved to help people. That's who I was, who I had always been, and who I would always be. Not even my foolish act could stop that.

I walked back to the defense counsel's table and shoved my folders into my oversized briefcase. While Bob, Mark, and I were fuming, the government leaned back and appreciated its handiwork. Over the course of three days, Steve Madison had taken John Macardican through countless tapes and transcripts. Each one of them reaffirming his central theme.

Standing stiff, staring straight at the jury's faces, Madison said, "Mayor Tucker was a corrupt politician, methodically going about the business of extorting money from this forthright businessman."

In the three days of Macardican's direct examination, there came even greater enemies—time and the press. With no cross-examination, all the press had to write about was incriminating evidence against me, brought to public attention by Macardican. The government was chalking up so many points that even my defense team and I almost cowered with concern that we were getting left too far behind to ever catch up.

Throughout Macardican's testimony, I glanced back and forth at highlighted passages in my Bible. No one could dispute that I needed all the spiritual help I could get. Madison said that in the week to come he and his partner, John Potter, would play further taped evidence, which they claimed showed me accepting a total of $30,000 from Macardican and $7,500 from Murcole. If there was ever a time for me to receive some special help from God, it was now. If there was ever a time for my defense team to answer the bell, this was the time.

CHAPTER THIRTY-FIVE

Fighting Back

J ohn Macardican resumed his place on the witness stand. On direct examination, he had appeared affable, but now it was time for cross-examination by the defense, and everything was about to change. The press knew it, the courtroom knew it, I knew it, and the government braced itself for it. I opened my Bible slowly to Psalm 91:

"He that dwelleth in the secret place of the most High shall abide under the shadow of the Almighty." (KJV Psalm 91:1)

Attorney Bob Ramsey took to the podium with his usual deliberate style, looking poised and patient. But underneath that laid-back exterior was a trained litigator, anxious to exploit any of Macardican's open wounds.

Although Judge Marshall hinted on several occasions to move the process along, my defense team and I knew that Macardican was the government's star witness, and we were not about to be bullied by the court into a curt and ineffective cross. Over the next three and a half days, the gray-haired, 57-year-old businessman often appeared combative, flustered, and evasive under questioning. Bob sought to expose him as an overzealous government informant who manipulated me into accepting money in exchange for serving as his business consultant. It seemed so logical. Who would be better than me to give advice about how to bring an important business proposal to Compton? I was not only a licensed attorney, but also the spokesman for the city who knew the key players and the way things were done in Compton.

Now it was our turn at bat and Macardican was fair game. Through our cross- examination, Macardican would find out how it felt to have his integrity put under the microscope. Bob aroused Macardican's ire early when he questioned him about his relationship with a young, attractive black woman, Helen Brown.

"What about your relationship with Helen Brown?"

The evidence had shown that Helen worked for the city of Compton's planning department until Macardican made her an attractive offer to come and work for his company. The clear inference was that Macardican was calculating and manipulative. He knew a former city employee, an insider, would help him push along his project.

"Mr. Macardican, you're a married man, right?"

"Please don't insult me, Mr. Ramsey," Macardican shot back. "I had a relationship with her like she was a sister."

Oh, please. Give me a break!

Bob, then referring to the transcripts, cited where Macardican had made reference to an unidentified man who came to his office trying to sell him something.

Macardican scoffed, "Can you imagine that guy trying to hustle me?" Once again, the implication was that Macardican prided himself as a "hustler" who could not be hustled.

"So, Mr. Macardican, you see yourself as a hustler?"

Trying ever so hard to retain his veneer of professionalism and integrity, Macardican responded, "That's a cheap shot."

Bob withdrew the question. Nevertheless, I hoped the innuendo had stuck in the jurors' minds. Then Bob turned his attention to the history of this whole matter.

"So, Mr. Macardican, you testified that in the eighties you made your first attempt to get the city to approve your project, but you ran into significant opposition, is that correct?

"Yes, that's true."

"In nineteen eighty-four, Congressman Mervyn Dymally solicited fifty thousand dollars from you in exchange for influencing the Compton City Council to approve your project, isn't that right?"

"Yes, that's right. Dymally told me, if you don't give me fifty thousand dollars, I'll kill your project."

"And did you pay the fifty thousand dollars?"

"No, I did not."

"And subsequently, your deal was killed, isn't that right?"

"Yes, they did a number on me."

As cross-examination continued, it became more and more clear that Macardican felt the Compton City Council wrongfully denied his project in the 80s and it seemed he had set himself on a course of vengeance against them.

"So, Mr. Macardican, after your project was killed by the city, you hooked up with the FBI, isn't that correct?"

"Well, I told them what happened."

Come on, Bob. You got him. Don't let him wiggle out of it.

"And you agreed to be a cooperative witness, isn't that right?"

"Yes."

"In fact, from nineteen eighty-four to nineteen ninety-one, you wore a body recorder four hundred and fifty to five hundred times, right?"

"Yes, that's about right."

Exactly what I thought! A real predator!

"It was during this time that you and an undercover FBI agent met with then Compton City Councilmen Bob Adams and Floyd James to discuss reviving the project?"

"Yes."

"And these two councilmen requested fifty thousand dollars to get the project revived and approved?"

"Yes."

"And former Mayor Walter Tucker, II wasn't privy to these conversations with you, right?"

"No, he wasn't."

"And his son, Walter Tucker III, wasn't a part of those discussions either, was he?"

"No."

"So, did you pay bribes to Adams and James?"

"No."

"Why not?"

"It just never happened."

Not that you didn't try.

"But on direct examination, you testified you made a political 'payoff' to Councilman Maxcy Filer, isn't that right?"

"Yes, but I was lying. I never made a payoff."

"Mr. Macardican, were you lying then, or are you lying now!"

"Objection! Argumentative."

"Sustained," said Judge Marshall.

Good one, Bob!

From the testimony given on cross-examination, it became apparent that Macardican's references to Compton politicians who allegedly attempted to bribe him all took place before I was ever a public official. Despite these multiple references to attempted bribery, Macardican insisted that he had no motive for revenge or entrapment of anyone, especially Walter Tucker, III. He was clearly lying.

As cross-examination continued, Bob then pounced heavily on the main issue of entrapment.

"Now, before your first meeting with Mr. Tucker, didn't you plan to entrap him?" Attorney Ramsey asked.

Macardican stiffened. "No, not true."

Yes, he did!

Bob took his glasses off and leafed through some papers. "But you did employ the former Compton Planning Director, a Mr. Bob Gavin, to steer your project through the city's bureaucracy, isn't that right?

"Yes, I hired Bob Gavin to help me."

"And he recommended that you talk with Mayor Tucker, correct?"

"Yes."

"So you took Bob Gavin's advice, correct?"

"Yes."

"Did Mr. Gavin tell you anything about the mayor before you met with him?"

"Well, he told me that the mayor was upset that I didn't support his campaign."

Upset? I didn't even know him.

"What else did he say?"

"Gavin said if he (Tucker) was going to support the project…the arrangement would probably be money…"

I never told Gavin that! If he did tell Macardican that, that was his own presumption.

"What exactly did he say?"

"He said, don't be surprised if he asks you for money."

"And you told this to the FBI?"

"Yes, I reported those comments to the FBI, and that is when they fitted me with the body recorder and authorized me to meet with Tucker for recording purposes."

See, he came after me with bad intentions.

Attorney Ramsey then pressed Macardican. "So, based on the information that Mr. Gavin gave you, you expected Mr. Tucker to hit you up for money, isn't that right?"

"No, not at all."

You can't have it both ways. Either you expected me to ask you for money or you didn't.

"Oh, then, despite what Mr. Gavin told you, you went to this meeting with no preconceived notions, with a clear mind, is that right?"

"Yes, that's right."

What a liar!

"So then, why did you immediately get fitted with a body recorder unless you expected Mr. Tucker to say something incriminating?"

"I was just following orders. I didn't expect him to say anything incriminating. In fact, I hoped he wouldn't, or else my project would be dead in the water."

This was never about your project; it was about revenge for something I knew nothing about!

"But you knew that the whole point of you being a cooperative witness was to make a case of bribery on one of these Compton officials, didn't you?"

"Well, to just see if they would bite."

Even though the jury's predominately white, they **have** *to be able to see through this guy!*

"And now that Mr. Gavin had told you what Mr. Tucker said, you had a pretty good idea that he would bite, didn't you?"

"No, not really."

Bob reared back in disbelief and asked, "You didn't really have any realistic hope in your project being approved, did you?"

"Oh yes, I did."

"No, you were too busy trying to get revenge for the enormous waste of time and money these politicians caused you before, when you tried to get your project approved."

"No, that's not true!"

"Well, how could that be, sir, when the moment you trapped Mr. Tucker or one of the other politicians, for all practical purposes, the federal government could no longer be a party to keeping your undercover status secret, thus exposing your project as nothing more than a device for a federal sting?"

"No, that's not true!"

You got him, Bob!

Macardican denied that the FBI told him what to do or say, or what to get me to say. On the other hand, he admitted, "They (the FBI) told me not to mention money. They told me to listen, follow his lead. If he wanted something, to find out what he wanted and when he wanted it."

Bob pointed out from the transcript that Macardican, in an exchange between him and his FBI handler, exclaimed, "I got him to say it, and I got him to say it strong!"

Anybody could see that round went to us. Entrapment—plain and simple!

CHAPTER THIRTY-SIX

Charging Ahead

N ow that Bob saw some daylight on cross-examination, he began to plow ahead through Macardican's defenses. When Macardican testified that he had told me of his admiration for my father, Bob cut him short.

"So you honored his father by trapping his son, isn't that right?" Bob asked sarcastically.

"His son trapped himself," Macardican fired back.

Not true! He already testified that he planned the whole thing out with the FBI.

But as Bob methodically plodded through the transcripts, seeking Macardican's interpretation on conversations between us, the inferences of foul play became more and more evident.

"Mr. Macardican, on page fifty-nine, line ten of the transcript, you say, 'I'll do whatever has to be done.' Isn't that right?"

"Well, yes, but…"

"And you were going to get somebody to take your money, right?"

"If I was, somebody shouldn't have taken it."

Come on, Bob. Don't let him off the hook. Don't let him revise what really happened!

The focus of the cross-examination became who was leading and who was following in the exchanges between Macardican and me. Bob pressed Macardican to admit that he sought and obtained "advice" from me. Macardican, under direct examination, had already testified that he had never engaged me as an adviser. Through cross-examination, the secretly-recorded meetings showed that Macardican did seek and receive my advice several times. Even when Bob confronted him with transcripts containing the word "advice," Macardican remained steadfast. He described his remarks as, "just words, just friendly words. I was trying to make him feel comfortable with me." At another point, he said, "He was telling me. He wasn't giving me advice."

What a bunch of bologna! When you give someone helpful information they don't know, it's advice.

Bob suggested that after Macardican paid me the first $10,000, the FBI pressured him to get an official act from me in exchange for it. Bob implied that Macardican insisted I vote on an Exclusive Negotiating Agreement.

Bob's high-intensity cross-examination of Macardican kept him on the stand for three and a half days. When it was all said and done, there were several glaring exchanges accusing Macardican of untruths. Macardican remained evasive. "I was not lying, just role-playing." All in all, our defense team counted twenty significant lies made by the government's star witness. Perhaps the biggest lie was that he was *not* out to get revenge on anyone, especially Walter Tucker, III. Bob pointed out that, as a businessman with a $250 million project lost, and millions already spent, Macardican had a healthy motive for revenge. He had spent four years as a cooperating witness for the FBI and had been rewarded with about $50,000 for his unrelenting tenacity.

It was a battle over credibility. The audio and video tapes that spoke a thousand words weighed heavily against my credibility. But Macardican's list of lies during cross-examination created serious doubt that he was a legitimate businessman, an innocent victim. If his company, Compton Energy Systems, was a legitimate company, what was its legal status with the state of California? Where were its offices, or bank accounts? Who were its Board of Directors, officers, and employees? And who *really* was John Macardican but a con man?

During the rigors of the cross-examination, the media became more engaged. Up to this point, the evidence had been rather one-sided. I was being publicly picked apart. However, for the first time since the news of the trial broke, there was another side to the story: TUCKER, VICTIM OF AN FBI STING? Should our government continue to induce its public officials to engage in crime?

I imagined the backroom whispers:

"Now you boys know that Washington is really keeping its eyes on this one. No screw-ups, or you'll be back pushing paper at a local precinct."

"No problem, boss. We'll get Macardican straight, and wrap Tucker up tight!"

One of the biggest issues surrounding Macardican's testimony had to do with whether I was legitimately advising him as a part-time lawyer. Bob was quick to point out on cross that the advice I gave Macardican was not a conflict of interest because it had to do with matters concerning the Compton School Board and not the Compton City Council. The Compton Energy Systems project had not yet been brought before the Compton City Council, but was projected to go before the Compton School Board. Through Macardican's testimony, Bob clearly brought out that the new proposed site for the project was on school board property. Without securing that property, there was, for all practical purposes, no viable project.

The fact that I, as a part-time mayor, may have given advice to Macardican was not enough to substantiate a case of "conflict of interest" or, for that matter, extortion. As a mayor who was also a lawyer, I could technically have been engaged to consult on matters in which the city had no vested interest at the time. The lines were muddled, causing the prosecution to scramble around on red alert. This became particularly true when Bob revealed on cross that Macardican's body recorder faltered at one point and there was a gap in the taping. It was somewhat reminiscent of the infamous 18-minute gap in the Watergate tapes.

Macardican attempted to explain that he had forgotten to activate the recording device, and was unable to do so in my presence. Once again, the questions hung in the air. Why was there a gap? What was really said during that gap? Isn't it reasonable to infer that those in control of a sting operation can control what they record, when they record, and what they provide to the defense, based on what they find to be the most incriminating recordings?

When one considers that Macardican lied over and over again on the stand, questions could easily become suspicions and suspicions could easily become doubts. Macardican admitted that the FBI told him not to bring up the subject of money, but in fact, he mentioned money first. "I have to squeak money out of my company and it'll have to be cash."

There—it's official! He spoke about money first! That was his pre-disposition, not mine!

Until then, I had only been responding to Macardican's overtures to provide campaign contributions. Up to that point in the conversation, I had not conditioned the campaign contributions on anything or on any official act at all. Nevertheless, the language used in the transcripts was often vague and interpretive. It was up to the jury to decide what the conversation between Macardican and me showed: A politician exploiting his office and manipulating a businessman, or a businessman under the manipulation of the FBI, skillfully exploiting a politician?

By the time my defense attorney was through with Macardican, his many lies were apparent. The *LA Times*, in an article appearing immediately after Bob's cross-examination, remarked that Macardican left the stand with a lot of lumps on his head. Perhaps even more damaging to Macardican was the resurfacing of an *LA Times* article dated September 5, 1994— "TUCKER: BUSINESS SPARKED BRIBERY PROBE, SOURCES SAY." In that article, the press uncovered that in 1985 Macardican and about a dozen associates were sued for allegedly bilking the state out of $7.4 million in bonds used to finance a Compton garbage facility that went bankrupt. Macardican was ordered by the court to pay a $130,000 judgment.

Unfortunately, Judge Marshall didn't allow that information into evidence, citing that it was prejudicial to the jury. *I can't believe that. It goes to the heart of this man's character and motives! Our justice system is broken. They can bring in all kinds of prejudicial history against the defendant, but none against his accuser.*

The same article further reported that there were other lawsuits, including one by a former attorney seeking $250,000 in unpaid legal fees and another by a posh hotel that claimed Macardican failed to pay $12,000 for his daughter's wedding reception.

"In light of the lawsuits against him, any government institution or body that did a check on him would realize he was not a reliable person to do business with," Richard S. Johns, who sued

Macardican on behalf of the California Pollution Control Financing Authority for his role in the bond debacle, said.

In the words of former Compton Congressman Mervyn Dymally, "That man is a pathological liar!"

The greatest problems of my past didn't compare to the struggles I was now facing. My past had its challenges, as I had made some bad choices. But by the grace of God, my good intentions always carried me through. That thought was about the only comfort I felt. I knew that no matter how bad things got, somehow God's grace and mercy would bring me through.

A verse from the book of Romans became my most important and favorite "Life Scripture." It was formed in my heart in the crucible of my criminal trial: *"For we know that all things work together for good, for those who love God and to those called according to His purpose."* (KJV Romans 8:28)

I had learned to stand on that Scripture. I knew I loved God and I believed I was called for His purpose. I wasn't sure back then what that purpose was, but I always felt God had a special one for me. As His power had d brought me through some tough situations before, I trusted Him to bring me out of this one. I trusted Him to use this trial to produce something good. Another scripture concerning the biblical character, Joseph, confirmed this in my heart:

But as for you, ye thought evil against me; but God meant it unto good, to bring to pass, as it is this day, to save much people alive. (KJV Genesis 50:20)

CHAPTER THIRTY-SEVEN

The Best Defense

Thursday morning, November 2, 1995. It was a typical overcast morning in Los Angeles. Tyrone was weaving Robin, Martha, and me through the northbound traffic on Figueroa Street. We couldn't be late for Judge Marshall's court that began at 8:00 a.m. We pulled up in front of the federal courthouse as usual, but the crush of reporters waiting right at curbside reminded me that this was a day in the trial like no other.

The night before, as I considered the mountain of evidence the government had brought against me, I decided I needed to take the stand; I resolved to fight to the end. Win, lose, or draw, my side of the story would be heard. Who else could really make the jury understand how I had been entrapped? Who else could really explain how I had no intent to extort money? I was going up there to tell exactly what had been in my heart and to clarify my intentions. I would bear the press' intense scrutiny of my testimony. Yes, I would let the court hear it, the press write it, and the prosecution try to kill it. But after their best shot, the truth from me would be public record for all times.

With my Bible clutched in one hand, and holding Robin's hand in the other, I rushed past the reporters and surged up the courthouse steps. With the press in close pursuit, I passed through the metal detectors leading into the federal courthouse. I never wanted to see that place again, but how else was my story going to be heard?

8:00 a.m. The bell rang, and I entered the ring again. I was bloodied and bruised, but far from being defeated. Walking by faith and supported by the love of family, I marched into a packed courtroom and took my seat at the defense counsel's table. The solemnity of our defense team was only exceeded by the arrogant appearance of the prosecution. With several court benches filled with their cronies, the prosecution stood, surveying the courtroom with a smug look on their faces.

"Attorney Ramsey, you may call your next witness."

"Your Honor, the defense calls Mr. Tucker to the stand."

"Alright, Mr. Tucker, please come forth."

Standing in my dark-blue suit and conservative paisley tie, I raised my right hand, took the oath, and mounted the witness stand. It was the answer to the question that pundits had asked all along: Would Walter Tucker take the stand in his own defense? There was no further need for speculation. There I was. It was like stepping into the lion's den, and hoping that God would do what He did for Daniel—keep the hungry lions' mouths shut. Nevertheless, I knew that taking the stand was my only hope.

With my life hanging in the balance, I took one careful look at the jurors and then watched my methodical attorney approach the lectern for direct examination. In our conference the night before, Bob and I decided it was important to first paint a picture of the man, Walter R. Tucker III, and then to address the more substantive areas of the charges. So, Bob began by asking me about my early life in Los Angeles.

"Mr. Tucker, where were you born?"

"I was born in Los Angeles, and raised in Compton, California."

I testified that I was the second oldest of four children, and a product of a strong, close-knit family. Bob offered the jury an image of a boy who was studious, obedient, morally-centered, and an achiever. From High School Valedictorian of Compton High School to Princeton University, to Georgetown Law School, to the Los Angeles District Attorney's Office.

Bob was experienced enough to know that the prosecution would certainly grill me about being fired from the DA's office and paint it darker than it was. Therefore, he approached the issue head-on before going any further.

"Mr. Tucker, why did you leave the District Attorney's Office?"

"I was terminated in the fall of nineteen eighty-six. I had a problem with a case I was prosecuting and made a mistake with that case."

"Would you elaborate, please?"

"Yes. I was single-handedly prosecuting five gang members accused of selling illegal drugs on the streets; fighting their five highly-skilled and vocal defense attorneys. I had one of my investigators take and blow up a photo of the crime scene. After I gave a copy of the photo to the defense and attempted to introduce it into evidence, the defense pressed me about when the photo was taken. I wasn't sure of the exact date the photo was taken, but when asked by the court I gave a date I recalled in my mind. At recess, I researched the matter in the Records Department and discovered I was wrong—the photo had been taken days earlier. In a state of panic, I altered the date on the public record to conform to the one I had given the court. I was charged with a making a false statement to the court—a felony. However, the DA agreed to my 'no contest' plea to a misdemeanor—altering a public document, and was fired from the DA's Office."

If I hadn't been so caught up in winning, I never would have made that stupid mistake. Nothing seemed more important at the time than stomping out drugs on our streets, drugs that destroyed entire families, and left them hopeless, helpless, and paralyzed from daily life. Then after I realized I had erred, panic blurred my good judgment, and I did that stupid thing. All I had to do was go back to the court and tell the judge I had made a mistake. Whether that crime scene photo was admitted into evidence or not was a minor issue to the case. I had allowed stress and fear to get the best of me. I hate what I did. God was trying to mold me into the man He wants me to be, even back then. Hindsight truly is 20/20.

"What, if anything did you do after the DA's Office?"

"Fortunately, because it was a misdemeanor, I didn't lose my license to practice law. So, after my time with the DA's office, I started my own criminal defense practice in Compton."

"At some point did you become a politician in Compton?"

"Yes, when my father, the mayor of Compton, died in October, nineteen ninety, I ran to fill his unexpired term and won. I became the mayor of Compton."

"Now, Mr. Tucker, let's talk about April of nineteen ninety-two…"

Bob took me through the period in my life when I was mayor of Compton and the L.A. riots broke out. He made a point of sharing with the jury how I served faithfully and saved Compton from destruction. Several photo blow-ups were offered into evidence, but Judge Marshall only allowed one—the one of me touring riot-torn South Central Los Angeles with President George

Bush and Governor Pete Wilson. It was the picture worth a thousand words. Then it was time to turn to the matter at hand.

"Now, Mr. Tucker, where did you first meet John Macardican?"

"At Congressman Mervyn Dymally's fundraiser in Beverly Hills, in May of ninety-one."

"How did you come to meet him?"

"My office landlord, Walter Cathey, one of Congressman Dymally's personal friends, introduced him to me.

"You hadn't met him before?"

"No. I knew the name because I'd seen it on my dad's campaign statements."

"Did you ever say to him, 'We need to talk'?"

"No, I said, '*People keep saying* we need to talk.' "

"What people were you referring to?"

"Pat Moore and Walter Cathey. They said, 'There's someone you should meet.'"

"And did you call him after that initial meeting at the fundraiser?"

"No. The next thing I knew I got a call from former city planner, Bob Gavin, for a lunch date. At lunch, I found out that Mr. Gavin was now working as a consultant for Mr. Macardican."

"When was this?"

"May twentieth, nineteen ninety-one at the Mustard Seed Restaurant, Long Beach."

Eventually, Bob directed my attention to the first meeting between Macardican and me at the City Grille in Long Beach. It was there where Macardican was strapped with a secret recording device, and we discussed the Compton Energy Systems project. It was our strategy to go through all of the transcripts from that meeting, and rebut, line by line, all the innuendoes the government had planted in the minds of the jury by Macardican's testimony.

What was at stake, from a legal standpoint, was the question of intent. The law on entrapment made it clear that the critical issue was the defendant's intent, not the intent of the person trying to entrap him. Did Mayor Walter Tucker intend to do an "official act" in exchange for payment? Did Mayor Walter Tucker intend to use his office, his position ("color of authority") to receive payments to which he knew he was not entitled?

First, Bob took me through a series of transcript pages that covered the beginning of the lunch meeting.

How I've been waiting for this! Now it's my turn to interpret those comments made in the transcripts.

"May I approach the witness, Your Honor?" Bob asked.

"Yes."

"Now, Mr. Tucker, on page two, line fourteen of the transcript, what are we talking about here?"

"Here, he's letting me know that he knew my father. He mentions that my father was a good man and that he supported the project."

"What was your reaction to that?"

"It made me feel good to hear that about my dad, but looking back, now I believe he wanted me to have a sentimental attachment to the project right off the bat."

"Had you heard of the project before?" Bob asked.

"Yes, vaguely, just by way of living in the community. I heard of some of the problems they had in nineteen eighty-four, but nothing in real detail. I just knew that Councilwoman Moore vehemently protested it and subsequently, the project died."

"When Mr. Macardican presented his project to you in ninety-one, did you have an open ear?"

"Of course. That was a different time, and now he was proposing a different site. And based on the fact that he was talking jobs, and addressing our public policy need to abate waste, I was all ears."

"Did you ask about the project, or did Mr. Macardican present it to you?"

"Once Bob Gavin explained the project to me in general terms, I asked him who was the developer. He said it was John Macardican, and that the developer could give me more information."

"And did you want to hear more about the project?"

"Yes, I thought that was the reasonable thing to do."

"Did you ask for Mr. Macardican's phone number?"

"No, I gave Mr. Gavin my phone number in case Mr. Macardican wanted to follow up with me."

"What number did you give him?"

"My law office number."

"Why?"

"Because I was mostly at my law office. As a part-time mayor, I tried to stay at my law office as much as I could to keep my practice afloat. At the same time, I would handle city-related calls as they came in. This is the way I saw my father do it before me. He practiced dentistry while being a part-time mayor, and very often had to handle calls related to city business from his dental office."

"Are you sure you didn't give him your law office number in order to conceal some illegal practice?"

"Of course, not."

Jab, jab, jab. Stick and move. Let's keep scoring points, Bob. I know we fell behind on points, but I feel a comeback comin' on!

Bob fumbled through his papers and appeared momentarily disoriented.

"Your Honor, in light of the time, would this be a good place to stop and pick it up tomorrow?" Bob asked.

No, no! We're on a roll.

"If there are no objections from the government..."

"No objections, Your Honor," Madison replied.

"Alright then, court is in recess until tomorrow morning at nine a.m."

Judge Marshall pounded her gavel and our momentum disappeared with the sound of it.

CHAPTER THIRTY-EIGHT

Life-Changing Lunch

L ater that night at home, I mused over my direct examination and reflected on the details of that infamous lunch with Macardican.

* * * * * *

The attentive waiter appeared at our table again. Seeing my water glass was empty, he asked, "May I pour you some more water, sir?"

"Yes, please," I replied.

He filled my glass, and I said, "Thank you." He departed.

I resumed speaking to Macardican. "Since the state is mandating cities to increase our capacity to reduce waste by twenty-five percent, by nineteen ninety-four, the project sounds great. If it passes environmental review and creates jobs, that's a winner. You should do fine."

"I wish it was that easy," Macardican said.

"What do you mean?"

I didn't want anything to be wrong with a project my dad thought was good for Compton. It could be a windfall that would benefit Compton far into the future. I visualized a new city that was economically and environmentally sound, one where every citizen would be an integral part of its soundness—a model of progress for other cities. I wanted to support that, but not seem overly optimistic.

"Well, I've been around the block a few times. In the eighties, I made a lot of mistakes. I crossed Pat Moore, and she didn't like that," Macardican said.

He was referring to Patricia Moore, the woman who served on the City Council with me. In the '80s, she made a name for herself as a fiery community activist, taking on anything she considered to be unjust.

"I had a good idea, and all things being equal, it should have passed the council then, but Pat Moore created the politics that did me in," he moaned.

"Well, it's all politics," I said, trying to sound savvy about such matters.

"I had a white New York banker and that bothered a lot of people, but I realize now that when you're a white person coming into a black community, it's not prejudice—"

"Just political reality," I interrupted.

"Yeah," he said, "you just don't know where to come from, or how to work it."

I nodded.

"You see, this time, I figure I'm gonna do it right. This time I'm gonna get with somebody like you and get some good advice; find out what I need to do to get to the right people. Have them on my side and make this happen."

I knew this businessman was trying to get me to help him achieve what he wanted. However, if his project could help my struggling city, I'd give him good advice to help him.

"Well, politics is a funny game," I said. "You definitely do have to know the players in power. With a project like yours, you want to do your advance work, touch bases with the people who make the decisions, and lay to rest any environmental concerns. You need to put yourself in a position where you already have support."

Because of the talks my dad used to have with me on Sunday afternoons, I sounded knowledgeable, like a seasoned mayor who could get things done.

"I'll do whatever has to be done," he said.

Although I had just been in office a few days and didn't know as much as my dad, I still knew it was all about the residents having jobs that could afford them a better life. It was about taking care of the citizens by creating a solid tax base in the city.

"So, what's the status of your project? Do you have a site? Is it up for a vote?" I asked.

"No, we're a long way from any vote. We've got our eyes on a piece of property that's owned by the school district, located at Central and Greenleaf."

"I know the area. Have you talked with the school board members?"

"No, that's where I need your advice. I don't even know where to begin. Who should I talk to?" Macardican asked.

"Well, it sounds like you've got your work cut out for you."

"Yes, and politically, who do I support, and how? I'm gonna tell you right now, I don't want anybody to know I supported anybody because that's like cutting your own throat," he said. As our conversation continued, Macardican restated his mantra, "I don't want anybody else to know, and I'll do whatever it takes to get it done."

Something stirred inside me. *I need to help him move this project forward.*

"Well, there are ways around that. You can get one of your relatives to give my campaign a contribution," I said.

I gave Macardican the political advice he asked for. I offered him an option based on what I had heard that some politicians would do. They would come as close to the line as possible to keep the press from killing a project before it got off the ground. Of course, my dad took no such chances.

By the time dessert came, I resigned myself to accept Macardican's support in exchange for my advice to help him navigate through the murky waters of Compton politics. I didn't see our conversation as one about him getting my vote for money, but about him getting a fair shake. If his project passed environmental scrutiny, I'd support it on its own merits. And that was that.

CHAPTER THIRTY-NINE

The Whole Truth

The next day, after a restless night's sleep, I was back on the witness stand to continue my direct examination. I knew that Bob's next series of questions would produce the most important answers and information of this entire case.

I've been wanting the jury to hear this from the very beginning.

"So, did you spend any time talking about the merits of the project with Mr. Macardican?" Bob asked.

"Yes. As you heard from the transcripts, we spent the first half of our lunch talking about the project, possible environmental issues, and political issues."

"Were you sold on the project?"

"No, but I liked what I had heard so far."

"What, if anything, did you understand Mr. Macardican to be asking you for?"

"A fair shake. He spent a great deal of time telling me how city officials had become jaded by the community protests, and he felt he never got a fair hearing."

"Alright, let's look at some specific references. What did you think he meant when he said, 'I'll do whatever has to be done'?"

"I believed he was referring to learning about the politics of Compton, lobbying public officials, and giving them campaign contributions."

"Did you understand him to also imply giving bribes?"

"No. I didn't think he meant anything illegal at the time. Since then, I see he meant something else."

"Objection, Your Honor."

"Overruled. The answer will stand."

"So Mr. Macardican said he never got a fair shake in the eighties?" Bob asked.

"Yes, he said the City Council voted *against* his waste project."

"And he indicated he was partly to blame?"

"Yes, he said his errors included not lobbying council members or supporting their political campaigns."

Bob repeatedly took me to places in the transcripts where, as far as I was concerned, Macardican and I had a misunderstanding.

"On this page here in the transcript," Bob pointed, "what did you mean when you said, 'get your ducks in a row'?"

"When I said get your ducks in a row, I meant he should lobby and educate people, not bribe politicians."

"Did you receive money from Mr. Macardican?"

"Yes, on a few occasions."

"What for?"

"For consulting, not for my vote."

"Did you ever specify as such to him?"

"Yes."

"Mr. Tucker, how can you explain why a conversation concerning your role as Mr. Macardican's consultant does not appear on tape?"

"If the prosecution doesn't have a tape of that conversation, it's either because they chose not to record it, or bring it to court. They've been in control of the tapes from the start, not me."

Absolute silence filled the courtroom. Bob removed his glasses and thumbed through some pages on his legal pad.

"So, Mr. Tucker, where did this conversation take place?"

"Outside of Macardican's office."

"When?"

"I don't recall the exact date, but it was about two weeks after the May thirtieth luncheon. I saw him walking in the parking lot near the stairs leading to his office, and I approached him."

"Why did you approach him?"

"I was feeling uneasy after the luncheon. His insistence that payments to me be made in cash instead of checks bothered me. I wanted to be sure he understood that while I was taking cash, it was for consulting and not for my vote."

"So what did you say to him?"

"I told him I needed to clarify our agreement. I said, 'Fine, it can be cash as long as you understand I'm earning it.' "

I also testified that not long after I took the initial $2,000 cash payment from Macardican there was another time during which I again sought to make it clear to him that the money I received was not in exchange for my vote.

"Where did this conversation take place?"

"In my car, in the parking lot between his office and mine."

"Who was present?"

"Just me, alone again with Macardican."

"What led you to clarify things again with him?" Bob asked.

"When he gave me the two-thousand-dollar cash payment, he made the statement, 'That should secure your vote.' That statement really threw me for a loop. It just came out of left field. As days went by, I reflected on it and realized there may be some significant misunderstanding that needed to be cleared up. So that's when I spoke with him about it in my car."

"What did you say?"

"I reiterated that my support was based on the merits of the project and while I supported the idea in general, the environmental impact report was key."

"What, if anything, was Mr. Macardican's response?"

"He said, 'This time I know everything's alright.' "

"Anything further, Mr. Ramsey?" Judge Marshall asked.

Bob tilted his glasses downward and flipped a couple of pages of his legal pad.

"No, Your Honor, I have nothing further for Mr. Tucker."

"Alright, in light of the hour, let us recess, and resume with direct examination tomorrow morning."

After I had gone through two long days of direct examination, I felt at peace. I had moved through the questions calmly and had given the truth, no matter what it looked like. I was glad to get off the witness stand and leave that courtroom for the moment. As I darted down the federal courthouse steps, heading toward my car, a crowd of reporters set out in chase. At the bottom of the stairs, they surrounded me.

"So the whole thing was one big misunderstanding then, is that right, sir?" a reporter shouted from the group.

"Why don't you think he understood you, Congressman?" another reporter called out.

"Do you blame Macardican for twisting things out of proportion?"

I felt overwhelmed with the questions as they melded together into one big white noise. Thankfully, my attorney interceded. "This young man has already answered all those questions on the stand today and I guarantee you, we'll be back here tomorrow."

Bob and Mark rushed me to my car and we sped off.

Before long we were back to the solace of the Tichenor house. But there was no peace at our dinner table that night. If the family wasn't discussing the finer points of the day's trial, we were watching snippets of it on the news.

"Daddy, Daddy, you're on TV again!" my seven-year-old son said.

Being on TV again was not a big deal for me. It was being on the stand again that made my heart race.

Wednesday, November 8, 1995, was my fourth and last day on direct examination. Under Bob's gentle questioning, I had jumped out in front on every major issue, except one—the infamous vote on the Exclusive Right to Negotiate. Now it was time for us to address it and complete my direct examination.

"Did you vote to give Mr. Macardican's company, Compton Energy Systems, an Exclusive Negotiating Agreement."

"Yes."

"Why?"

"I voted for it because it was the right thing to do, not because I was given twenty thousand dollars by Mr. Macardican. If the project was going to sink or swim, it would do it on its own merits," I said. "The Exclusive Negotiating Agreement would permit Mr. Macardican's company to proceed with a feasibility study, and to have the city consider its plan for six months to a year, exclusively. But the agreement did *not* bind the city to approve the project, nor grant permission to build."

A sudden cough sounded in the courtroom, and my statement seemed to resound in the ears of the audience. Nevertheless, through Macardican's testimony, the government had presented that three days after the approval of the Exclusive Negotiating Agreement, Macardican delivered a $10,000 check to me. Bob confronted me with that fact on the stand.

"Now, Mr. Tucker, shortly after the approval of the Exclusive Negotiating Agreement you received a check from Mr. Macardican for ten thousand dollars, correct?

"Right."

"What was that check for?"

"Based on our consulting relationship, I asked Mr. Macardican for a loan. I did not consider it as payment for my vote."

"And in a secretly recorded meeting between you and Mr. Macardican, did you tell him he should 'make some small but rather significant contributions to a couple of key pastors in Compton as insurance for his project'?"

This is a "no-brainer." Churches in inner cities have always helped to educate the citizens about political issues that affect their lives.

"Yes, I recommended that he make contributions to some key churches to establish educational forums so that all Compton citizens could have a better understanding of his project and its benefits to them and our community. I thought it would be good for the people to know about this project."

"Now, Mr. Tucker, as to the issue of your taxes, you have been charged with willfully falsifying your nineteen ninety-one and nineteen ninety-two tax returns, did you?"

"No, my records were boxed up and left behind when I was elected to Congress in nineteen ninety-two and moved from L.A. to Washington D.C. My life was a whirlwind and admittedly some things slipped through the cracks. Mr. Macardican's payments to me over a two-year period didn't show up on my tax returns due to my own negligence. But I have since found my records and amended my tax returns."

Bob displayed a blown-up photo of a disorganized assembly of boxes from the Tichenor house garage that contained my financial records.

"Sir, showing you Defense Exhibit thirty-five, do you recognize this photo?"

"Yes, that's a photo of my many boxes of paperwork from my law office, mayor's office, and personal finances." I shrugged. "I should have done a better job of keeping records."

Bob glanced at his notes, then looked up, "That's all that I have for direct examination, Your Honor."

"Alright then, will the government be ready for cross-examination tomorrow?"

"We will, Your Honor."

"Court is adjourned until tomorrow morning at nine," Judge Marshall rapped her gavel.

CHAPTER FORTY

Rolling with The Punches

Thursday, November 9, 1995, separated the men from the boys. It was time for cross-examination. I braced myself for the worst because I had an idea of what was coming. I hoped I'd still be standing after it was all over. There would be no more hand-holding from my attorney. No more friendly faces. No more foreknowledge of what questions were coming. The gloves were off, and Assistant U.S. Attorney Madison was waiting in his corner, positioning himself, ready to charge forward at the sound of the bell.

Like a confident boxer, he seemed to be visualizing every stinging blow he was about to deliver. First, a few left jabs, then a right, then a left again, then an uppercut. It promised to be a brutal, bloody, and oh-so-exhilarating spectacle. Not many could say that they had the opportunity to pounce on the likes of Walter Tucker—an ex-deputy district attorney, former mayor, and current congressman. I could see the adrenaline flowing over Madison's face as well as the venom dripping from his mouth.

My family and I—Robin, Martha, my sisters, and brother—huddled in the side hallway in prayer. We knew these next few days would be trial by fire. But I'd come this far by faith, and I knew the only way I could possibly see the light and the truth at the end of the tunnel was to stay in the lion's den and have faith that God would not allow them to consume me. My black Bible lay open to Psalm 57 on the defense counsel's table. Just the memorizing of it encouraged me:

"Be merciful unto me, O God, be merciful unto me: for my soul trusteth in thee: yea, in the shadow of thy wings will I make my refuge, until these calamities be overpast." (KJV Psalm 57:1)

I had faced challenges from Attorney Madison on multiple fronts—all designed to damage my integrity while I was mayor of Compton. Now, I expected that he would attack my prior misdemeanor conviction while I worked in the District Attorney's office. That's exactly what he did.

"Mr. Tucker, when you were a deputy district attorney and altered a public document, that wasn't a mistake, was it?" Madison asked.

"I made a mistake in judgment," I answered.

"In fact, it was a series of intentional acts—the mistake was an intentional act on your part, isn't that right?" Madison charged.

"I made a mistake and the mistake was followed up by a wrongful intentional act. We sometimes make mistakes in life, then make things worse by trying to fix them instead of humbling ourselves and owning up to them. I didn't go to court that day thinking, 'I'm going to lie to the court and the defense.' In the heat of trying to convict some drug dealers, I made a huge error in judgment. Then, realizing what I had done, I panicked and tried to cover it up. Obviously, I only made a bad situation worse," I admitted.

Not getting all the damage he wanted out of that line of questioning, Madison then hammered away at my statement that I acted as a consultant for Macardican.

"You advised Mr. Macardican to make illegal campaign contributions through other people, isn't that right?"

"No, I just told him to encourage his friends to contribute to campaigns, not to funnel his money through them."

"But you never phrased your advice to Mr. Macardican that clearly, now did you?"

"I could have said a lot of things. But I said what I said, and I meant what I meant."

At times, the calm demeanor I had maintained during the five days of my attorney's direct examination now cracked with agitation. At one point, I challenged Madison, saying, "That misstates the evidence, sir," and was admonished by the judge for shooting back at Madison.

"Mr. Tucker, your job is to answer the questions, not to ask them," Judge Marshall offered.

"Yes, Your Honor."

Next, Madison tore into the matter of the parking lot meeting I had with Macardican two weeks after our initial lunch meeting.

"Why didn't you telephone Mr. Macardican at his office right after your May thirtieth lunch, since you were concerned about your understanding with him? Why did you wait two weeks to confront him?"

"I was busy with a lot of things, but I did eventually clarify things with him."

"Show me any reference of this meeting in the nearly thirty hours of tapes submitted by the government."

"I didn't make the tapes, the government did. They don't reflect all the conversations that Macardican and I had, and they know that! I can't control what they decide to bring into court and what they decide to leave out."

"Isn't it true, Mr. Tucker, that a parking lot meeting where you discussed your consulting services never occurred?"

"No, that's not true. His office was right next door to my building. The parking lot is the one I walk through daily to go to court. I simply ran into him."

"Do you know whether or not he even had the keys to the office?"

"No, I do not...neither did I know his office was a front for an FBI sting operation!"

A favorable groan seeped out of the audience.

When Madison asked me about areas in the recordings where I failed to clarify what Macardican's payments were for, I became argumentative.

"If I knew you all were trying to set me up, then I wouldn't have said, 'Okay, uh-huh, all right.' Like I said before, I never agreed with Macardican's money-for-votes comment. It came out of the blue and went straight over my head. But as I testified on direct examination, I set him straight days later when I talked with him in the car."

Unfortunately for me, the conversation in the car was not recorded. The two FBI agents who had monitored that conversation disagreed with my version of it.

"Are you saying they're lying?" Madison asked.

"I'm not calling them liars, but they're mistaken."

At the end of the day, Madison fought hard to destroy my defense team's portrayal of me as an inexperienced politician who was led astray by a slick and overzealous FBI operative. Madison noted that I had worked in my late father's political campaigns, and was not that innocent.

Before he concluded his cross-examination, Madison turned his attention to the issue of my tax returns.

"Isn't it true, Mr. Tucker, that Mr. Macardican's payments to you over a two-year period didn't show up on your tax returns because you knew they were ill-gotten gain?"

"No, as I explained on direct examination, it was bad record-keeping on my part. As I testified, I have since amended my tax returns to reflect those payments and some other income that I neglected to report."

Madison's cross-examination proved to be high drama for the U.S. Attorney's office. It was like a public execution with no shortage of spectators. More than 40 prosecutors and staffers stopped by Judge Marshall's courtroom to see at least part of it. But after it was all said and done, I was still breathing, and still standing. I had been knocked down, but now I was on my feet, taking a standing eight count.

During the final day of my cross, Madison tried to strike the final, knockout blow by convincing the jury that I solicited a $250,000 bribe from Robert Kilbane, an FBI agent posing as Robert Kelly, Macardican's financier. Nevertheless, in my answers to Madison's questions, I believed I proved that it was the government's operatives who were trying to entrap me. I testified that Kilbane left messages for me at my law office in an attempt to entrap me, but I didn't return his calls.

Madison accused me of lying, saying that my secretary didn't take messages on the type of notepads I had described. When challenged to produce the messages, I said, "I have been searching for them, but I cannot find them. I turned everything over to you and the FBI."

Spectators amongst the government's camp snickered.

"Anything further, Mr. Madison?"

"Nothing further, Your Honor."

"You may step down, Mr. Tucker."

Madison sat with confidence at the government's table as I left the witness stand for the last time. He had given me his best shots, and though they were powerful I did not fold; I did not break. Madison's posture seemed to say he had done enough damage to sway the jury.

Bob leaned over and whispered to me, "You took his best shot."

I whispered back, "I hope so."

The next day the government picked up where it left off. They called FBI agent Gary Will as a rebuttal witness. Bob's cross-examination of Agent Will was brief and pointed. "So, Agent Will, after Mr. Tucker's testimony yesterday, did you review the documents more thoroughly?"

"Yes."

"And what did you discover?"

"I discovered a phone message from Agent Kilbane."

"Written on the type of notepad Mr. Tucker described, and during the period of time to which he referred?"

"Yes," Agent Will replied reluctantly.

"May I have a moment, Your Honor?"

"Yes."

Bob pivoted back to me at the defense counsel's table.

"Anything else, Congressman?" he whispered.

"And they said I lied about that too. That notepad is proof they were chasing me down, trying to tack on even more bribery charges against me," I whispered back. "No, nothing else. The point is made."

It was one of those special moments of validation in this long, arduous trial.

Bob returned to the podium. "No further questions for this witness, Your Honor."

"Anything further from the government?" Judge Marshall asked.

"No, Your Honor."

"Defense?"

"No, Your Honor."

"Alright, I'll expect closing arguments bright and early tomorrow morning. Court adjourned," she rapped her gavel sharply.

Those were the words I knew would one day come in this protracted trial. I was happy to gather up my belongings and leave that dark, repressive courtroom. When I walked into the crowded, buzzing halls, I overheard Madison giving his daily update to the press.

"Attorney Madison, the defense's case ended on a high note for them, don't you think?" the reporter asked.

"The truth about one single message slip will be of little help to Mr. Tucker. Bottom line, he's buried under a mountain of evidence that we've presented."

Bob passed by and quickly a female reporter grabbed for him.

"Oh, Attorney Ramsey, I'd love to have a quote now that you've finished presenting your evidence to the jury?" she asked.

"Well, as it has been said, it's not over till it's over. Mr. Tucker is going home to spend some quality time with his wife and kids, and then we're going to get ready for closing arguments."

Bob shot me a look and then we both walked defensively through the crowd. I was already pressured about the weight of tomorrow's closing remarks. How would my mild-mannered attorney stand up against the giants that faced us? Only tomorrow would tell.

CHAPTER FORTY-ONE

Offspring

Exhausted by the legal marathon, my only solace was spending time at home with my wife and two children. As I watched Robin making dinner, Walter and Autumn chatted with each other at the table, as if nothing had changed from our joyful beginning.

* * * * * *

Just ten years ago my life had been so simple and settled. The girl of my dreams was now the wife of my youth. Robin and I rented a lovely little apartment in Paramount, California. I was working downtown in Central Trials, where all the big trials were making headlines. One day, I was certain to be a part of that. Life was good.

In November of '85, I got a call at work from Robin saying she had been sick at her office that morning. Without questions, I rushed home and found Robin already sitting on the sofa looking drained.

"You alright?" I asked.

She nodded as I sat beside her.

"What happened?"

"All of a sudden I felt queasy. I ran into the bathroom and almost passed out."

"I hear the stomach flu is going around—"

She looked straight into my eyes and said, "Honey, I think I'm pregnant."

"Pregnant?"

Suddenly, it hit me. *Is this real? Am I really about to become a dad?*

After a trip to the gynecologist, it was confirmed. My wife was pregnant! The months that followed brought a whole new experience for us: morning sickness, unpredictable moods, and shopping for the baby. We were excited and fearful at the same time. The whole family was excited for us, especially since this would be my parents' first grandchild. Naturally, I wanted a boy because he could carry on the family name and follow in his dad's footsteps. But after reading *Daddy's Girl*, a poem about a father's love for his daughter, I romanticized that our first baby would be a girl.

We couldn't resist the temptation of modern medicine, so an ultrasound gave us the gender of our unborn baby.

"You will be the proud parents of a baby boy. See there, his little, bitty penis right there."

We were going to have a boy! We had already agreed that if it were a boy, we would name him after his granddad and me—Walter R. Tucker, IV.

One night, in the last month of Robin's pregnancy, we were eating a delicious fried chicken dinner that Robin had cooked especially for me. Suddenly, Robin looked at me and said, "Honey, something's wrong. I feel like I pulled something when I brought the groceries up the stairs today."

We made a wild dash to the hospital. It seemed like, in no time, we were inside the hospital room and a sense of relief took over, seeing Robin surrounded by nurses.

"Robin, do you need anything?"

"Just call my mom and dad let them know I'm here at the hospital."

I rushed to find a phone and brought Robin's parents up to date. "She's fine. Probably a false alarm."

When I returned to Robin's hospital room, everything had changed. I found myself in a thick air of tension. Robin was breathing heavily and the nurses were running around in panic mode.

"What's going on?" I asked one of the nurses.

"Your wife's placenta separated from her uterus."

"Can you give that to me in layman's terms, please?"

"We lost the baby's heartbeat and the doctor decided to break your wife's water so we can hurry up and get him out."

I started praying, "Oh God, please don't let anything bad happen to my wife or my child, in Jesus' name."

Just then, all hell broke loose. Robin began to have close and hard contractions while hyperventilating. Seeing her writhing with pain, I tried to encourage her to focus.

"Honey, remember Lamaze class," I said. "You've just gotta breathe. Hee-Hee-Hoo, Hee-Hee-Hoo. Focus!"

Before I could get the next round of breaths out of my mouth, Robin slapped me. *Pow!*

"Don't talk to me about focusing! You did this to me!" she screamed. I reared back for safety.

What in the world! I've never seen my wife act like this!

"Okay now, Robin, you're going to have to push," the head nurse said.

"I am!" Robin yelled.

"Breathe, and push harder!"

"Oh, God!" Robin held her breath and pushed.

In the midst of this intense drama, I was seeing our son, Walter, slowly enter the world. It was the most incredible sight I had ever witnessed. No film or class can truly prepare someone for such a moment. Finally, he was out, covered with blood and fluids. The doctor asked if I wanted to cut the cord. I did while reeling, and about to faint. The nurses quickly cleaned our baby up and lay him on Robin's chest. She held him lovingly. What came next was one of the most important moments of my life.

"Mr. Tucker, would you like to hold him?" the nurse asked.

While I was nervous that I might drop him, I extended my arms and held the tiny little guy, gazing at him with great pride. Walter R. Tucker, IV, my namesake, my son.

What will he grow up to be? How tall will he be? Will he one day give us grandchildren? Suddenly, those questions were silenced by one single thought: *I've gotta be the best father in the world.*

I whispered into Walter's ear, "I promise to be the best dad for you. I will protect you, direct you, and be a godly example for you so that you can be everything God called you to be."

Walter holding his son, Walter R. Tucker, IV, after his birth.

I handed Walter back to the nurse, then leaned in close and kissed Robin on the forehead, whispering, "You did it. I love you."

She shot me a look that said, *"Right now, I love you and I hate you all at the same time."*

Nevertheless, I was excited to have a son with her. I knew she would be a great mother. Any fantasies I may have had about living an entertainment lawyer's lifestyle were put to rest. No late nights, socializing with the rich and famous and flirting with a world of temptation. I was now a dad, a man responsible for a family. I would continue to work at the DA's office to maintain a sober and secure future for them.

In 1988 my family and I moved from our two-bedroom apartment in Paramount to a two- bedroom townhouse in nearby Bellflower. We opted for a townhouse because it had an attached two-car garage and we needed some storage space. On April 4th of that year, I was defending a client in a felony trial in downtown L.A. We had just picked a jury, and the prosecution asked the court for a short recess. Seeing that it was already afternoon, the judge decided to put the case over to the next morning, and have the evidence start fresh. I was happy for that unexpected break, so I checked in with Robin at home, since we were getting close to our second baby's due date.

"Hi, honey, everything alright?" I asked.

"I think I need to go to the hospital," Robin said.

I picked up Robin from home and still in my suit and tie, rushed her to the hospital. Robin was relieved to see the doctor.

"Thank you, Doctor, for seeing me on such short notice. This is my husband, Walter."

The doctor looked me up and down. "So, Mr. Tucker, what kind of job do you have that you can be here at this time of the day?"

"I'm a defense attorney on recess from a felony trial in downtown L.A. We start back up tomorrow morning," I said.

"Oh, my," he said. "It's time to have this baby."

Robin shot the doctor a look, but before she could marshal an objection, the doctor prepped her and induced labor. Robin writhed in pain and started hyperventilating, but this time I knew better than to try to tell her how to breathe. Instead, I offered my hand.

"Honey, squeeze my hand when it hurts."

She grabbed it and squeezed until it was numb.

As the contractions came quicker and stronger, I said, "Push, honey. Push!"

I guess it's easy for me to say the second labor was not as long or as difficult as the first. But Robin said she'd rather walk barefoot on hot coals than go through childbirth again. All I knew was excitement. I was finally holding our baby girl in my arms—

Autumn Mone't Tucker. She was the most beautiful baby girl I had ever seen.

I whispered into Autumn's ear, "I promise to be the best dad for you for your entire life. I will protect you, direct you, and be a godly example for you so that you can be everything God called you to be."

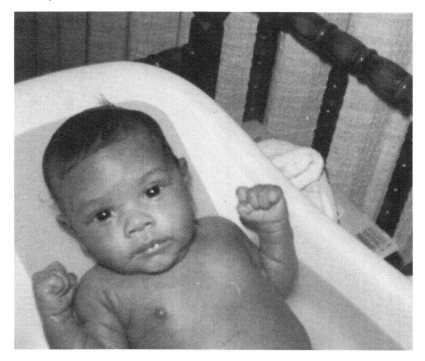

Autumn in her crib.

Robin's sister, Nedra, had all girls, and her brother, Mark, had all boys. We had secretly hoped we would have one of each. Robin and I looked at each other with a joyful grin as if to say, "We're done."

Being the father of two children motivated me to kick things up a notch. I had been working from my home, but within a couple of weeks, I rented office space in downtown Compton, hung out my shingle, and added a legal staff, which consisted of my friend, Wanda Williams, as my legal secretary. The Law Offices of Walter R. Tucker III was born.

I was no longer a smug college kid who wanted to be rich and famous by the time he turned thirty-five. I was a young father who wanted to earn enough to provide for his family, send his children to college, and ensure that their future would be filled with great opportunities. There was a "Tucker name," a legacy, to uphold, and I wanted to make sure they upheld it.

My children were tiny then, but oh how I wanted them to know about their great legacy! They were too young to know that their great, great grandfather refused to be a slave, and started our family on a journey of academic excellence. They were too young to understand that their granddad was the first black man ever re-elected mayor of Compton. They were too young to appreciate that he didn't get to be mayor overnight. They were too young to appreciate the many sacrifices I was making for them and would continue to make for them until their adulthood. But one day I knew they would know and understand and it would affect their lives in a positive way.

* * * * * *

Now as I continued to watch my nine and seven-year-old chatting at the dinner table, their laughter quickly turned into an argument over a bottle of ketchup.

"Daddy, Walter's not leaving me any ketchup."

"Son, you have to learn to share."

As I settled their dispute, I realized that the verdict, which could come now at any moment, could greatly affect my son and daughter's future. If I should lose the case, I wouldn't be around to help them with their increasingly difficult math homework, celebrate their birthdays, or cheer them on at their graduations. I think they had only a vague understanding of what was happening to our lives. But no matter which way the road of life turned, I still wanted to be the best dad in the world for them. I still wanted to make good on the promises I made to them when they were born.

CHAPTER FORTY-TWO

Final Round

Thursday, December 1, nine o'clock am: It was time for closing arguments. Not one seat in Judge Marshall's court-room was empty. People even crowded against the back walls. That day no one could say whether this high drama would lead to a verdict of not guilty, or guilty.

My wife, mother, and siblings braced themselves in the first row. Some of my supporters held Bibles and wore solemn faces; others stretched to see every one of the attorneys' moves and perched to take notes as soon as the arguments began. As usual, my black Bible lay in plain view on the defense table in front of me. I felt that all eyes focused on me as I turned toward Robin and the family and gave a nod of reassurance.

Suddenly the bailiff belted out, "All rise!" The crowd stood in unison. I too rose with my attorneys flanking me on each side.

"You may be seated," Judge Marshall stated.

After seven weeks of evidence, it had all come down to this—the battle of the mouthpieces, the tango of the trial attor-neys. As most legal experts know, it is the summations by the opposing counsels that can easily determine the outcome of a case.

Would my political future be delivered or destroyed? With blood-shot eyes and unsteady hands from pulling an all-nighter, my mind instinctively darted back to last night.

I had been so busy preparing notes for Bob's closing that, unlike the typical defendant, I had no time to think about the outcome. Those early morning hours were like the last minute of a 12-round heavyweight bout. I kept bobbing and weaving, trying to deliver a knock-out to replace the rather mild closing that Bob had written.

Yes, I was exhausted, bleeding, and possibly losing the fight, but none of that mattered then. This was "do or die." The only thing that mattered was our last chance to sway the jury to our side. I needed one more chance to land the knockout blow. One more chance to fight my way out of the pitfalls of my past and land into the liberty of my future. Because this was for all the marbles—freedom, family, life, liberty, and the pursuit of happiness—I had to punch with everything I had left in me.

Super-human adrenaline tore through the fear in my veins until it was twelve o'clock a.m., then three, then five. Finally, I finished a draft I felt good about. Everything was in clear, plain language. There were also several clever sound bites the jury would be able to hold onto; language I strongly felt would guide them to a not-guilty verdict. I only wished we had more time for Bob to mull over it, practice reading it before his presentation.

Although Bob had lived with my case for months, I didn't trust his ability to hold a narrow focus on the entrapment issue in the closing argument. My testimony during the trial had made an undeniable case for entrapment. And, if guided properly, the jury would see and understand that this whole matter of me receiving money from Macardican was initiated by him and not me. I had been undeniably targeted. It was clearly a case of entrapment, and Macardican's past, even before I was elected mayor, proved that.

As I worked on those notes to highlight Macardican's culpability, my thoughts also morphed into the truth of my own mistakes. When I met Macardican, I was still mourning my dad's death and I was vulnerable. I never should have trusted him, no matter how he tried to present himself as my father's friend. Talk about a lapse of judgment—somehow I had strayed so far from the things my father taught me along the way. "Have your own program and don't let anybody program you." I had no intention of extorting money from Macardican, but the moment he mentioned "cash," I should have stopped him in his tracks.

Technically, I knew I could argue this case and win it. On the other hand, I knew that as long as I was the client, I couldn't win even one count. As it has been said, "A lawyer who represents himself has a fool for a client."

I now sat in the courtroom, so frustrated that I unloosed my tie to get some air. As soon as Bob entered the courtroom, I placed my final draft of the closing argument in his hand. He sat down and poured over it, page after page. I tried to release it, but my mind kept wandering back to what I had written.

From my past experience with Bob, I knew he didn't perform at his best when using notes I prepared, even though they were well-organized and comprehensive. Nevertheless, the thought of not helping Bob bring out the most compelling arguments in the most important case of my life was totally unacceptable. I didn't regret wanting Bob to use my notes as long as he read them the way I wrote them. I was convinced they would provide the jury with a clear roadmap to an acquittal.

Now the most important thing for Bob to do was to convey the evidence and the arguments to the jury with a convincing demeanor; to have good eye contact and connect with the jury. The jurors not only needed to hear what my attorney was saying, they also needed to feel it, and believe it. They needed to rely on his integrity as he pointed out the government's questionable evidence. Surely enough discrepancy lay open in the government's unrecorded conversations between Macardican and me to create reasonable doubt.

As was the usual procedure, the prosecution went first.

"Alright, counsel, are you ready?" Judge Marshall asked Attorney Madison.

"Yes, Your Honor," Madison answered.

"The government may proceed."

When all the cards are laid on the audience's conscience, this case will come down to a question of who was really on trial: An inner-city mayor for extorting bribes from a businessman or the U.S. government for entrapping an inner-city mayor?

The government portrayed me as a corrupt politician who betrayed his sworn trust. But my counsel portrayed me as the victim of an illegal entrapment by the FBI and a vengeful manipulative informant. The only thing the two sides agreed on was that the public's trust had been violated, for one side or the other.

"Ladies and gentlemen of the jury," Madison said, "you must strike a blow for honest government. The defendant sold out his office and his constituents by literally taking thousands of dollars in cash in back rooms. Fortunately, there were cameras and microphones in those back rooms, and the defendant's corrupt actions have been exposed."

As soon as it was my attorney's time to answer, Bob came out swinging. "It was the FBI and the office of the U.S. Attorney that committed the crime by targeting, misleading, and eventually entrapping Mr. Tucker. Therefore, I urge you, ladies and gentlemen of the jury, to be a buffer against an overzealous government. Please consider the proof of this case and allow Mr. Tucker to return to Washington, D.C. to continue serving his country and community."

Because both Madison and Potter had been assigned as my prosecutors, Madison sat down and it was John Potter's turn to take the floor. Assistant U.S. Attorney John Potter hailed Macardican as a responsible citizen who agreed to work undercover for the FBI to stop corruption.

"Macardican believed corruption was wrong and he tried to do something about it," Potter said.

Bob rebutted, "Mr. Macardican was a shrewd, street-savvy businessman who manipulated his taped conversations with Mr. Tucker to give the appearance that they were talking about trading money for votes."

Potter criticized my attorney for questioning Macardican's motives.

"When they met for lunch on May thirtieth, nineteen ninety-one, it was Walter Tucker who initiated the first discussion of illegal conduct when he advised Mr. Macardican on how to launder campaign contributions to political candidates. And when Macardican asked if it was advisable to give cash to candidates, Tucker told him to decide that on a case-by-case basis. The first piece of advice that the mayor of Compton gave to John Macardican was to violate the law," Potter argued.

Madison returned to the podium, "Attorney Ramsey's telling you not to believe what you see here. He is telling you to disbelieve the hard evidence. He is telling you to accept the images and the understandings he says he had in his head. Images and understandings that contradict the evidence."

Bob countered, "The FBI scripted the conversations, and set up Mayor Tucker! They set up the meetings, as they knew what they wanted to get. They orchestrated the whole thing. Carefully review the tapes and consider what Tucker, not Macardican, was thinking at the time. The law instructs you that the elements of the crime are based on what Mr. Tucker was thinking, not what Mr. Macardican was thinking. Mr. Tucker never intended anything sinister or illegal. What was in Mr. Macardican's mind, Mr. Tucker didn't know. Was Mr. Tucker supposed to know Mr. Macardican was talking about bribery?"

Bob flipped a page in his notebook then continued, "Mr. Macardican's motives weren't genuine at all. He held a grudge against Compton officials for not approving his previous incinerator proposal in the early eighties. Working with the FBI, he kept plotting until the nineties when he saw a thirty-three-year-old rising star come on the Compton political scene. The government proved to be persistent in their focus on Mr. Tucker. You tell me, why did federal officials wait three years, when Mr. Tucker was in Congress, to file charges stemming from incidents that occurred in nineteen ninety-one and nineteen ninety-two? They were hoping to build an even bigger case against him. They were hoping to catch him in some other alleged criminal activity, but there was none to be found. They wanted a big fish. The mayor of Compton wasn't big enough, but a U.S. congressman would be the catch of a lifetime."

Bob closed the notebook, "Bottom line, Mr. Tucker was the victim of illegal entrapment by the government, and there was no evidence presented that Mr. Tucker had agreed to perform any official act in return for his vote."

Potter countered, "Not true! We have offered considerable evidence showing that the defendant willingly sold his vote for money."

Potter played relevant portions of the FBI video tapes.

"See, Mayor Tucker responded affirmatively at several meetings when told he was being paid for his vote or some official action. Remember the June twenty-sixth, nineteen ninety-one meeting when he visited Macardican's office to collect a two-thousand-dollar installment on the ten thousand dollars he was promised.

"It was at that meeting that Mr. Macardican said, 'That, plus eight we agreed on should secure your vote' as he handed over the money. And Mayor Tucker said, 'We'll be friendly definitely.' He took the money, got up, and left."

Every time I heard that quote, I winced inside. As the old adage goes, "Perception is reality." It sounded and looked very bad. Looking back on it, if I had it to do over, I certainly would have done and said that differently. It sounded like a definite "quid pro quo," but I meant that this time his project would get a fair hearing. No one in their right mind could promise unconditional support without seeing an environmental impact report! Why in the world did I say that?

Bob argued that just taking the money was not enough.

"The law says there must be an exchange, a quid pro quo—something given or promised in return for something received. Nowhere in the transcripts do you see that! There was no reason to go after Mr. Tucker. There wouldn't be any problem in Compton if the government hadn't gone out there paying money to entrap him. Compton wasn't bothering anybody, so the government "created" the house of cards...."

Potter was steadfast, speaking even more confidently, "Compton was seeded with corruption well before Tucker took over the city's helm, and that corruption needed to be ferreted out by the authorities."

"Even so," Bob argued, "Walter Tucker was not the culprit of any wrongdoings that caused the government to run into Compton and protect it…" The government has stated that Mr. Tucker was a corrupt politician who swiftly betrayed the public's trust upon entering office—"

While Bob was speaking, I was really hoping he would stop removing and then replacing his glasses. It seemed to reveal some inner nervousness, some lack of confidence in what he was saying; it prevented him from establishing any real eye contact with the jury.

"If that is true," Bob continued, "then where is his track record of having betrayed the public trust as a public official? Under the best of circumstances, he didn't have enough time to build that kind of a track record. The truth is the government has no evidence that Mr. Tucker was predisposed to extorting bribes because he was a young man who had just assumed office. Walter Tucker, III, who inherited the mayor's office from his late father, was dedicated to public service. He was proud of himself, as he was proud of his dad, and dedicated to helping the people of Compton and all the cities in his district."

At that moment, my mother, Martha, who had sat quietly taking notes throughout the trial, left the courtroom sobbing, with Robin scurrying after her. Later, I remember her explaining it to me, *"I couldn't help but cry because it was apparent they targeted you before you ever got into office. And you were so young, with such a bright future."*

Madison, representing the government, got the last word.

"Mr. Tucker wants you to believe he is the victim of a massive conspiracy, a phenomenal series of plots and coincidences, all aimed at wrongly attacking Walter Tucker. It's absurd to presume that he just kept taking all the money and playing along with no real idea of what was going on. Contrast the gullible image of Tucker with the one displayed during the trial. Remember, he was determined to respond to questions by prosecutors in his own way, even if the answers were not responsive.

"It was Walter Tucker who often fed his attorney's questions to ask witnesses during the trial. He even went out of his way to correct me when I mispronounced the name of the street he lived on. This defendant is someone who must be in control. This is a man who enlightened the President of the United States and Governor of California, but wants us to believe that suddenly he becomes putty in the hands of the trash man from El Monte? C'mon, ladies, and gentlemen. What Mr. Tucker did, he did wittingly, intentionally, and deliberately."

Man, he's pulling no punches!

"Ladies and gentlemen of the jury, that concludes the closing arguments from the attorneys," Judge Marshall said.

The judge then began to read the lengthy jury instructions, as the droning sound of her words gripped my body and mind into a moment of climactic terror.

Well, we had the last hour to give our truth. We scored a lot of points, but every time we scored, the big boys knocked us down again. It was 'six of one and half-a-dozen of the other.' And Bob kept lifting his horn-rimmed glasses on and off his eyes during his argument. It seemed to interfere with his flow. I just hope it didn't cause him to appear less than confident to the jury. But we can still win this case based on the issue of "entrapment." I release it; I let it go. Whatever decision comes now is just a matter of fate.

I heard snippets of the jury instructions, but as the judge concluded her remarks, I heard her command.

"The jury is now dismissed for deliberation. Court adjourned."

She pounded her gavel and a kind of finality resounded across the courtroom. Now my future rested in the hands of twelve icy-faced jurors that sneaked a glance at me as they walked out for their deliberation.

CHAPTER FORTY-THREE

Pins and Needles

F riday, December 9, 1995—a day that will be forever stamped in my mind. I sat in the burgundy executive chair in my congressional district office trying to stay busy, shuffling papers, checking upcoming appointments. I was trying to keep my mind from focusing on the obvious— TIME—but the gold, art deco clock on the opposite wall wouldn't allow it.

The jury had been out now for nine days and during that time, they had sent seventeen notes to the judge. In those notes, there was one question stood out: *Explain to us again the law on entrapment?* Judge Marshall had responded by sending the relevant legal language. Still, there was no indication of what they were thinking or how long they would stay out.

The last nine days had been a black hole, a blur for me. How does one wait gracefully for a jury's verdict that can change your life in a moment? It wasn't like any criminal case I had tried as a prosecutor or defense attorney. This time, I was the defendant. This jury's decision wasn't about my won-loss legal record or my ego; it was about my life. Everything was riding on it.

In those last few days of the jury's deliberation, my mind raced back and forth over all the legal issues and their many possibilities. I studied the jury sheets, made notes on the jurors, tried to predict how they might vote, and why. At this stage, it was an exercise in futility, but then what else could I do? There was no way to clear my mind of the issues for more than a minute at a time. I waited at my desk while "Mr. Clock" ticked on the wall.

When would the jury come back? If they came back early, would that be a bad sign? Or, what would it mean if they stayed out long? Legal pundits would have varying opinions. And what if there was a hung jury? I used to think that all I wanted was a hung jury, but now the thought of it was like purgatory! You're not in hell, but you're surely not in heaven. A hung jury meant a retrial. While I had held up strong during the last several months, I couldn't imagine going through that kind of ordeal again. It would be worse than a guilty verdict. It would just delay the inevitable. All those thoughts looped and twirled in my brain as Audrey entered my office wearing a solemn look. "Congressman, it's the court. Line 2."

The jury had finally reached a verdict. I gathered the troops—Robin, my mom, and Tyrone and we weaved in and out of morning traffic to the downtown Los Angeles court house. Sitting in the backseat, my mind was in turmoil. The saga had come to an end, and there was nothing more I could do but face the outcome. Whichever way the verdict went, I felt my life would be new, somehow. I leaned back, looked out my window and sighed as life moved quickly by. Everything was silent.

Verdict

"Each day brings a world of new possibilities, but one day brings a moment that changes your life forever."

After being away from the courtroom for nine days while the jury deliberated, I found myself back at court, sitting between my two attorneys. The tension in the air was heavy. I was on pins and needles, tapping my fingers incessantly on the mahogany defense table. Everything began to move in slow motion—the court personnel, the government, even barely visible movements of the audience. My family huddled together in their usual spot on the first row. Other supporters filled the rows behind them. The government sat at their counsel table with an air of certainty in front of the crowded federal courtroom. Suddenly Judge Marshall stepped into the courtroom and the bailiff called, "All rise!"

My attorney quickly leaned over to me and whispered, "Here we go." We stood.

Everyone stood at attention until the judge calmly took her seat on the bench.

"You may be seated," she said.

Then Judge Marshall turned to the jury foreman.

"Have you reached a verdict?"

The foreman stood with the verdict sheet in his hand. "We have, Your Honor."

The court clerk walked over to the foreman and received the verdict sheet, then she took it to Judge Marshall. She reviewed it stoically and handed it back to the clerk.

"Will the defendant please rise," she summoned.

Terror beat in my chest as I breathed deeply, pushed upward, and rose to face my fate. I gripped the edge of counsel table and silently prayed that my legs would allow me to stand tall, no matter the verdict. I prayed that if I was found guilty, Robin would still love me; that Walter IV would still respect me; that Autumn would never lose faith in me; that my family would one day be proud of me again; that constituents wouldn't harshly judge me and ultimately forgive me for taking them through this ordeal.

"You may read the verdict," Judge Marshall nodded to the clerk.

It was time for the verdict and the hush was unbearable. After seven gut-wrenching weeks of litigation, after living with this sword over my head for almost two years, the conclusion was finally at hand. It was hidden on that sheet, but it would soon be revealed.

"In the matter of the United States of America versus Walter R. Tucker, III, as to count one: a violation of eighteen U.S.C. Section nineteen fifty-one, we, the jury…"

That second seemed like an hour or a day, or even a lifetime. It was the proverbial field goal attempt from fifty yards out with no time left on the clock in the championship game. The ball floats slowly in the air. Maybe we would win, maybe we wouldn't. It would all depend on where the ball would land; on who had convinced the jury to agree with their version of the facts and how they applied to the law. It would depend on the perspective of this predominately white jury. One way or the other, the next few seconds would change my life.

"…find the defendant…"

The still small voice of God I had heard from last night rose inside me again.

"If it doesn't work out like you think, remember, you are still mine, and I still have mighty plans for your life. They are for good and not for evil."

I believed so strongly in the omnipotent power of God that I knew if I was convicted, it would be because God allowed it and my purpose in life would be fulfilled through it.

"…guilty as to count one, a violation of eighteen U.S.C. Section nineteen fifty-one…"

I clenched my teeth and fought back tears.

"Oh, God!"

"No!"

My wife and mother shot a scream through the courtroom, then a deafening hush filled the room. And just like that, my life had changed. The clerk continued to read the rest of the counts.

"As to count two…guilty…as to count three…guilty…as to count four…guilty …"

I was numb, but somehow, I managed an encouraging glance at Robin, meaning, *Please don't worry, it's going to be alright. You're going to be alright, the children are going to be alright. The great work I started in Congress to create jobs, reduce crime, and provide quality healthcare and education for all the residents of my district will get done—somehow.*

A surge of strength swept from my feet to my head. Stability settled in my brain. *It's done. No more waiting and wondering—it's done*. I had hoped and prayed for the best, but ultimately I was prepared for the worst.

When the clerk finished reading the verdict, I had been found guilty of seven counts of bribery in violation of 18 U.S.C. Section 1951 and two counts of filing false tax returns, in violation of 26 U.S.C. 7206 (1).[21] The two counts accusing me of bribing Murcole Disposal, Inc. and the one accusing me of demanding a $250,000 bribe from undercover FBI Agent Kilbane (representing Compton Energy Systems) deadlocked 11-1 for guilty. Mark had done a good job of defending me on the Murcole counts. Thank God he had convinced at least one juror that they had no merit.

I was later told that the lone black juror, Wanda Flagg, held out on those three counts and wouldn't budge. One part of me was overjoyed that she took an unwavering position on those counts. It was a moral victory if nothing else. At least someone saw that what I'd been saying was true. Still, another part of me was highly disappointed. All she had to do was be firm on the other counts to cause a mistrial. But recalling the dreadful ordeal of this trial, I conceded that anything was better than a retrial. It was time to move on.

"Sentencing will be held in thirty days, January fifth. The defendant shall remain free on bail until that time," Judge Marshall said.

Even that announcement is God's favor. I don't have to go to prison today. No, not right away.

I stood motionless as Judge Marshall made final remarks. All I heard was my private conversation with God.

Did they get it right? Am I the calculating, greedy politician they've made me out to be? No, I was just looking for another contribution to retire my campaign debt. Isn't that what politicians do? Did I ask for cash? No, but I was all too willing to receive the cash he offered to me. I let my need for cash blur my better judgment. I listened to the wrong voice and departed from my character. Yes, if I had to do it all again, I would do things differently.

I gave Macardican advice that was worth far more than the small amount he paid me, but I never should have taken cash and not documented it. God, you know the truth—I was set up! But, of course, I didn't have to take the bait. My impatience caused me to compromise the principles I grew up on. I realize that impatience is something I'm going to have to overcome. God, I'm sorry!

God whispered back in the most comforting voice I had ever heard, "Son, I forgive you." My soul felt relieved.

In the blink of an eye, I was standing on the federal courthouse steps holding my briefcase and Bible, surrounded by my wife, my attorneys, my family, and the few supporters I had left. Cameras flashed lights in my face. Reporters hurled indistinguishable questions.

Suddenly, I felt as if I was outside of my body, looking down on this frantic scene on the courthouse steps. I could still hear everything being said.

"How are you feeling right now, Congressman?"

"Congressman, what do you think about the verdict?"

"Do you have anything to say to the jury, Congressman?"

"I believe the jury made the wrong decision. I know what happened. The government knows what happened. It was entrapment."

I spoke calmly from a new peaceful place.

"I still believe God has a master plan for my life. 'All things work together for the good to those who love God...' He will work even this verdict together for my good."

I was no longer afraid, ashamed, angry, or agitated. I resolved to see things from a spiritual perspective in spite of pain, guilt, or sorrow. I kept speaking above the barrage of questions the press was asking.

"I believe God wants me to start my ministry now. Apparently, He wants me to start with prison ministry."

The crowd chuckled politely.

My mom burst through the crowd and hugged me tightly. Then, teary-eyed she whispered in my ear, "This too shall pass, my son." Seeing that she was overcome with grief, my sister, Keta, put her arm around her and said, "Come with me, mom." Keta shot me a look and I gave her a nod. With Richard, Kenneth, and Camille joining her, Keta led Mom away.

Walter with Bible in hand, addressing the media after the verdict

(flanked l to r by Attorney Bob Ramsey, Camille Tucker, Attorney Mark Smith, Kenneth Tucker, and Robin Tucker)

Just then, Bob took center stage and addressed the media, "Ladies and gentleman, that is all Mr. Tucker has to say today."

"But counselor does this mean the congressman's going to resign?"

"What prison do you think he'll be sent to?"

With that, Mark put his arm around me and I grabbed Robin's hand firmly to steady her in her highly emotional state. Her face revealed a depth of hurt and anger I had only seen in her at my dad's funeral. Our world, our life, had just been rocked and I knew she needed my support as we walked carefully down the courthouse steps. With members of the press still hounding us, we made our way to the street and saw Tyrone with the Town Car waiting at the curb. Mark ushered us into the back seat and Tyrone whisked us away. Now alone with Robin in the backseat, still holding her hand, I stared into her watery eyes and allowed my silence to assure her.

Walter getting into the Town Car outside U.S. District Court, Los Angeles

As Robin's eyes searched for answers, I believe she saw strength in me that I had never possessed on my own—a steadiness despite knowing that I'd soon have to leave her, our two young children, and my family. Surely, it was the power of God.

"Where to, Congressman?"

"Home."

"Man, what a raw deal!" Tyrone blurted out.

"Hey, life happens, but God is still good. Thanks for having my back, T."

As Tyrone maneuvered through the surface streets toward the Harbor Freeway, my cell phone rang, and I answered it. It was Marcus calling from D.C.

"Congressman, we all watched what happened. We're so sorry it didn't go your way."

"Thanks, man. Please give the staff my deepest thanks for all their prayers and support."

"I will."

"Talk soon."

I hung up the phone and Robin leaned back in her seat and closed her eyes. She seemed utterly exhausted. I carefully removed my hand from hers, then leaned my head back on the seat, took a deep, slow breath, and exhaled abruptly. As I stared through the window at the Los Angeles landscape passing by, I rested in thoughts of my past.

My life had always been one of service—whether teaching students in Compton public schools, practicing law at the Compton Courthouse, or responding to the needs of constituents in my congressional district. I had not only talked the talk about empowerment, I took young black men and women who had worked my congressional campaign and hired them as congressional staff. I exposed them to a world of opportunities to elevate their lives to new heights. As the youngest mayor in Compton's history and the youngest African-American ever elected to Congress from California, I had become a poster boy for what hard work and discipline could achieve.

Having put so much of my time on fixing things to benefit the lives of others, now I considered my own future, stretching far beyond the horizon.

Maybe it's my destiny to be the one to show millions of black men in prison how to get out and stay out; how to stay the narrow path, overcome their past, and become God-fearing, productive members of society.

Maybe I'll be the one to offer an inside look on rising and falling and getting up again.

Maybe I will show that the principles of God—faith, hope, and love—can bring victory and freedom, as nothing else can. Maybe.

CHAPTER FORTY-FIVE

Beyond The Horizon

A pril 17, 1996. After fighting through the reporters and processing through security, I was back in Judge Marshall's packed courtroom for sentencing. 1996 would be unlike any year in my life. For the first time—I would come to know what it's like to lose my freedom.

"All rise," the bailiff called out.

Everyone stood at attention until the judge took her seat.

"You may be seated," Judge Marshall said.

There was deafening silence while the jurists glanced down at the papers before her.

"Will the defendant please stand."

I marshaled the strength, and for the last time in that courtroom, rose to my feet with Bob and Mark on each side of me.

"This is the sentencing in the matter of the United States versus Walter R. Tucker, III. The court has reviewed the verdict, the law, and all the relevant reports from the Probation Department. Having heard the evidence in this case and based on the totality of the circumstances, I have my own opinion about what his sentence should be. However, the sentence for these charges is governed by federal guidelines. Based on these federal guidelines, the Probation Department recommends that the defendant serves between thirty to fifty-seven months in federal prison. However, it is the position of this court that based on this being the defendant's first felony conviction and the conviction being of a non-violent nature, and in light of his public service, and the more than two hundred letters of support submitted by his constituents, he should be sentenced to the lower range of the guidelines—a twenty-seven-month sentence, of which he will serve eighteen months at the Federal Prison Camp at Lompoc, California. Mr. Tucker, this court will give you time to prepare for this transition, but you must report to Lompoc on June sixth. The Probation Department will be in touch with you with the details. I wish you good luck," Judge Marshall said and rapped her gavel. It was final; it was done. All those months of wonder about the trial's outcome had disappeared, but there was still a lot of wonder about what was to come.

I turned to Bob and shook his hand for the last time.

"Congressman, I'm sorry. I wish I could have done more."

"You did what you could. Thank you."

I turned and hugged Mark and said, "Thanks again, brother, we'll talk soon."

"You know it, homeboy."

With Robin on my arm and my mom and siblings close behind, we maneuvered through the crowd of reporters in the hallway. They wanted one more quote, but as far as I was concerned there was nothing more to say.

Once outside the courthouse, my family and I gathered in a place around the corner from the courthouse entrance.

"Mom, are you going to be alright?"

"Yes. Let's pray."

We formed a prayer circle and I gave Mom the nod to lead the prayer.

"Father, in the name of Jesus, we thank you that Your word says 'weeping may endure for a night, but joy comes in the morning.' It seems very dark right now, but by faith, we declare that beyond this darkness joy will return to our family… Amen."

We hugged and then Robin and I went our separate way. Since I had resigned from my congressional seat on December 15, 1995, Tyrone was no longer there to drive us home. I helped Robin into a rental car and drove off. As I headed to the freeway, I remembered the words of the beautiful poster that hung on the wall in my Capitol Hill office: *'Faith is not knowing what tomorrow brings, but Who brings tomorrow.*

Despite all the uncertainties of tomorrow, I was ready to trust God's grace for the next leg of my race. Deep inside, I sensed that it would bring great value to humanity, something greater than anything I had ever known. About that time, I rolled off the Harbor Freeway and into Compton.

I don't remember how I got to Angeles Abbey Cemetery, where my father's body lay in a crypt. All I knew was that I found myself standing with Robin in a long, quiet hallway in front of Dad's crypt. The high, marble ceiling was far above us, and a slice of sunlight beaming through the skylight was upon us.

"Honey, I'm gonna give you some time alone with Dad. I'll be in the car."

I appreciated that. I could feel Dad's presence as I walked up to the crypt and slid my fingers across his bronze nameplate. Suddenly, the burden of my heart rose in my chest.

"Dad, I'm so sorry. Everyone said you were honest to a fault. I now understand that's not a bad characteristic to have. I'm truly sorry for this moment in my life... I promise to never do anything that would bring shame to your name again."

I turned, walked back down that long hallway, and rejoined Robin in the car.

"You alright?"

"Yeah, I'm gonna be alright."

Robin leaned over and delivered a comforting kiss on my cheek.

I headed home through the streets of Compton, seemingly on "auto pilot." When I turned onto Tichenor Street, I felt like I was turning to the real purpose of my life. I felt a resolve that was far greater than the one I made when I ran for mayor, greater than when I decided to run for Congress. Actually, the resolve had come the night before the verdict. I had promised God that I would love him by faith and serve Him with my whole heart—no matter the verdict.

I recalled the prayer I had prayed, "Father God, if you will always provide food and shelter for my family and me, I will serve you in full-time ministry."

I was ready to make good on that vow, but now that I was on my way to prison I had no idea how God was going to provide for my family. Nevertheless, my dad's favorite Scripture came back to my mind and brought me comfort:

"Seek first the Kingdom of God and his righteousness, and all these things shall be added to you."(KJV Matthew 6:33)

My life was no longer about me; about the pursuit of fame, fortune, and power. I would no longer seek to rack up countless personal awards, no longer work tirelessly to please a myriad of political contributors, or try to maneuver my way to the political mountain top. I had served the world, but now I was fully committed to serving my Lord and Savior Jesus Christ.

I had made many stump speeches, preached political empowerment, but now it was time for me to preach the gospel of Christ; to seek and save those who are spiritually lost.

Despite the prison sentence I was about to serve, I had peace. The Apostle Paul, who experienced prison on more than one occasion, called it "the peace of God, which passes all understanding."

I had no idea what Lompoc was like. I had no idea how challenging the next leg of my race would be. All I knew was that one day the world would be a better place because of God's grace on the new race I was about to run for Jesus Christ.

Footnotes

1. "Oath of office: Federal Executive and Legislative Branch Oaths." *U.S. Code, Title 5, Section 3331*

2. Wikipedia contributors. "Compton, California." *Wikipedia, The Free Encyclopedia*. Wikipedia, The Free Encyclopedia, 9 June 2016. Web. 11 June 2016.

3. Wikipedia contributors. "Douglas Dollarhide." *Wikipedia, The Free Encyclopedia*. Wikipedia, The Free Encyclopedia, 31 Jan. 2017. Web.

4. Wikipedia contributors. "Lionel Cade." *Wikipedia, The Free Encyclopedia*. Wikipedia, The Free Encyclopedia, 11 Jun. 2017. Web. 21 Jun. 2017

5. Tina Griego, "Tucker Rolls With Punches," 28 June 1992, *Los Angeles Times*: B1

6. "Election Returns: Compton: Mayor." *Los Angeles Times*. Los Angeles Times, 17 Apr. 1991. Web. 13 June 2016.

7. Wikipedia contributors. "Compton, California." *Wikipedia, The Free Encyclopedia*. Wikipedia, The Free Encyclopedia, 9 Jun. 2016. Web. 16 Jun. 2016.

8. Joe Davidson, "Targets for Scrutiny," October 1996, *Emerge*

9. Joe Davidson, "Targets for Scrutiny," October 1996, *Emerge*

10. Angel Jennings. "Compton Illegal Pay." *LA Times*. 20 August 2015. Web. 11 June 2016 http://www.latimes.com/lo-cal/lanow/a-me-ln-da-compton-illegal-pay-20150820

11. Tina Griego. "Elections/U.S. House of Representatives; Stormy Race for 37th District Seat Steals the Thunder," 31 May 1992, *Los Angeles Times*: J1.

12. Tina Griego. "Aftermath of the Riots," 7 May 1992, *Los Angeles Times*: B1.

13. "California House: CA 37," 3 June 1992, *Hotline*; http://www.sos.ca.gov/elections/prior-elections/statewide-election-results/primary-election-june-2-1992/statement-vote

14. "California House: CA 37," 7 June 1994, *Hotline*; http://www.sos.ca.gov/elections/prior-elections/statewide-election-results/primary-election-june-7-1994/statement-vote

15. Committee on Standards of Official Conduct, "Historical Summary of Conduct Cases in the House of Representatives," available at http://ethics.house.gov (accessed 26 March 2007); Michael Janofsky, "California Congressman Indicted by U.S.," 12 August 1994, *New York Times*: A12; Ron Russell et al., "Rep. Tucker Indicted on New Charges," 2 June 1995, *Los Angeles Times*: B1; "2 in Congress Attend Court on Charges," 23 August 1994, *New York Times*: A13.

16. Jim Newton and Emily Adams, "Rep. Tucker Is Indicted; Denies Bribery Charges," 12 August 1994, *Los Angeles Times*: A1.

17. Wikipedia contributors. "Bill Clinton." Wikipedia, The Free Encyclopedia, 10 Jun. 2016. Web.11 Jun. 2016

18. Committee on Standards of Official Conduct, "Historical Summary of Conduct Cases in the House of Representatives," available at http://ethics.house.gov (accessed 26

March 2007); Michael Janofsky, "California Congressman Indicted by U.S.," 12 August 1994, *New York Times*: A12; Ron Russell et al., "Rep. Tucker Indicted on New Charges," 2 June 1995, *Los Angeles Times*: B1; "2 in Congress Attend Court on Charges," 23 August 1994, *New York Times*: A13.

19. Wikipedia contributors. "Geronimo Pratt." *Wikipedia, The Free Encyclopedia*. Wikipedia, The Free Encyclopedia, 23 Jul. 2016. Web. 28 Jul. 2016.

20. Wikipedia contributors. "Bill Clinton." Wikipedia, The Free Encyclopedia, 10 Jun. 2016. Web.11 Jun. 2016

21. Kathryn Wexler et al., "Rep. Tucker Convicted of Extortion; Congressman Took Bribes While Mayor of Compton, Calif.," 9 December 1995, *Washington Post*: A1